BEYOND THE NORTH-WEST FRONTIER

Travels in the Hindu Kush and Karakorams

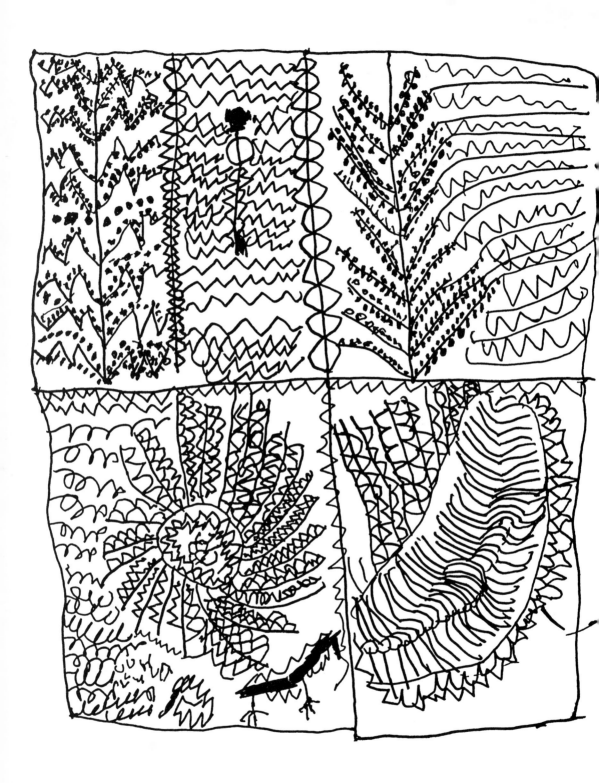

Drawing done by a Kalash girl.

BEYOND THE NORTH-WEST FRONTIER

Travels in the Hindu Kush and Karakorams

MAUREEN LINES

 The Oxford Illustrated Press

© 1988, Maureen Lines

ISBN 0-946609-68-3

Published by:
The Oxford Illustrated Press Limited, Haynes
Publishing Group, Sparkford, Nr Yeovil, Somerset
BA22 7JJ, England.

Haynes Publications Inc., 861 Lawrence Drive,
Newbury Park, California 91320, USA.

Printed in England by:
J.H. Haynes & Co Limited, Sparkford, Nr Yeovil,
Somerset.

British Library Cataloguing in Publication Data:
Lines, Maureen
    Beyond the North-West Frontier : travels
    in Hindu Kush and Karakorams.
    1. Description & travel – Personal
    observations
    I. Title
    915.49'1045
    ISBN 0-946609-68-3

Library of Congress Catalog Card Number:

Contents

Dedication

To Saifullah Jan.

May the Kalash people of Birir, Rumbur and Bumburet survive and preserve their culture and continue to resist conversion and avoid further exploitation. It is also hoped that the Pakistan government will continue to help them in their endeavour. If they should lose the battle, man will have destroyed another part of his true heritage. The end of the Kalash will further diminish the life of man on this planet.

'You are a traveller who once or twice has glimpsed a distant land and consciously or unconsciously searches to find it again. This land does exist, it is not an illusion. Persist in your quest and sooner or later you will find the path which leads to it.'

Taken from: *The Beckoning Land* by Rowena Farre (Hermit Fo speaking on island of Lanto).

Acknowledgements

I should like to thank Dr Raoul Desmaras Luzuriage, the former Argentine Ambassador, for his assistance and kindness to me while in Islamabad; Mr Shakil Durrani, the former Deputy Commissioner of Chitral and now Commissioner for Kohat, for his co-operation and assistance; Mr Qutubuddin Aziz, former Minister of Information at the Pakistan Embassy in London and former Chairman of the National Press Trust of Pakistan, for his patience in answering my many queries. My thanks, also, to his successor, Mr Ruziuddin Shaikh.

I am indebted, too, to all those officials, hotel workers and the people of the country I met along the way, who treated me with courtesy and kindness and gave me hospitality. A special thanks to Haider Ali Shah and Abbas Bhatti of the Mountain Inn and all my friends in Karachi.

My thanks also must go to my editor, Jane Marshall, for her patience and encouragement.

Lastly, but by no means least, I am indebted to Mick Lighten for developing my black and white photographs, my mother for typing the final manuscript, Richard Easterbrook for his drawings on pp 91 and 97 and Patrick O'Brian for his photos on pp 224 and 231

Foreword

Nowhere in the whole of British India was there a region that could stir the blood of an officer of the Raj more than the wild North-West Frontier. Its ancient capital, Peshawar, lies in the heart of the tribal belt, where Pukhtunwali, thé way of the Pathans, is still the guiding force. Here the government holds little sway away from the confines of the main roads, and tribal skirmishes and blood feuds are as common today as in the past.

Once the crossroads for caravan routes from Central Asia and the Middle East, Peshawar was notorious for the intrigue that infested its bazaars and the numerous murders committed in its narrow alleyways. Today, Peshawar is not only the chief Pathan city, but is also the headquarters of the Afghan Mujahideen. In the Old City, spies and assassins still lurk within the shadows of the bazaars which seethe with whispered rumours. North of Peshawar, the former princely state of Dir, now a Merged Area,* is still a backward and festering region active in the growing of opium.

In the far north of Pakistan, the North-West Frontier merges with the Northern Areas. This vast region (bordered on the west by Afghanistan, in the east by Indian-held Kashmir, in the north-west by the Russian-controlled Wakhan Strip and in the north-east by Chinese Turkestan) has always been a volatile political area. At the end of the last century, E.F. Knight wrote a vivid narrative about his travels in the region in his book *Where Three Empires Meet—Britain, Russia and China*. The Great Game between British India and Russia was at its height and the trade route from Kashmir to Kashgar was unimpeded by sealed borders. Now in the late 1980s, it is a question of everything changes but everything remains the same. Now, two of the powers are still Russia and China but

---

*Pakistan is made up of the provinces of Sind, Baluchistan, Punjab, N.W.F.P, and the Northern Areas. The 'Merged Areas' are former princely states which have now been integrated with one of the four main provinces.

the British have gone, and, in their place are two others who have stakes in the region: India, who lives uncomfortably with the Chinese to the north, and, squeezed in between them all, American-backed Pakistan.

The northern region of this little-known country is a land of rugged high mountains (the highest cluster in the world), mighty glaciers, desolate landscapes, lonely snow-covered passes and sunlit fertile valleys, and is home to one of the great rivers of the world, the Indus. Now that the Khunjerab Pass is open and travellers can once more journey to China, the area's main town, Gilgit (a former staging post on the old Silk Road and the most northerly outpost of the British Raj), is again a bustling trading centre.

Even though northern Pakistan lies at the crossroads of history and its borders reach up to Central Asia, little is heard or written about this beautiful and fascinating land, other than newspaper reports about border skirmishes. Few, outside Pakistan, know about the many ethnic groups that inhabit the region, or about their history which stretches back to the time of Alexander the Great and before; they are a tough, stoic mountain people, still strong in culture and tradition.

And in this unique land, in the former princely state of Chitral (also a Merged Area), there exists a special people—the last to withstand conversion to Islam. For here, close to the Afghan border and high up in the rugged mountains of the Hindu-Kush, live the 'Kafir' Kalash. These people number approximately four thousand and live as they have done for centuries in the three remote valleys of Bumburet, Rumbur and Birir.

In my travels over a period of thirteen months, on three different visits, I covered more than three thousand miles (not including many mountain flights and the long train ride from Karachi to Rawalpindi) by wagon, bus, jeep, raft, on foot, on horseback and even for a short distance on a bulldozer.

This book is not an anthropological study or university thesis, it is purely one woman's account of her adventures, travelling through this still untamed land. For those readers wishing for a more academic study of the various peoples and history of the region, I have included a bibliography of books dating back to the time of the British Raj.

The Birth of a Dream

I awakened at dawn. From the verandah of the Kalash 'hotel', I watched as night faded from the valley. Behind me the sun burst over the distant rim of the mountains, bathing the opposite ridge and tree-dotted slopes in a blaze of golden light. I pushed aside my sleeping-bag and, sitting on the edge of my *charpoy*,* gazed out over the lower mountain slopes of green corn and ripening wheat and groves of mulberry, apricot and walnut trees. I knew that soon the women would be out hoeing in the fields while the men reaped the wheat and tended to their livestock. Below me, I could hear the welcome sound of an axe on wood. I was thirsty for my morning tea, but I had first to make a trip to the river to carry out my morning ablutions.

I left the verandah and stepped out onto the mountain track, which led to the roof of a large storehouse usually used as a threshing floor, but at that particular moment serving as a wrestling ring for two small boys dressed in ragged *shalwar-khameez*.* I paused to watch. The youngsters were unaware of their solitary and silent spectator envying their innocence as they rolled and tumbled amidst the wheat stalks and animal droppings. Above their shouts of laughter, the sudden snapping of twigs made me turn and glance upwards. Through the trees, I could see a group of women leave their small mountain-top village and head towards me down the slope. As the black-robed figures emerged from the cover of the foliage into the dazzling sunlight, their numerous rows of red and white beaded necklaces, their many silver and bronze bangles and their head-dresses decorated with cowrie shells and red and white buttons, turned the scrub and rock-strewn mountainside into a canvas of bright colour.

Charpoy—string bed common on the subcontinent.
Shalwar-khameez—the long, tailed shirt and baggy pants commonly worn in Pakistan. (See glossary.)

When they reached me, the women smiled and called out: '*Ishpata, Baba!*'* The bells on the end of their long-tailed head-dresses rang out sweetly in the quiet of the early morning. On their backs were cone-shaped baskets, made from willow and goats' hair, in which they carried bread for the afternoon meal and their hoes for working in the fields. When they returned in the evening, they would be carrying kindling wood in their baskets, and would have to face an arduous climb back to their village.

I followed the women down to the front of the hotel, where a number of men were chatting together on the porch. Reluctant to make straight for the river bank and broadcast my intentions to this small gathering of strangers, I turned right instead and carried on along the jeep track, which ran past the porch and led out of the valley, thereby, as is often the way at such moments, drawing attention to myself.

I had walked but a short distance when I saw a convenient and secluded grove of trees on the banks of the river, the other side of the cornfield. I stepped off the track and walked on through the tall corn, jumped over a low stone wall and passed by a small house built of cedar wood and stone. As I entered the trees, there was a sudden sharp cry behind me: '*Bashali! Bashali!*'

I stopped immediately and turned around. A woman, dressed in the customary black robes, was waving at me frantically. Momentarily I froze, realizing I had entered the grounds of the Bashali House, where women passing through their menstrual cycle or about to give birth were confined. Inadvertently, I had violated the ancient code of the Kalash. With mounting unease, but reflecting that I was, after all, a female, I put my hands to my head in a gesture of dismay. The woman smiled, but her anxiety was still painfully obvious. Hastily, I jumped over the nearby wall and into the cornfield.

When I arrived back on 'Main Street' in front of the hotel, I saw my guide and interpreter, Saifullah Jan, the leader and official representative of the Kalash, standing on the porch in earnest conversation with a tall, stern-looking man whom I had noticed there earlier. They both stared at me as I approached. When I offered my hand to Saifullah in greeting, he looked embarrassed and gave me the wrist of his right hand, in which he was holding a lighted cigarette. I looked from him to his companion.

Saifullah read the query in my eyes. 'You have made a big mistake,' he said.

I felt myself flush and the proverbial butterflies flutter in my stomach.

'I'm sorry! I did not know that was the Bashali House. I'm truly sorry.'

---

*'*Ishpata, Baba!*'—'Hello Sister'.

Saifullah turned unhappily to speak to the man standing beside him and then back to me.

'This is the priest. He saw you. I told him you did not know, and now he blames me for not telling you. We must sacrifice a goat. It is the law.'

Relief! I was not going to be thrown out of the valley. I was, however, a little bewildered.

'But, I don't quite understand. I am a woman. I thought from what I learned last year that was okay. Doesn't that make a difference? I . . .' My voice trailed off.

Saifullah shook his head. I thought I had detected a glint of amusement in his eyes, but, when he spoke, his voice was flat and expressionless.

'It makes no difference—you did not wash from head to toe or change into clean clothes before entering the grounds of the Bashali House, nor did you leave without purifying yourself first.'

Now I understood. I was impure, and, unless a goat was sacrificed to quell the wrath of the deities, I should contaminate all whom I touched.

Taking a deep breath, I asked: 'How much is a goat?'

'It will only be a kid. About fifty rupees.'*

I received the news with mixed emotions. I hated to think I had caused offence and that I should be responsible for the imminent demise of some hapless goat.

'Right. Tell the priest I shall pay for it.'

Saifullah translated.

There was an audible sigh behind me. I turned to see a small group of women, children and old men staring at me. Five rupees seemed a small price to pay for violating one of the greatest taboos of the 'Kafir' Kalash.

Thus began my stay in the Kalash valleys in 1981—not an auspicious beginning, but one which was to herald discoveries and lead to love and to the birth of a dream. For a dream to become a reality, it must have constant nurturing, for dreams are fragile—contingent upon cause and effect and circumstances beyond our control. When I left in the autumn of that year, I little thought that in the pursuit of that dream, my life would undergo a profound change.

Rupee—approx 17 rupees to the dollar.

13

The City of Flowers

To visit a place, to hunger after it upon leaving and then finally to return, is exhilarating. To make that return in an uncomfortable and undignified manner, however, does not inspire geniality, and I felt positively hostile towards the driver, as the nerve-shattering and bone-jarring rickshaw came to a sudden halt beneath the high pinkish walls and towering minarets of the Sunehri Mosque in the Peshawar Cantonment.

'Hotel opposite very cheap, very clean,' the teenage driver grinned, though I noticed the brown eyes regarded me shrewdly.

'I know,' I muttered as I slid out of the doorless and windowless vehicle and nearly landed in a ditch of running water that smelt suspiciously like a sewer. I pulled my rucksack out and, bending down, handed the driver a five rupee note.

'No five rupees! Ten!' he said, pulling a white head-cloth tighter around his ears and throat, leaving only a trace of gold skull cap still visible.

'No ten rupees,' I stated firmly, handing him just two more.

'*Tikay** I come for you one hour.'

My cry of 'no' was lost beneath the sound of the engine. Then, to my frustration, he sent the flimsy, three-wheeled, multi-coloured rickshaw, sporting designs of birds and flowers, shooting across the wide street in a U-turn right in front of the hotel. Why hadn't he done that with me still inside, I wondered, cursing inwardly as a bicycle, made for one and ridden by two, swerved past within inches of my face. I quickly leapt over the ditch onto the pavement and, making to run across the road, stepped in front of a bullock-cart and just missed being knocked down by a motor-bike with a mother, carrying a baby, sitting side-saddle on the pillion, the folds of her *burqa** draping over the rear wheel. For a moment I stood still, stranded in the middle of the road. An empty tonga pulled up, froth flowing from the horse's mouth down the legs of my

---

Tikay—okay.

15

A bazaar in the Peshawar Cantonment.

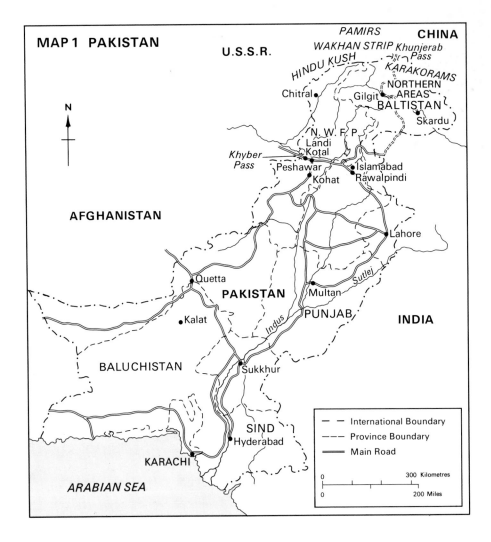

MAP 1 PAKISTAN

jeans.

'You want tonga?'

'No!' I yelled, trying to peer through the horse's legs and carriage wheels to see the oncoming traffic. I made another dash and safely reached the hotel. I climbed up the steps, past some interested young boys (and some who were not so young but still interested, if for different reasons), and dropped my rucksack down onto the tiled floor. The hotel

---

*Burqua—a tent-like garment which has just a small opening for the eyes, covered with a type of thin netting. In Pakistan, purdah (the seclusion of women from men except close male relatives) is strictly observed in the villages and towns. In big cities, the more 'modern' woman has discarded 'the veil'; but when she returns to her family, she is likely to revert to tradition.

16

sweeper moved silently past me on his hunkers, whisking away the dust with his short-handled broom.

I booked in and after a quick wash and brush up, I left the small, simple, but clean room and went out again, eager to rediscover the city that had so thrilled me in 1980 and 1981.

The late afternoon sun was hot through the dusty haze, which always seemed to envelop the city, as I drove once again through the tree-lined avenues of the Cantonment, delighting in the massive Victorian bungalows, their gardens filled with flowers and shrubs. At the entrance to the Old City, I left the rickshaw and walked into the Khyber Bazaar.

Every city has its own ambiance, its own distinctive characteristics. New York throbs with energy, London tantalizes the spirit with its grandeur beneath grey skies, Paris evokes passion and art, Rome conjures up ancient history, Jerusalem is swept by religious fervour and political ferment, New Delhi proudly displays its colonial heritage, and in Athens, a feeling of despair prevails as the present clashes with the past. Here in Peshawar, it is a sense of the past being at one with the present that stimulates the imagination.

Peshawar, which derives its name from the Sanskrit word 'Pushapur', meaning 'the city of flowers', is overwhelming to the stranger both in its exciting and ancient history, dating back over 2,500 years, and in its colourful and pulsating atmosphere. Capital city of the Pathans and the meeting place for the various groups of Mujahideen, it is also the capital of the North-West Frontier Province. It is a city which has seen Chinese Buddhist pilgrims and many an invading army, including those of Alexander the Great, Genghis Khan, Tamerlane, and Babur the Mogul. In relatively recent times, it has been occupied by the Sikhs and by the British. Strategically located, only some dozen or so miles from the Khyber Pass, it was once the crossroads for caravan routes from Persia, Turkestan, Arabia and China. Now it is the north-western terminal for the subcontinent's railway system and marks the western end of the Grand Trunk Road, which crosses through cities such as Rawalpindi, Lahore and New Delhi. Close to the Durand Line, separating Pakistan from Afghanistan, Peshawar is the gateway to the mountains of the Hindu-Kush to the north, which give way in turn to the Pamirs separating Pakistan from Russia and China. To the east the Hindu-Kush emerge into the Karakorams which lead into the Great Himalaya, while in the south lie the Suleiman Range, Baluchistan and the Persian Gulf. With the war now in Afghanistan (formerly a buffer state between Britain and Russia), Peshawar is still in the forefront of modern history, for it is poised precariously between the spheres of Soviet and Western influence. Spies and assassins still lurk in its furtive alleyways, while armed tribesmen from both sides of the border walk its ancient streets. The presence of Red Cross workers and United Nations officials and the greater volume of traffic, however, are the only obvious signs of change.

The enormous influx of Afghan refugees* has had a strong impact upon the citizens of Peshawar, as they have practically taken over the running of the city's transport system as well as the market for labourers, but it is not obvious to the casual visitor, for the camps are on the edge of the city, and many of the refugees belong to the same tribes as the indigenous population.

Again, to the stranger not accustomed to the vicissitudes of the city, the spirit of the Frontier makes Peshawar a romantic and exciting place.

In the West, the thought of towns and cities often conjures up high-rise apartment buildings, towerblocks, look-alike houses and supermarkets— drab, depressing and soul-destroying. Here, at the beginning of the Khyber Bazaar, the scene before me was a kaleidoscope of colour. Nearby was an oil tanker; painted on its rounded rear-end was a fairy-tale scene of a white castle overlooking a bright blue lake, surrounded by tall, green pines with an orange sun beyond distant snow-capped mountains.

I was fascinated by the people's dress. The *shalwar-khameez*, in an array of different colours, flashed before my eyes, interspersed with the common grey, apparently the accepted 'uniform' of the young male. Grizzled old men in stark white, baggy pantaloons and long shirts called *kortas*, ambled by, adorned with *loongis** wrapped around stiff-domed caps. There was also an abundance of armless jackets of varying checks, or heavy woollen waistcoats skilfully embroidered. Brown Afghan blankets and white or checkered cloths (such as the Arabs wear as traditional headgear) were slung over the shoulder or draped around the head and clutched at the throat, as protection from the dust raised by the horses' hooves.

The headgear was just as varied—white and gold skull caps, some multi-coloured with intricate designs; woollen Chitrali berets common to both sides of the frontier; and wound around the head in a variety of styles were turbans of every colour. Even footwear was far from uniform, although the famous Pathan *chaplis** were most in evidence. Long Afghan oriental shoes with curled-up toes, rope sandals, leather boots, and smart Western shoes caught my eye, and, in some instances, there was no footwear at all.

---

*There are now well over three million Afghan refugees in Pakistan.
*Loongi—Puggaree-type of turban worn around another form of headgear such as a domed cap.

I stood for a moment, listening to a cacophony of horses' hooves, the crack of a whip, the jingle of harness and the creak of carriage wheels which mingled with the ring of a modern bicycle bell and the unmuffled roar of a rickshaw engine. Merging with all these noises was the timeless cry of the vendor selling his wares.

Faces passed with strange, beautiful, unfamiliar features. I saw the aristocratic glance of a Pathan with those famous piercing eyes, the hawk nose and the strong chin; I was aware of fair-complexioned men from the north, and the flat Mongol faces with oriental eyes and wide foreheads beneath their thick turbans of the men from far beyond the Durand Line. Occasionally, like a ghost, a woman in a white *burqa* flitted past, her voluminous garments sweeping the dusty ground.

A small boy tugged at my sleeve, I stared at his cheeky grin but before I could take his photograph, he had fled, reminding me of Western children who ring a neighbour's door-bell and then scamper out of sight. Looking about me, I realized I was in that part of the bazaar devoted to leather goods—primarily the Pathan *chaplis*. I had walked down here on my previous visits. Now I noticed that money-belts, bandoliers, and gun-holsters were even more predominantly displayed beneath the ragged awnings of the little shops. I passed a small stall dealing only with padlocks, varying from the size of a thumbnail to that of a book. Then, turning a corner, I came upon a couple of men on either side of a big metal pan on rockers, which they pushed back and forth to make crushed ice. Farther along was a stall displaying cooked goats' heads and on the other side of the bazaar was a shop devoted entirely to tinsel decorations used for ceremonies such as weddings. Gaily-coloured garlands of gold and silver with red and blue geometric patterns, fringed with white frills, hung over the darkness of the interior. In front, a small boy sat on a cane chair with his bare feet on the rung of a crude wooden table weighted down with pink, orange and white plastic flowers spread out on green plastic leaves.

Soon I found myself walking beneath low, rickety wooden balconies. Mingling with the smell of fresh horse-dung and diesel oil, came a whiff of charcoal, kebabs, fresh unleavened bread, ripe fruit and the aroma of cardamom. Green tea scented with this fragrant spice is one of the pleasures of the Frontier, and I stopped to enjoy a cup at one of the numerous tea-stalls, where the vendors sit next to large copper samovars, their bare feet resting amongst the round handleless china cups and blue enamel teapots.

I was now in the famous Qissa Khawani Bazaar, Street of Story-

---

Chaplis—strong leather sandals.

Tellers, where, in former times, professional raconteurs would entertain the citizens and travellers would gossip and exchange news. I knew that farther on to the left was the Bazaar of the Coppersmiths, where trays, samovars and vases were made with loving skill and farther on still was the Chowk Yaad Gar, the central square and general meeting place of the Old City. Leading off from this scene of many a political rally, was the Bazaar of the Silversmiths and beyond that soared the white minarets of the Mosque of Mahabat Khan, dating from the seventeenth century.

I turned back; I would explore further another day. Any more, and I should get cultural indigestion. To explore Peshawar fully, or, in my case, to rediscover the city after five years' absence, needed time not to mention energy.

The next day a bomb exploded in one of the bazaars in the Old City, killing six people and injuring a number of others.

Not far from Peshawar lies the historic Khyber Pass, the smugglers' haven of Landi Kotal and the small town of Darra, notorious for its gun factories.

In 1986, the notoriety of all three was beginning to be recognized worldwide. Accompanied by an Afridi tribesman as bodyguard, I revisited Darra to find little obvious change. The gun shops were still markedly in evidence; men still walked through the bazaar carrying rifles and revolvers (Kalashnikovs, however, were now more numerous), and the air still reverberated to the sound of gunshots, but there was a sense of depression among the gun merchants.

'The government is closing down our factories,' complained one merchant bitterly. Another said 'Why should we receive all our weapons from China and the United States when we can manufacture our own?' As he spoke, he showed me a copy of an old Lee Enfield and a modern Kalashnikov. The men of Darra boast that there is no gun in the world they cannot copy, and, seeing the variety of weapons for sale manufactured locally, I saw no reason to disbelieve them. Their *pièce de résistance*, however, was a small gun in the shape of a biro pen. Only its heavy metallic texture belied its innocent appearance.

Back in the car, my bodyguard assailed me with stories from Afghanistan.

'The Russians attack the Afghan convoys. They order the people to give up their valuables and their produce. If the people don't obey they are shot. You can't believe how inhuman the Russians are. Over half a million Afghans have been killed, but the Afghans will always retaliate. They will never give up and they are clever, too. Now the Mujahideen inject water-melons with heroin, so, when the Russians stop a convoy of

20

The Khyber Pass: the starkness of those desolate mountains touched my soul immediately.

Landi Kotal stands at the highest point of the Khyber Pass and is reputed to be a haven for smugglers.

arable produce, they are paying a heavy price.'

He paused and went on:

'Peshawar is going to be another Beirut if the government doesn't take care. Over eight thousand refugees a month are pouring into Pakistan, and there are various factions, all of whom are being stirred up by foreign agents. Aside from agents of Afghanistan's Khad, we have spies from all the major Western powers here. A recent story going the rounds is of a French woman, working for the West, who married a German reputed to be in the pay of Russia. When she had obtained proof of his secret activities, she shot him dead. In the confusion of the arrival of the police and neighbours, she slipped away to an airstrip where a plane was waiting to whisk her away to the West.'

As we sped on to Jamrud Fort at the entrance to the Khyber Pass,* my mind went back to a time five years ago, when the modern heroin trade was in its infancy and when tribal skirmishes were a rare event.

A bargain is appealing to most people whether they are born in the materialistic West or in the esoteric East (where haggling is a way of life), and in 1981, 'armed' with the information that I could buy a short-wave transistor radio very cheaply in Landi Kotal, a small town situated in the Khyber Pass, I set off for the bus station on the edge of the Old City.

As I squelched through the churned-up mud, admiring the glistening chrome buses decorated with baubles, tassles and plastic flowers, I found myself surrounded by a crowd of potential passengers. Some carried sacks slung over their shoulders, while others balanced old suitcases, tied with string, firmly upon their heads. As I stopped at each bus I called: 'Khyber Pass?' until a small boy, standing on the steps of one of these colourful conveyances, pointed to the bus in front. When I looked hesitant, he jumped down and taking me by the hand led me to the bus he had indicated. This caused considerable merriment among the passengers leaning out of the windows of both buses. As I got on through the rear door, he called out: 'Goodbye, English!'

I waved farewell and dropped into a vacant spot next to some women on the back seat, beside the open door—a marvellous choice from the point of view of photography. The youthful conductor and my fellow passengers tried to persuade me to move to the front, but, knowing the back seat of buses, unlike in the jeeps and wagons, was generally reserved for women, I chose to stay where I was.

As I leaned back against the old cracked and stained leather, and new passengers brushed past me with milk churns, baskets, sacks of grain,

---

*Khyber Pass and Darra—closed to tourists since 1982, because of smuggling and the resulting lawlessness.

dirty bundles that contained God knows what, and the inevitable squawking chickens tied by their feet, I soon realized why I had been urged to sit elsewhere. It was not long before my knees and calves were bruised and my fawn slacks blackened with dirt. But it was not only my legs that were bruised. Psychologically, I was taking a beating. Phobic fears of dirt and disease, added to a phobia of being shut in and trapped, were almost overwhelming. Perhaps, if this ride up the Khyber had not been in some small way a personal pilgrimage, I should have fled.

My female companions kept gesturing to me, but trying to communicate with them behind their dusty *burqas* was almost impossible. When, however, the bus moved out of the 'station' (once a resting place for camel caravans), the woman immediately next to me boldly lifted the visor of her *burqa* and pushed it over her head. Her large deep blue eyes smiled at me in curiosity. Her face was strong and her features aristocratic, but her skin was so brown and weather-beaten from toiling in the fields that it was a mass of tiny lines. As her smile deepened, so did the lines, becoming like the cracks upon the leather seat beneath us. Her hair was long and dark, and looked thick and coarse. As I stared at her, taking in every detail of her face, I realized that this fascination was mutual. She reached out a boney hand and stroked my hair, which was very fine and bleached from the hot sun of Sind and the Punjab. All the while, she kept up a running commentary for her companions. I wondered to which tribe she and the other women belonged.

The Pathans, who form the largest tribal society in the world and inhabit over 100,000 square miles of territory, covering an area on both sides of the Durand Line, actually consist of a number of different tribes each with their own *khels* or clans. A fiercely independent and individualistic people, they are renowned for their tenacity and warlike spirit. Their way of life, built on the principles of revenge and honour in respect of *zar*, *zan* and *zamin* (gold, women and land) and hospitality, still exists to this day. It has been written that they are descendants of the ten lost tribes of Israel—a legend propagated by the Pathans themselves and further endorsed by Mogul historians, as well as some enthusiastic nineteenth-century English scholars. This theory, however, is disputed by Sir Olaf Caroe, the last governor of the N.W.F.P. before independence.* Whatever their origin, they were already converted to Islam by the end of the tenth century, and today they, remain staunch upholders of the Islamic faith.

Admired by the British, who were constantly at war with them, the Pathans still exercise their own laws (except in the 'settled areas') beyond

---

*See *The Pathans* by Sir Olaf Caroe (1958).

the jurisdiction of the government of Pakistan. As under the British, this generally applies to anywhere in the tribal belt away from the confines of the main roads.* In areas where foreigners are allowed, they are always cautioned not to wander far afield. Like their semitic Arab brothers, the Bedu, Pathan hospitality is such an integral part of their code of honour, that, if by some ironic twist of fate, a man should find himself seeking refuge in hostile territory, not only will he be granted sanctuary but he will be defended from his pursuers. Once he leaves, however, the original feud with his former adversary (his recent protector) will resume.

I had already had cause to enjoy that famous Pathan hospitality the previous day when I had been driven along a narrow country road to a small Pathan homestead. Behind the walls of a compound, where water-buffalo and goats lay tethered in a courtyard, I had been welcomed into a solidly built house of mud and stone. Although, to my surprise, it contained simple Western furniture (in the main room were a double bed, couch, chairs and a table, with pride of place given to a refrigerator), there was no plumbing. Electricity had been thought a necessity, but sanitation had not yet become a priority, and, when I needed to relieve myself, I was taken out into the yard and shown a small mud hut, which was filled with clean-smelling hay. When I declined a proffered rag and brought out a tissue, I caused much laughter among the family (some twenty souls in all), who had accompanied me into the yard.

The most notable and interesting feature of the house itself had been the turret on top. The head of the family led me up there via a tall wooden ladder, made from the branches of a tree. The turret was large and square, with slit-like openings from which we could see for miles around. Beneath these slits were a number of rifles and rounds of ammunition. At no time, however, did I feel in any danger—riding pillion on the son's motor-bike, while he talked over his shoulder to me, had been more hair-raising than the sight of that arsenal of weapons.

Jamrud Fort came into view. Built by the Sikhs, it is now the home of the frontier force, the Khyber Rifles.* We stopped just before the modern Bab-el-Khyber gateway to the pass. A slightly arched battlement spanned the road between two rounded towers, twenty to thirty feet high, each of which had a small cannon mounted on top. In the

---

*The tribal areas are administered by the Federal Government, through its agent, the Governor of N.W.F.P.

*Khyber Rifles—a frontier force made up of *levies* (local conscripts), formed by Robert Warburton in 1879.

brickwork of the towers were the customary slits, and from the small battlement flew a flag with a crescent moon and star—the universal emblem of Islam. As we stopped however, my attention was diverted to the open doorway of the bus and the passengers who were getting on and off. Here, as in Peshawar, they wore a variety of colourful dress, but not a man or youth passed me who was not wearing a bandoleer strapped across his chest, a revolver at the hip or a rifle slung over the shoulder. Indeed, many were weighed down by all three.

I was fascinated by these men as I had been with their Arab brethren. Unlike most of the Bedu, the Pathans have retained their way of life and have been little affected by twentieth-century progress. They still live unfettered by Western conformity, and their code of honour has remained inviolate, even if transistor radios and refrigerators are sometimes to be seen in their homes. These are a people who refuse to be subjugated. Glimpses into their way of life, and that of the Arabs in the sixties in Syria, make me wonder if man, in the pursuit of the comfortable life, loses something intrinsically valuable.

The bus moved off between the towers, and soon we were twisting and turning as we climbed up the fabled Khyber Pass. Much has been written about this notorious rugged defile, which has been trodden by many an invading army. Books on the British in India are full of heroic stories of skirmishes and battles fought for its control, and the very name Khyber summons forth all sorts of romantic images. Having read so much about it, I was prepared to be disappointed. I had been afraid I might find it a dull, and, perhaps, after all, an uninteresting place, but the very starkness of those desolate, barren mountains, with barely a tree or shrub to relieve their inhospitable slopes, had touched my soul immediately. The lonely picket posts on lofty crags all seemed to call out to the past, and the occasional train of pack horses or camel caravan, winding its way along narrow tracks worn into the sides of the mountains, evoked a time when life was lived at a more leisurely pace.

The great red walls of Shagai Fort, also built by the Sikhs, came into view. The defile narrowed and the crests of British regiments, carved and painted onto the cliff face, became clearly visible. The higher we climbed, the more the horizon was taken up with numerous fortifications on lonely promontories. Then we reached the highest point of the pass— the small town of Landi Kotal, which marks the end of the transcontinental railway.

Although set amidst a vast barren land, as well as astride the annals of history, Landi Kotal did not appear to suffer from the sleepy, small-historic-town syndrome. As soon as I jumped down off the bus, the usual contingent of small boys grabbed at my arm or danced in front of me, pointing to my camera with the inevitable older youth intervening on my behalf. Sent off giggling, they stood about in the shadows of the awnings overhanging stalls where huge wicker baskets invitingly displayed all manner of fruits.

Having come to the end of my film, I looked around and spotted the small *chai**-shop I had patronized the year before. Close by were the steps which I knew led down into the bazaar, where, along with the old stalls, were modern ones filled with an unbelievable range of electronic goods. I sat with my back to the daylight, sipping the fragrant green tea, aware of the interested and curious glances of the old men on a few wooden benches in the darkened interior.

While changing the film in my camera, I recalled the time a year before, when from this very *chai*-shop, I had boarded a pick-up truck to take me to the frontier some five miles distant. Moments later, the truck had been involved in a head-on collision. Although both vehicles had been severely damaged, no-one had been injured. Squeezed between the driver and his companion, I had had all the breath knocked out of me, but except for a few bruised ribs, I had not suffered from the incident. I had been struck though by the speed with which the matter had been settled (the paying over of a number of rupees by the guilty party on the directions of the crowd that had quickly gathered), and also by the attitude of the elderly man who had taken charge and the drivers and passengers involved in the accident. There had been no 'post mortem' they had simply gone about their business with a philosophical air, and I had been given a seat on another pick-up

At Torkhum, the hotel and P.T.D.C. had been closed, although the border was still open with both pedestrians and trucks passing through in each direction. Leaving the company of a youth, who was eagerly trying to sell me whisky* and hashish, as well as telling me how I could smuggle out a pound of heroin, I had wandered across to a knoll overlooking the mile-long 'no-man's land' into Afghanistan. At my feet had lain three playing cards—the Queen of Hearts, the six of Spades, and one face down. The last one I had left undisturbed.

On returning later to my hotel in Peshawar, I had felt compelled to open my journal at the page where I had copied down a poem from a framed parchment hanging in the manager's office of a hotel in Rawalpindi:

Chai—tea.

*Pakistan is a dry country and it is forbidden for visitors to import any type of alcoholic beverage. Alcohol is only sold to Christian inhabitants and non-Moslem foreigners on purchase of a liquor permit. Tourists can only obtain these at First Class hotels and the amount of alcohol is restricted and expensive.

Torkhum marks the frontier with Pakistan and Afghanistan.

The Clock of Life
The clock of life is wound but once
And no man has the power
To tell just where the hand will stop
At late or early hour.
Now is the only time you own.
Live, love, toil with a will
Place no faith in tomorrow, for
The clock may then be still.

The Road North

I was bound for the Kalash valleys near the Pak-Afghan border.

There are two ways to reach Chitral from Peshawar and either one is a gamble. If you prefer to gamble with time, there is the uncertain flight with the extra hotel bills if the weather is inclement over the mountains, if, however, you prefer to gamble with your life, to go via the Lowarai Pass (a two-day bus and jeep ride) is the obvious choice. It was not the Lowarai, though, which I was worried about, but having to break my journey in Dir—a place with a bad reputation.

The bus ride began at five in the morning. Being the only woman on a crowded bus, I was obliged to take the 'honoured' seat up front with the driver. This was a debatable privilege, as I was practically on top of the leaking fuel tank and had an unrestricted view of the road ahead. As soon as we moved out of the station, the driver's desire to break all records in reaching his destination became evident. Assailed by petrol fumes, I was to spend most of the journey shutting and opening my eyes as the bus's wheels narrowly missed cyclists, dogs, cats, goats, chickens and children; one poor duck was the exception.

We sped through the somnolent outskirts of Peshawar to stop just after sunrise at a teahouse for breakfast. There, Gerard (a French journalist and the only other foreigner on the bus) and I became acquainted when he introduced me to a Pakistani dish similar to American French toast (pieces of bread dipped in a liquid of egg and milk and then fried), but without the maple syrup and cinnamon. Then the bus raced on through the Vale of Peshawar—a veritable bread-basket for the North-West Frontier.

This fertile area, ringed by mountains, stretches to the Khyber in the west, to the Kohat Pass to the south, in the Indus in the east and the Malakand Pass in the north. It is a region of orange groves, rice paddies, and alternating with the seasons, fields of wheat, barley, maize, corn and sugar-cane. Out of the side window, I gazed upon a pastoral scene of cultivated fields, streams, rivers, and small villages tucked away among the orchards. Every so often, when the bus was forced to slow down, I was rewarded with glimpses of daily life—a naked boy standing before a communal tap, splashing himself with water, his young limbs sparkling in the sunlight; an ox pulling a cart heaped with produce, the driver nodding on his seat, the end of his whip lazily draped over the animal's back; the white minarets of a tiny mosque, half-hidden by a grove of lush green trees.

Sometime just before noon, we came to a halt at a railway crossing. As we waited for the train to pass, I noticed a truck, colourfully decorated as usual, waiting on the other side of the track. The road, at this point, was very narrow, and I doubted that the truck and the bus would be able to pass one another. The train rumbled through. I glanced at the driver. His face was set with grim determination. As soon as the last coach had passed, both vehicles moved forward and came to an abrupt stop, bumper to bumper. The driver of the truck glared at us through the windscreen, gesturing wildly, but we remained motionless and eventually he gave way. A little farther on, we made a halt at a bus station to have the fuel tank checked, and I took the opportunity to buy something to eat and drink from the vendors selling *chai*, soft drinks and samozas (spiced vegetable pies). A number of passengers muttered to one another and gestured towards the bus. I wondered if they mistrusted its capabilities. Their places were taken by some armed police with two prisoners in chains.

The torment continued as we hurtled across the Fusufzai Samah—a vast plain irrigated by water canals (channelled from the Swat River), and diverted through a man-made tunnel beneath the Malakand Pass. Then we were among the foothills and were making the gradual ascent towards the narrow cleft of the Malakand Pass. The Malakand, although greener than the stark barren ridges of the Khyber Pass, was almost as rugged and, like that famous pass, was notable for its battles. I knew that the surrounding area, too, was full of historic interest, as two major battles between the armies of Alexander the Great and the local inhabitants had been fought in this region

As we sped on towards Dir, through mountainous country dotted with narrow terraced fields and over the Panjkora River, I remembered that the Malakand had not only been important to the early invaders, and the Moghuls, but also to the British. In 1895, the first battle for the Malakand Pass had taken its place in British military history, and, later, in 1897, a big uprising had occurred among the tribesmen of the Malakand. It was during this period that Churchill, while serving in the Malakand Field Force, was stationed at Chakdarra—an occasion commemorated to this day by a notice outside the fort which is strategically located on the banks of the Swat River, where the road to Upper Swat diverges.

Here there was a checkpoint, but when the bus came to a halt, I was disappointed to find that we were not allowed off, as I should have liked to photograph the picture-postcard fort. Within moments of the police coming on board with their registration book for me and Gerard to sign, the bus was again on its way.

Until the siege of Chitral in 1895, and the first battle for the Malakand, the British knew little about the country around the Malakand Pass, as the region north of the Lowarai (north of the Malakand) had not yet been penetrated by them. Up until then, the farthest outpost in that whole vast region was to the north-east in Gilgit. Events leading up to the siege read like a Shakespearian tragedy (with overtones of farce), full of sibling rivalry, betrayal and murder, but if you do not share my enthusiasm for learning about such 'goings on', I suggest the next page or two be skipped.

In the 1870s, Chitral lay at the extremity of the territory governed by the British. Its capital, also named Chitral, was situated less than fifty miles from the main water-shed of the Hindu-Kush, from which flowed the Oxus into Turkestan (already being swallowed up by Russia) and Central Asia, and the Chitral River which flowed on into Afghanistan to become the Kunar. For some years, the British, nervous of Russian intentions on the other side of the buffer state of Afghanistan, had wanted to control the external affairs of Chitral and have guardianship over its northern passes. With this in view, Major Biddulph was sent, in 1877, to Chitral to establish friendly relations with the Mehtar, but nothing concrete came of the mission. In 1885, fearing that a Russian offensive was imminent, another mission headed by Sir William Lockhart, was despatched to Chitral. This time, friendly relations were established with the old Mehtar, and Lockhart spent a year in Chitral and the neighbouring territory, checking out its defences.

Although Aman-ul-Mulk was a ruthless ruler, putting down his enemies with intrigue and murder, he was both an astute and forceful character and strongly supported by the people of Chitral. While he stayed on the throne, the British were confident Chitral would remain loyal to them. When however, in August 1892, the old Mehtar died, the British looked on with growing concern at the anticipated upheaval in the royal family of Chitral. At the time of his father's death, Nizam-ul-Mulk, the elder of the two sons (out of seventeen offspring of the late Mehtar's four legitimate wives—and those who were not so legitimate) most favoured to take ove the throne and subsidized by the British, was in Yasin, as governor to Chitral's north-eastern territory. His younger

30

brother, the other heir-apparent, Afzul-ul-Mulk, seeing his opportunity, grabbed the throne, murdered most of his brothers and marched on Yasin, sending Nizam fleeing to the safety of the headquarters of the political agent in Gilgit. With the people of Chitral supporting the new claimant to the throne, the British gave him their recognition. Two months later, however, an uncle, Sher Afzul, an old enemy of Afzul-ul-Mulk's late father, left Afghanistan, where he had been in exile, hot-footed it across the Hindu-Kush with a band of followers, shot the governor of one of the valleys en route and arrived at the walls of Chitral in the dead of night. The commotion aroused the young ruler who, upon investigating the disturbance, was immediately shot down. Once more the Chitralis supported their new ruler, and the British felt obliged to stick to their principle of recognizing the will of the people.

It was not long, however, before Nizam, hearing of the death of his younger brother, decided to claim the throne for himself. Promising the British, among other things, that they could station troops in Chitral, Nizam received the doubtful consent of the political agent in Chitral, Colonel Durand, to go about his business. Crossing over into Upper Chitral, Nizam collected a large force of Chitralis from that region and marched on Mastuj. Troops sent by Sher Afzul to repel the enemy promptly went over to Nizam and Sher Afzul fled back to Afghanistan. Once in control, Nizam asked the British for one of their officers to be stationed in Chitral. So, in January 1893, another mission was sent to Chitral, to report on the situation. Although Nizam was not a model ruler, he appeared to be a loyal ally of the British and to be firmly in control of Chitral. At the end of May, Robertson retired to Gilgit, and, in September, British troops were withdrawn to Mastuj (sixty-five miles north of Chitral), designated as the future headquarters of the political agent, and, for the next ten years, all was peaceful in Chitral.

Unfortunately, for Nizam, knowing the British looked upon such acts unfavourably, he refrained from murdering the remaining brother who posed a threat, thereby sealing his own fate. On the first of January 1895, Nizam was shot dead, while out hawking, on the orders of his half-brother Amir-ul-Mulk. The British, worried about this new development and with only one officer and a small escort in Chitral, sent troops to reinforce those at Mastuj; and Major Robertson, now the political agent in Gilgit, set out once more for Chitral.

Meanwhile, still more skulduggery was afoot.

To the south of Chitral, on the western fringe of the State of Dir, lay the Pathan state of Jandul. Umra Khan, the chief of that state, who had also gained power by murdering his brother, decided that this would be an opportune moment to expand his growing territory. To this end, and with a force of 3,000 men, he marched on Chitral, despite the Lowarai being covered in snow. At first these forces were met with strong resistance by the Chitralis, who regarded the Pathans as hereditary enemies, but Amir-ul-Mulk was a weak ruler, unrecognized by the British and ready to change his allegiance at any moment to suit his purpose. Consequently, lacking leadership, the Chitralis became divided among themselves, and, as the British did not want to intrude upon a domestic 'squabble' without instructions from their government, Chitrali resistance collapsed, and Umra Khan succeeded in capturing Kila Drosh, the principal fort on the southern frontier of Chitral.

It was at this inauspicious moment for the British, soon after Robertson had arrived in Chitral, that the arch-villain, Sher Afzul, appeared on the scene again. Getting wind of events going on in Chitral, he 'escaped' from the confinement imposed on him by the Amir of Kabul (to please the British), and joined up with Umra Khan in Drosh. The Chitralis, demoralized, defected to Sher Afzul, and, with the forces of Umra Khan, advanced in a wave towards Chitral.

In the meantime, Amir-ul-Mulk had been deposed and held in custody by the British, who had ignored the demands of the enemy to withdraw to Mastuj, and the young Shuja-ul-Mulk, a mere boy, had been recognized as the provisional Mehtar of Chitral. Robertson, with four hundred men, under the command of Captain Colin Campbell, had occupied the fort. Unknown to the British Government of India and to the forces of Chitral, however, two detachments despatched from Mastuj with ammunition and engineering supplies had been ambushed en route for Chitral. A British officer had been killed along with a number of sepoys, another was wounded and two British officers were captured by Umra Khan. Communication with Mastuj had been severed.

On the 3rd of March (in Robertson's words, 'a fateful day')* a strong reconnaisance party under Captain Campbell and accompanied by Robertson, left the fort. In the ensuing battle, Campbell was shot through the knee, two Kashmiri officers and a number of sepoys were killed, and a British officer fell mortally wounded, later to be carried heroically back to the fort by his comrade, Surgeon-Captain Whitchurch. Under heavy fire, Robertson rode post-haste to the fort to raise the alarm. With the aid of a contingent of Sikhs, Campbell and his men were able to withdraw to safety within its walls. And so began the siege of Chitral, which was to last forty-seven days and nights.

On the 7th of March, news of the siege reached the Government of India, which promptly tried to negotiate with the enemy. On the 14th of

*Chitral: A story of a Minor Siege by Surgeon-Major George Robertson.

32

March, the last ultimatum was sent to Umra Khan, ordering him to quit the country forthwith. If he did not withdraw by April 1st, he would be compelled to, and the British made ready for the relief of the garrison. When news filtered through about the ambush of the two detachments and the capture of the British officers (later released unharmed by Umra Khan), the British ignored their ultimatum to Umra Khan and speeded up their plans.

However much one may condemn colonization and its inherent evils, there is no doubt that the North-West Frontier attracted men of exceptional valour and leadership. To this day on the Frontier, the British are remembered with warmth, as was proved to me, when, in Chitral, one old man with tears in his eyes asked me why the Queen did not send troops to fight the Russians in Afghanistan and protect Pakistan from a possible invasion. But it was not only courage which marked the defence of the fort and the subsequent battles and relief of the garrison, but also the remarkable planning of such an operation. In the depths of winter, a small contingent, under the command of Captain Kelly, was sent from Gilgit across the Shandur Pass, over 12,000 feet high, while a much larger one was sent from Peshawar. This southern force, under Major-General Sir Robert Low, had to build bridges over turbulent rivers, ford mountain torrents and cross over high ranges of mountains. Just to mobilize such an army, equip it with its own food and supplies and send it into unknown territory, heavily defended by the enemy, was no mean feat.

At the Malakand, the British met with strong opposition. In the ensuing battle, a detachment of the Frontier Guides turned the tide by scaling and holding onto the heights—known to this day as Guides' Hill. Then, fearing that a large army would not be able to arrive in time to relieve the garrison before supplies ran out, General Low despatched a small force of levies on ahead to cross over the Lowarai with the help of the Khan of Dir. On the 13th of April, Colonel Kelly reached Mastuj, having made his famous crossing of the Shandur Pass. On the 17th of April, Umra Khan, abandoning the siege, made his last stand against the British and on the same day, Lieutenant Harley, who had covered the retreat of Captain Campbell and his men on the eve of the commencement of the siege, led a successful sortie outside the fort. On the 18th of April, Umra Khan retreated to Afghanistan with a hoard of treasure, and Sher Afzul was captured by the British. The siege was over. Two days later, Colonel Kelly, after much hardship and engaging the forces of a local Chitrali chieftain, arrived at the fort in time to share in the rejoicing at the relief of the garrison.

It was not only the British who displayed courage, as they were the first to admit, but the enemy as well. Umra Khan, the Pathan leader, true to his code, had defended the two captured British officers when they were in danger from fanatical and backward tribesmen in Dir. Two stories, related by George Younghusband in *The Relief of Chitral*, can still be heard in Chitral to this day. One tells the tale of a young Pathan boy who went to watch the battle for the Malakand. Shot in the arm, he was told by the British surgeon, who feared gangrene would set in, that his arm was beyond saving and that he had two choices—amputation of the limb or death. The boy chose the latter, but the arm healed and the boy lived. The other remarkable tale tells of a drummer who kept drumming under fire of the British. Every time he was shot down, he rose to his feet and went on drumming until death finally released him. The siege and relief of Chitral was an heroic story.

Arriving in Dir, I forgot about history; my mind was on the present, preoccupied with the town's reputation and wondering what I would find there.

From a distance, the small town of Dir, nestling in the foothills below the Lowarai, looked attractive in the late afternoon sunshine. When, however, the bus pulled up at the one and only hotel, I felt apprehensive. The three-sided, two-storied building looked derelict and uninhabited; many cracks showed in the dirty white-washed walls, and the fading dark green paint was peeling. The garden, filled with rose bushes, fruit trees, shrubs and conifers, was overgrown. The fountain in the centre was still and the water at its base looked stagnant. A number of local inhabitants were lounging around the fountain, viewing myself and Gerard with lustreless eyes. We turned to the bus driver, who had accompanied us into the grounds, and checked again to see if this was indeed the only hotel in Dir. As the driver confirmed this was so, a man appeared on the balcony above, holding a bunch of keys, and gestured for us to join him. We stepped onto the porch, through a tumble-down doorway, climbed up a steep, broken spiral staircase alongside a completely destroyed wall, and out onto the ramshackle balcony. Dressed in a very unkempt grey *shalwar-khameez* and wearing a gold skull-cap, the manager shuffled forward. He was short in stature, and his crafty evil-looking eyes gleamed out of a sallow face partially hidden by a pointed, thick, black beard. The face of the devil, I murmured to myself, aware of the men below gazing up at us, their ill-concealed curiosity temporarily overcoming their lethargy.

The manager opened the doors to two rooms and stood watching us with a sly grin on his face. I felt instinctively that Gerard also was uneasy and was no more eager to discover the merits of our accommodation than

I. Gallantly he offered me first choice of the rooms, though there was little to choose between them; neither had seen a duster or broom in weeks, if not months. I walked cautiously into the shower-room, with its antiquated plumbing and cracked Asian toilet, and turned on the tap. No water. I turned to the manager.

'Yes! Yes! *Pani** will come!' The grin broadened and became more satanic.

I shuddered, noticing the bed with its dusty quilt and the broken-down chest below the closed painted-over windows that led to a rear balcony, The broken-down table at the foot of the bed confirmed the furniture was in keeping with its surroundings. When the two men left, I tried the tap again. I was longing for a shower after the long day's travel. In the West, people generally give little thought to the act of taking a bath or shower and changing into clean clothes—but for me it is a compulsive necessity. One, two, sometimes even three or four showers a day plus a constant changing of clothes is the norm. Now in this dirty room and the stressful atmosphere of the hotel, my desire for a shower was threatening to open the flood gates of my phobia against dirt. For some years now it had been successfully held in check, but every so often there were moments when those familiar feelings of panic would start the heartbeat racing—and this was one of them.

When the water came, it came in a trickle and I just managed to complete a wash-down and to fill a bucket for later before it went off again. Feeling refreshed and decidedly happier, I joined Gerard on the main balcony where he was looking quite relaxed, reading a paperback. He smiled and waved me to an old wooden chair next to him.

'I had a look at the bazaar. Nothing to note. Now I've ordered some *chai*,' he said contentedly.

I flopped down, noticing the broken cane seating and the grimy surface of the small table in front of us. The tea, when it came, was brought by a small boy who looked no more appealing than the youths still lounging around the fountain below. The blue enamel teapot ran true to form and was badly chipped as were the thin china cups. To say there was an air of decay about the place would be an understatement.

At least the tea was hot, and, as I sat drinking it, I studied Gerard. He was not a good-looking man in the accepted sense, but he had a kindly rugged face and an easy confident air about him, which I found reassuring. I was glad of his company. Usually, I prefer to travel alone, but the atmosphere here made me feel uneasy and unsure of myself. Gerard had already made a crossing of the Lowarai a couple of years

---

* *Pani*—water.

before and was well used to the vicissitudes of the subcontinent, having opted to live in Kathmandu.

After a while, he suggested that we go into the bazaar in search of food. Not trusting the local inhabitants (the first time I had experienced such a feeling when travelling in a Moslem country), I carefully made sure the door to the balcony was locked and then hesitated. Should I leave my new Nikon in the room or take it with me into the bazaar? A quick flash of a knife in the darkness and my camera would be gone. Leaving it in my camera-bag, wrapped in a sweater, I rejoined Gerard on the balcony. I was not looking forward to our sortie into the bazaar of Dir.

Over the Lowarai

Dir, which is the capital of the State of Dir, now one of the Merged Areas, appeared to consist of one jeep station, the bazaar, the hotel, and a closed government resthouse, where Gerard had stayed on his previous trip as a guest of an official from Peshawar. Perhaps, as it was dusk, I was blind to the town's attractions. The bazaar was devoid of people, and the shack-like booths were nearly all closed.

At the farthest end of the bazaar, we came to a small *chai-khana**serving kebabs and tea with a samovar and brazier at the entrance. The two main walls of the long narrow room were lined with threadbare and very dirty *charpoys*, and, in front of them, were two long, wooden tables. We sat close to the entrance, preferring it to the claustrophobic depths of the interior. Next to me, a young hippie-style Westerner sat eating a kebab. From time to time, he tried to converse with me, but as he was obviously high on drugs, I found it difficult to communicate. Opposite us sat two men whose tattered clothes and unkempt appearance made me to turn to Gerard, who appeared to have lost a little of his earlier aplomb. I was just about to speak to him when the characters opposite us started spitting. Spitting is not an unusual habit in the East, but that they should do it inside an eating establishment and not into a spittoon, was most unusual; then, too, that they should spit across the table, so that their spittle hit the mud floor at our feet, seemed doubly offensive. I felt Gerard recoil beside me. It was as if the men had been deliberately placed there, by some inventive film director, to emphasize the broken-down atmosphere of the town.

The kebab, when it came, was practically inedible, and both Gerard and I pushed away our plates after only a couple of bites and ordered tea. Meanwhile, the 'hidden film director' added another touch to his scenario. A handsome, dark-skinned young man with bushy hair that hung down to his shoulders, and wearing a threadbare loin-cloth that

Chai-khana—Tea house.

37

revealed naked buttocks, came in to beg for food. His eyes held a crazed expression. Gerard seemed as mesmerized as I. The beggar took the bread offered to him and sat on the ground; between mouthfuls, he lifted his face to the moon and howled. Gerard and I stood up; I shivered as we passed. If Gerard had not been clutching his camera bag I think I might have taken hold of his hand. The evil lurking in the shadow of that bazaar was tangible, horrifying and all-powerful.

Later, when I was to relate my experiences of Dir to Chitralis and other travellers, I received knowing looks and similar stories of harrowing experiences. Nowhere, since I was once stranded in the Medina of Marrakech, where the severed heads of the executed were once impaled on spikes in the Djema'a el-Fna, have I experienced such a feeling of physical fear—a fear brought on solely by the sense of evil. The history of the State of Dir, with its endless bloody feuds and backwardness, and the cruel reign of the late ruler made me wonder if the evil of man leaves its mark on the very stones where he has walked.

Arriving back at the hotel, Gerard and I retired to our rooms for an early night—we would have to be up early the next morning in order to catch the jeep for Chitral. As soon as I entered my room, I was aware that something was wrong. Switching on the dim electric light, I saw that the door to the balcony was ajar. I snatched at my camera bag, but it was empty; both my camera and travelling alarm-clock were gone.

Poor Gerard. Knowing he could speak the language, I knocked on his door and together we marched into the garden, where the manager was talking with some of the locals. The sly grin never left his face as I related what had happened and Gerard added a few sentences in Urdu.

To our surprise, the Police Chief, a thin, unattractive middle-aged man, accompanied by what seemed an unnecessarily large number of subordinates, arrived within minutes. He was obviously eager to dispense justice as soon as possible. Sending his men in all directions, he accompanied me and Gerard to my room. It did not take him many seconds to discover that one of the windows which had been painted over had a weak bolt. Obviously it had been forced open, for on the bed beneath the sill was a tell-tale dusty footprint.

The Police Chief turned to me with a smile, which lit up his dark pock-marked face. 'I think this man is a very social thief, don't you?' and he burst out laughing.

I laughed, too—in spite of my frustration—and my heart warmed to this man, who, so far, was the most human individual we had encountered in Dir.

Besides Gerard and myself, there was only a German couple staying in the hotel. The police poured into their room to ask them some questions, while Gerard and I halted hesitantly on the threshold. The boy, fair-haired and bearded, lay in one bed, while the girl sat shivering on the other. Scraps of food, dirty plates, mugs, empty cigarette packs, fruit peelings and toilet tissues littered the table and floor. They knew nothing about the burglary, and I was inclined to believe them. I doubted whether either of them were capable mentally or physically of carrying out the theft—their addiction was too far gone. I left the room, wishing I could leave Dir there and then.*

Obtaining a police report for my insurance, I told myself I was lucky I had had the foresight to leave my other camera in the care of the manager of the hotel in Peshawar. If luck was with me, I could easily fly there from Chitral, collect my camera and return the next day. Conveniently, I forgot about the gamble when it came to flying. Telling myself tomorrow would be a better day, I said goodnight to Gerard.

Although I was up early the next morning, Gerard told me it was unlikely we should leave before noon, as the jeep owner was waiting for more passengers. While I drank endless cups of tea, Gerard spent the next three hours making trips to the jeep-station, to haggle with the jeep owner. It turned out there were only two other passengers wanting to make the trip, and, according to Gerard, the longer the owner held out, the more impatient we would become, and the better price he would be able to obtain from us.

Finally, Gerard, perhaps thinking I might just take the jeep without him, agreed a price and I sighed with relief. I couldn't leave fast enough and not even the sight of the antiquated jeep with its cracked windscreen could bring my spirits down now that I knew we were leaving Dir.

Preferring not to be squashed in the middle, I was delighted when Gerard volunteered to sit next to the driver. In the event of the jeep going over the edge of a precipice, at least I would be able to jump clear, I thought unrealistically. Our two other passengers, clean-shaven and with smiling faces, arrived on the scene. They were better dressed than any of the men I had seen so far in Dir, and their Chitrali caps were set firmly upon their heads. Loaded down with sacks of merchandise, they climbed into the back, while I got in beside Gerard and waited expectantly.

*Peter Mayne in his book *The Narrow Smile* said of Dir: 'Dir is a sad, furtive, enclosed little state for all the beauty of its valleys . . . Dir has a feel of sullen nothingless, and I was glad to go . . .'

Fosco Maraini, too, described Dir in disparaging terms and at considerable length. On arriving in the district of Chitral, his final comment was most pertinent. 'Even the features and expressions and gestures of the people we met seemed to reflect a less tragic and tormented spirit than that prevailing among the folk beyond the pass in the land of Dir.'

'What's he waiting for?' I asked looking in the direction of the man we had paid.

'He only owns the jeep. He doesn't do the driving.'

'Oh.'

At that moment, a young man with a short wiry body sauntered up. His intelligent brown eyes gave us a quick once-over, and as he stroked his small clipped moustache, he said something to the owner and then climbed in behind the wheel. I was sure he could not be older than eighteen.

At last that evil town lay behind us and the depression that had enveloped me for the past eighteen hours began to lift. The narrow, steep mountain track climbed and twisted around hairpin bends. The air was fresh and filled with the scent of pines. Even the loss of my camera did not now dampen my spirits.

Sometime in the early afternoon, we came to a wide, fast-flowing torrent which swept right across the track. No doubt it was similar to one of those that General Low and his troops had had to ford in their effort to reach Chitral; I wondered what it must have been like in the depths of winter in that difficult spot. I also wondered how we were going to make the crossing, seeing that not only was the current strong, but everywhere large boulders and rocks were sticking up out of the surface. I gave an involuntary gasp as the driver changed gears and plunged in. Half-way across, the jeep came to a standstill. The driver and the two Chitralis motioned for me to stay in the jeep while they clambered out, but I decided against it—my weight would either prevent the vehicle being moved at all, or cause it to be rocked over on its side with me in it.

It astonished me that within moments of our being stuck, both police and the army were on the scene to give a hand. At first I tried to lend my weight to shifting the jeep while Gerard busied himself taking photographs, but with my boots full of water, I soon stood back and let them get on with it.

Gerard seemed unperturbed. 'We were stuck in the same place the last time I came over the Lowarai,' he said. 'I expect it happens to every vehicle. They'll get it out somehow. But if there are landslides the other side of the Lowarai, we could get held up for hours.'

I was not reassured. As we talked, I noticed that a little way up a mountain slope, there was a pile of thick wooden planks cut from recently felled trees. Touching one of the soldiers on the shoulder, I pointed to them. He had a word with the driver and within minutes, they had scrambled up the slope and dragged one down. Using it as a lever, they soon had the jeep free and once more we resumed our journey.

Now the pines gave way to deodars, the fragrance of which I inhaled happily. I was at last beginning to enjoy myself again; my old adventurous spirit was returning.

As we continued to climb steadily, I thought of the number of people who had asked me why I liked to journey to remote and desolate regions of the world, where there are few amenities and I have to put up with constant discomfort and the possibility of danger. Like other travellers, it is a question I often ask myself when the going gets tough; but ever since I can remember, I have been restless, forever questioning things, always searching for an elusive something and never being happy unless on the move, experiencing the new, the strange and sometimes the dangerous. Goals such as a home, security and a career have never been mine, for I have no belief in the permanence of things. Such was my personal makeup, that at school, in a narrow post-war xenophobic Britain, I was not a favourite among my teachers. Being expelled from school for rebellious behaviour did not endear me to my father either. And in spite of (or because of) his penchant for philosophical wanderings among literary essays, it was not long before I began my own wanderings both literary and physical. The highs and lows of travel can be equated with the wonder, joy and pain of growing up—perceptions are sharpened and awareness becomes greater. Some cynics, whose goals in life are always equated with material assets, say that to travel is to try to capture one's childhood—and perhaps they are right. But the joy comes from the constant 'rebirth', from seeing new horizons in the landscape and in the mind as well; making new discoveries, having new ideas.

Still wrapped in thought, I noticed, without even flinching, the outside wheels skim the very edge of the precipice.

Just before the Lowarai Pass, we stopped for a break. The tea-house, built of cedar, was a simple affair with a stone floor and rough-hewn tables and chairs also made from cedar. As the tea was brewing, Gerard and I watched a group of men travelling along the track beyond the open door.

For the first time since leaving England, I experienced that familiar feeling of unreality when I am suddenly plunged into a world which is not only foreign to me, but also seems to transcend the barriers of time.

Dressed in homespun wool and animal skins with a bare arm or leg showing here and there, the men passed by, either walking or on horseback. Those on foot carried huge axes—executioners' axes, I thought, giving an involuntary shudder, though they were obviously to cut wood. Most had ancient-looking guns (they may well have been old muskets) slung over their shoulders. One, I noticed, wore animal skins wrapped around his feet and calves. How I envied Gerard with his two Nikons!

Remembering how during the siege of Chitral, Umra Khan had to defend his two British captives from the backward and fanatical men of Dir, I asked Gerard, who seemed to know much about the region's history, if they were local inhabitants.

Gerard shrugged his shoulders. 'I'm not sure. Probably. They're not Pathans. We're now really beyond the tribal belt. These people are mostly of mixed blood. Very backward and primitive. Dir is an unattractive place in my book. An official in Peshawar told me that not so long ago they had to bring helicopter gunships to subdue the populace. How true that is, I don't know. From all accounts the last Nawab was a cruel ruler and half crazy. He loved to seduce women and kept hundreds of ferocious guard dogs. Have you heard the legend of Shabeena? It's supposed to have happened in living memory.'

I shook my head, and Gerard told me a story I was to hear several times more. It is a tale Chitralis relish, though details of the account differ, depending, I suspect, upon the story-teller's imagination. The version given to me by Gerard runs as follows . . .

> Shabeena, whose name means 'Flower of the Night', was the beautiful younger sister of one of the Nawab's wives. While on a visit to the palace *zenana*,* Shabeena was unfortunate enough to come to the notice of the Nawab. Knowing her husband's lecherous ways, the wife sent word to her father, who brought the girl home and immediately went in search of a husband. But promises of a rich dowry did not bring forth any suitors, for the Nawab's retainers had been sent out in advance to intimidate all eligible men. In desperation, the father turned his attention to a wild and notorious outlaw, a Pathan named Motamar. This fearless man, having heard of Shabeen's charm and beauty, consented and promised the father he would kill his bride before ever allowing her to fall into the hands of the perfidious ruler.
>
> Shortly after, the young couple, with Motamar's two brothers, his father and a few followers, were forced to flee over the border into neighbouring Chitral, where they were given sanctuary in a house belonging to the ruler of that state. The Nawab now resorted to bribery and trickery. He sent word to the political agent in Chitral that Shabeena was really married to one of his men and that Motamar had kidnapped her. The outlaw soon found himself in jail, pending an enquiry into the legality of his marriage, and local soldiers were sent to separate Shabeena from her husband's father and two brothers and remove her to the palace. The soldiers met with stiff resistance, and, in the ensuing fight, Shabeena fired on them with a pistol. One of Motamar's brothers, fearing the worst, upheld the family honour and shot Shabeena dead, before he himself fell mortally wounded.

*Zenana—women's quarters.

42

It is said that all the inhabitants of Chitral attended Shabeena's funeral, and that some Chitralis composed a song equating Shabeena with a swallow who flew over the Lowarai, never to be seen again because she lay buried in Chitral, where, at night, mysterious lights were to be seen over her tomb. Motamar, who had escaped from jail on hearing of his wife's death, was captured en route to Dir, to seek revenge, and jailed again. He was finally released, whereupon he and his family were given a generous piece of land in Chitral. Shabeena's death, in true Pathan fashion, had saved the family honour, and the story of her beauty and virtue soon took its place in the folklore of the Frontier.

When Gerard came to the end of the story, I turned to see our driver sitting by the open fire, a few feet away. He had a rolled cigarette paper in his mouth and was drawing on some tobacco which lay in the palm of his hand. Having only had a few puffs, he got to his feet.

'Okay,' said Gerard. 'Let's go.'

'You mean, he's going to actually smoke it while he's driving?'

Gerard looked at me indulgently. 'What's the difference?'

I shrugged my shoulders. Somehow, it seemed that to drive and smoke hashish at the same time was rather like driving with one hand on the wheel and the other clutching a bottle of Scotch.

'With luck we should reach Chitral before dark,' Gerard remarked hopefully.

'*Insha'Allah!*' (God willing), I murmured under my breath as I climbed up beside him.

We crossed over the Lowarai Top at an altitude of over 10,000 feet. There was nothing particularly outstanding or hair-raising about the gradual ascent, but, cresting the top, the view of the valley below, stretching into the distance with the mountain slopes on either side deep with pines and deodars, was breath-taking. As far as the eye could see in all directions the mountains continued unbroken. To the west, I knew, was the turbulent land of Afghanistan, to the east, Upper Swat, and to the north lay Chitral. Not only was I struck by the grandeur and beauty, which, at such moments, like Churchill, I find hard to describe, but I was also overwhelmed by the sense of geography and history that the Lowarai inspired in me. Early invaders must have seen it as I now saw it; their eyes had beheld the same folds and ridges of the mountains, those same pine-dotted slopes, sometimes in the snow, sometimes, as now, bathed in summer sunshine. I wondered what thoughts they had harboured as they had journeyed north.

Then we were winding down the other side. True to form, we ran into the inevitable landslide and its attendant bulldozer, leaving me wondering how long it had taken to drive the heavy ponderous vehicle to that spot. I remembered hearing that the government, with the army and help of the Chinese, had once started to build a tunnel under the Lowarai, but that it had been abandoned because of lack of funds.* It is the avalanches and the landslides that makes the Lowarai so dangerous, and which cause Chitral to be cut off from the outside world for six months of the year (except when the 'plane can get through).

Stopping for a hurried meal of curried chicken at another roadside tea-house, we dropped down into the valley and to the small town of Drosh, which seemed to consist mainly of a long bazaar through which we went at a cracking pace. Then we were out on the track once again.* Now the road was on the flat, running alongside the river. Unlike General Low and his men, we did not have to build bridges when we came to cross those rushing, turbulent waters.

As we continued on, only a few feet above the water, great overhangs of rock towered above us, barely inches from the upper rails of the jeep. Then over a suspension bridge and before us there rose up, in the distance, the snowy summit of the magic mountain of Tirich Mir. We had arrived in Chitral. At the jeep station, Gerard and I parted company. I could not help but feel the poor man was glad to be rid of a relative novice to the subcontinent.

---

*The tunnel is again under consideration.
*In 1987, the road was metalled from Drosh to Chitral but although Afghan buses and wagons now endeavour to make the trip, many break down. The journey can still take one or two days, with the inevitable stop in Dir, which has not improved with time.

Chitral

Chitral lies in the heart of Marco Polo land, nestling between the rugged mountains of the Hindu-Kush—'Slayers of the Hindus'. According to historians, many slave children brought from Kashmir and beyond died on their winter slopes. The game of polo* is said to have originated here (at least the inhabitants of Chitral say this—those of Gilgit tell a different story). The town was the birthplace of the Chitral Scouts, British troops were besieged in the Mehtar's fort in 1895, and, if this isn't enough for Chitral to lay claim at history's door, Churchill slept here.

On a summer's day in 1981, a few days after arriving in Chitral, I set off along the main thoroughfare towards the bazaar, and looked across the yellow wheat fields to the red-hued walls of the fort and the chalk-white minarets of the Grand Mosque and the place beside the river where I had walked a year ago. The Chitral River runs through the wild rugged countryside until it meets the Kunar and flows on into Afghanistan. Beneath the crumbling walls of the fort lay the tents of the dispossessed Afghans and I could see smoke rising from their camp fires. Even as I stood there, an Afghan thundered by on his large white pony, with the tail of his turban and his cloak-like blanket billowing out behind him, sending me straight into a time warp which was broken only by an antiquated jeep hurtling towards me, overloaded as usual. Made to seat six, or eight at a pinch, the roofless and doorless vehicle screeched past, with its fifteen or so occupants clinging to one another with arms, legs and cloaks seemingly flying in all directions.

I continued walking until I saw a man standing on the dusty roadside, selling slices of water-melon. He beckoned me over and grinned, showing a row of gleaming white teeth tipped with gold as he did so. Pointing the tip of his long curved knife towards the juicy red and green slices lying in the dust, he suggested I try a piece but the dust put me off. I

Polo—Probably really originated in Persia around 500 BC.

The Grand Mosque and the Old Fort, Chitral.

Chitral fort on the Chitral river, scene of the famous siege of 1895.

lingered for a while as he served others less squeamish than myself. The tail of his dark blue turban, flecked with gold, hung down beside his lean sunburnt cheek. As with so many Afghans, his intense brown eyes were the most arresting feature of his face, almost eclipsing the scarred cheek, the long hawk nose, the sensual lips and thrusting jaw. Dressed in blue pants, long-sleeved shirt, and black embroidered waistcoat, he was a handsome vital figure. No doubt, before long, he would become a freedom-fighter and return with the Mujahideen across the high dangerous passes of the Pak-Afghan border. All too often, these passes are booby-trapped by the Russians. I had heard a number of stories of children's toys, cigarette-lighters and other such eye-catching articles left lying on the ground, which, when picked up, exploded in the person's face.

A little way on, I reached the main part of the bazaar. On either side of the narrow dusty road, the small wooden shacks, with their open fronts, were drab, greying in colour and without decoration. Unlike the souks of the Middle East and North Africa or the bazaars of the big cities of Pakistan, this market was without many of the exotic smells of the East, and most of its goods seemed mundane; but it was not entirely without colour. The rays of the sun streamed across the road landing on bolts of brightly coloured cloth, some edged with silver and gold. In front of them tailors sat cross-legged on the ground, turning the handles of old Singer sewing machines, while customers waited patiently.

I quickened my pace—I needed a permit from the Deputy Commissioner to visit the Kalash valleys and it was getting late. If there were too many people before me, or the D.C. had to attend court, the afternoon siesta would intervene, and another day would be lost; I had already been twice before.

Out of the corner of my eye, I could see the old man who sold apricots and walnuts, and the occasional lapis lazuli brought in by the Afghans. He waved. I paused. I could not ignore him, and there was no way, even if I could speak Chitrali,* to explain this insane Western compulsion to get things done, which I have always felt is symptomatic of a materialistic society. I gave in and smiled. '*As salaam Alykum*,'* I said and shook hands.

'*Alykum—salaam.*'

He dusted off the top of a sack of walnuts and called out to a young boy who was rolling the frame of a bicycle wheel down the incline of the bazaar, to get us some tea from the nearest *chai* shop. Then, placing a

*The other name for the Chitrali language is Khowar. It is a spoken language belonging to the Dardic group of Indo-European languages.
Salaam Alykum—Peace be upon you.

small stool in front of me, he passed a grimy hand across his watery bloodshot eyes, and, smiling again, patted me on the shoulder and told me to sit down. Rummaging through another of his sacks, he pulled out some apricots and thrust some in front of me. His hands were filthy. I swallowed hard. My stomach seemed to turn over and my heart-beat accelerate. I could feel beads of sweat beginning to form on my brow and the palms of my hands go moist—my phobia of dirt and disease was threatening to take over, but I was trapped. I could not refuse for I knew that to do so would give offence.

My father, who speaks to me only on the 'phone, is often fond of quoting a certain philosopher who said that to reach a state of grace in 'heaven', one should conquer at least one fear a day. By that reckoning there is no doubt in my mind that Valhalla will be my final destination. As any phobic personality will know, life between rising and going to bed at night (unless one is afraid of sleeping lest one should never awaken) can be one long adventure full of pitfalls and dramas.

Generally speaking, though, when I am travelling, I am not afflicted by my phobia, for whatever may have produced it in childhood, it is now a symptom of acute emotional stress aggravated by too many outside pressures. The difficulties I run into when travelling do not usually provide me with stress—they are merely a challenge. Having said that, there are always those unexpected moments, generally exacerbated by something else, such as the evil atmosphere of Dir or the fear of being trapped which I felt on the bus ride to the Khyber, which will suddenly press the panic button—and this was one of those moments.

I gulped down the tea as quickly as etiquette would allow and rose to my feet, having feigned eating the apricots but in fact having hidden them in my pocket. The old man, delighted at my accepting his hospitality, shook my hand in farewell.

Passing out of the gloom into the sunlight, two young girls collided with me. They looked up with a giggle and scampered away. In the bazaar of Chitral, women above the age of puberty are literally conspicuous by their absence.*

I walked on past a *chai* shop where a young boy was sitting amidst the tea-cups, and on past the kebab stand around which Chitralis sat gossiping. Near the top end of the bazaar, I passed a group of Afghans bestowing their favours upon a shoe-shine man and came face to face with a large placard which displayed Persian script and the drawing of an eye. Smiling at me, the man wearing the placard took hold of a youth to examine his eyes. I grinned and continued on, wondering how many patients the 'eye doctor' would treat during the course of the day and

*See Chapter One.

49

The main bazaar of Chitral with Afghan horsemen in the foreground and Tirich Mir in the background.

Above: The Afghan Mujahideen displaying their bandoleers.

Facing page: An eye 'doctor' in the bazaar of Chitral.

Below: An Afghan customer waits patiently by his tailor in Chitral bazaar.

remembering how, the year before, I had come across a travelling 'dentist' in the valley of Bumburet. Not only had he had a most horrendous collection of lethal looking instruments, but also, a number of sets of false teeth. To my Western mind, it seemed inconceivable that such a charlatan ever had any patients, but such rogues prosper in an area where medical facilities are poor.

Walking on, I came to the wooden bridge which spanned the *nullah*,* virtually cutting Chitral in two. As I crossed over I could not help but notice the severed heads of goats (a delicacy in these parts), with their eyes still open, stuck to the girders at the base of a large telegraph pole.

Once on the other side, I turned right and began the climb to the D.C.'s office. I wondered how long a stay he would grant me in the Kalash valleys. The year before I had only been given ten days. The new D.C., who had not long been in office, was reputed to be favourably disposed towards the Kalash, and I was hopeful that my request for two weeks would be granted.

I waved to the *dhobi* (laundry man) who was beating clothes in a stream on a rock, and then stopped to gaze out over the Chitral Valley, to the majestic summit of Tirich Mir which at 25,230 feet, is the highest mountain of the Hindu-Kush. Regarded as a magic mountain that is inhabited by 'fairies' (supernatural beings), by the locals, its solitary peak now shone brilliant white in the early morning sunlight. In the evening, under a clear sky, its snowy crest would turn a soft pink, reminding me of the topping on a strawberry ice-cream cornet.

As I continued on up the hill, I mused that if I were lucky enough to get permission for two weeks in the Kalash valleys, it was still a pitifully short time. After my visit, I intended to follow the route of Marco Polo and cross the Shandur Pass to Gilgit and then go on to Hunza and Skardu. Aside from wanting to travel over the pass and see these various places, I was also interested in discovering if there were any traces of the Kalash outside the valleys, as at one time, in the distant past, their territory had reached as far north as Mastuj.

This time, my visit to the D.C. was successful beyond my wildest expectations; he gave me a permit to spend one month in the Kalash valleys. Returning to the P.T.D.C.,* I found a dinner invitation awaiting me.

One of the most endearing traits of the Chitralis, besides their love of music and dancing—for which, next to polo, they have an abiding passion—is their hospitality to the foreigner. Not even the Pathan could be more generous. During both my long stays in Chitral, merchants,

Nullah—dried up river-bed.

53

Goats' heads are a delicacy in Chitral.

peasants, officials and hotel owners had all made me welcome in their homes.

Prince Burhan* was a portly, bearded man with a merry twinkle in his eyes, but a man it seemed, who did not take too kindly to Western women. Each time we had met (we had met several times but that was my first invitation to his house), I had received a courteous bow, but, unlike other Chitralis, he never offered me his hand in greeting.*

Situated on a small plateau, shaded by elm and poplar trees, Prince Burhan's home overlooked the valley and the town of Chitral, some seven or eight miles to the south. Although he kept cattle, his pride and joy was a Markhor goat, an animal native to the mountains of the Hindu-Kush and now almost extinct (although it is still possible to obtain a permit to shoot one of these rare creatures). Three times the normal size, they have long cork-screw horns instead of the usual small ones; the coat is soft and furry with a long ruffle coming down over the neck and chest, the beard is long and the face, more refined than the domestic variety, is enhanced by large intelligent eyes. The prince only had one of these splendid animals left, having given away the others, as although rare, they are apt to strip everything green within reach. He had tried to cross-breed them with the ordinary goat, but the result of this experiment seemed small and puny in comparison with the majestic Markhor.

Once the sun had set, the view from the plateau had been duly admired and the Markhor photographed and extolled, I was led into a small cabin-type house, nestling among several buildings and outhouses. I am not sure what I expected on that first visit, but I was certainly surprised.

To begin with, I was not required to leave my shoes outside the door as is customary in most Moslem houses. I entered a small white-washed room, where gaily coloured curtains decorated the small windows. The two main walls were lined with couches, and down the centre was a long table covered with a white linen cloth, on which was a tray of glasses and a large glass pitcher filled with a pinkish liquid. At the far end of the room, on wooden pedestals, were two life-sized statues of a Samurai warrior and a Geisha girl. On the wall, virtually hidden by a protective covering, was a Samurai sword. From the plain cedar wood beams overhead hung twinkling Japanese lanterns, glinting in the electric light. Beside me my escort, Sharif, a young Chitrali administrative official, whispered into my ear that during World War Two, Prince Burhan was reputed to have fought on the side of the Japanese.

---

*Pakistan Tourism Development Corporation.
*The title of Mehtar expired when princely privileges were abolished in 1972.
*In Pakistan, one can still meet elderly orthodox Moslems who will frown upon shaking hands with a woman who is not a close relative.

54

Prince Burhan's Markhor goat.

'He's absolutely crazy about the Japanese,' Sharif added, quite unnecessarily, as I surveyed the room and smiled at two 'hijacked' Japanese tourists.

As I sat down opposite Sharif, another Chitrali official and an English diplomat from Islamabad, Prince Burhan enthusiastically handed the two Japanese beside me a heavy volume of photographs. Not surprisingly, they contained snap-shots of his trip to Japan, which he spoke about with enormous enthusiasm. How ironic that here was I, hungering for everything his country had to offer, while he, in turn, hungered for another culture further east. His princely kingdom was not enough for him, as indeed my country was not enough for me.

Dismissing the bearer, he dispensed the drinks himself in the same way a Pathan or Beduin host would do, all the time keeping up a stream of conversation.

'You know, experience is the best school, but the fees come high,' he said, handing me a glass of what I guessed was fruit juice.

'You won't believe this, but I am really the reincarnation of Jesus Christ. It comes to me in my dreams. The world is crazy. Politics are nothing but publicity and complicity.' He paused and looked at me, his eyes twinkling. I wasn't sure if the prince was having us on, or whether he really believed what he was saying, but the elderly Englishman sitting opposite me looked ill at ease.

'I think all men are equal and the same. It is only climatic conditions that change the colour of a man's skin. All men are brothers. The United Nations should be for peace, not a political arena.'

When Prince Burhan had finished serving drinks, the bearer came in with tea and biscuits and a large iced cake, which the prince again insisted on serving himself. Then, as so often happens in any Chitrali gathering, whether it is in a peasant home, or in the upper echelons of Chitrali society, some form of music was to be enjoyed. While we sipped tea, Sharif was called upon to sing. Usually attired in a safari suit, and invariably carrying a baton, Sharif cut a sharp figure whether imperiously riding in his jeep through the bazaar, shaking hands with the populace, or riding his grey-white stallion down to the polo-ground. Dressed now in a pink safari suit, his mop of fair hair and nordic blue eyes shining brightly, he cut a handsome boyish figure as he stood before us singing some popular Chitrali folk songs, and I noticed that even the staid English diplomat relaxed under his charm and mellifluous tones.

As in an Arab household when the talking and entertainment was over, there came the serious business of eating. Unlike every other household I had entered in Chitral, where you sat on the floor and dined off a cloth laid at your feet, we were led into another room where a dining-table was laid for us.

As is the custom, hardly a word was spoken as we enjoyed potato croquettes, rice, dhal, Lady's Finger (a vegetable which looked and tasted like a cross between eggplant and squash) and curried chicken that were placed before us. To round off the evening, we adjourned back to the Japanese room for a dessert of stewed dried apricots (native to the area), apples which had been stored over the winter, and a delicious pink custard—the last being a very popular dish in Pakistan. (Later, when travelling in the Northern Province, I was to find a small establishment given over solely to the sale and consumption of this delightful dessert.) Once the meal was over, the visit came to an end. Such was an evening at the home of Prince Burhan.

56

The Road to Upper Chitral

My month in the Kalash valleys went all too quickly and I returned to Chitral sorry that I could not have stayed all summer. After my initial blunder of violating the taboo surrounding the Bashali House, I had been accepted by the community, although the short time available did not afford me the chance to get to know the people well, except for Saifullah the leader and official representative of the Kalash. He had been my guide and interpreter and had quickly become my friend. My knowledge of their customs and way of life was necessarily seen through Saifullah's eyes, rather than through personal experience, and my notes for a possible book were sparse. I needed no cajoling to plan a return visit if I should be allowed to renew my permit.

Now to travel north into Upper Chitral would give me the chance of seeing if there were still signs of Kalash culture outside the valley, as, according to Saifullah, his people had at one time inhabited the entire region up to Mastuj. I was also curious to see if there was any evidence of the Kalash culture on the other side of the Shandur Pass which cuts through the mountains of the Hindu Raj—a natural barrier between Upper Chitral and Pakistan's most northerly province.

Some people collect rivers, others mountains. Since arriving in Pakistan I had developed a 'thing' for passes. I had already been up the Khyber and had crossed over the notorious Lowarai. Now I was keen to cross the historic Shandur to Gilgit where I would be travelling in the footsteps of Marco Polo (Colonel Kelly and his men had marched in the opposite direction to relieve the British, besieged in the Mehtar's fort in 1895).

I remembered the first part of the journey well, as I had travelled the road the previous autumn on my way to Kosht,* a few miles south-west of Mastuj. Then I had been in the company of the tourist officer of Chitral, who was taking advantage of the Moslem holiday, Eid-ul-Azha,*

Kosht—the name means 'hidden valley'.

57

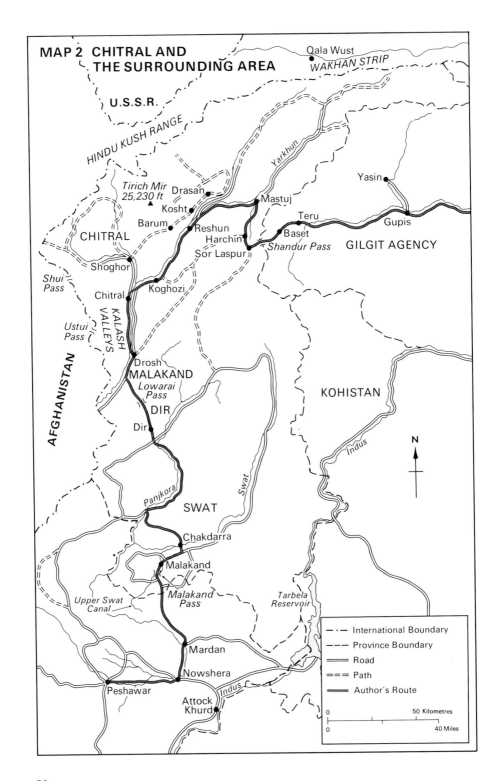

MAP 2 CHITRAL AND
THE SURROUNDING AREA

U.S.S.R.

Qala Wust
WAKHAN STRIP

HINDU KUSH RANGE

Tirich Mir
25,230 ft
Drasan
Kosht
Barum
Reshun
Harchin
Sor Laspur

Mastuj
Teru
Baset
Shandur Pass
Yarkhun

Yasin
Gupis

CHITRAL

GILGIT AGENCY

Shoghor
Shui
Pass
Koghozi
Chitral
Ustui
Pass

KALASH VALLEYS

KOHISTAN

Drosh
MALAKAND
Lowarai
Pass
DIR
Dir

AFGHANISTAN

Indus

N

Panjkora

Swat

SWAT

Chakdarra
Malakand
Malakand
Pass

Tarbela
Reservoir

Upper Swat
Canal

Mardan

Nowshera

Peshawar
Attock
Khurd

Indus

-·-·- International Boundary
- - - Province Boundary
——— Road
=== Path
▬▬▬ Author's Route

0   50 Kilometres

0   40 Miles

58

to make one of his infrequent visits home to see his wife. An intelligent and informed man, he had been a mine of information about the terrain we were passing through.

The road ran through the lower part of the bazaar, below the P.T.D.C., over the stone bridge across the Chitral River, and on into narrow gorges, running just above and parallel to the river. Then we began to climb. Every so often, the mountain of Tirich Mir would loom up on our left, its glistening peak seeming tantalizingly near, then we would again drop down and pass into its shadow, as the track wound its way through some narrow defile, only to twist around and meander up into the sunlight once more.

Approaching the village of Reshun, we entered a narrow gorge with the turbulent river on our left and inaccessible cliffs on our right. An ideal spot for an ambush, I thought, remembering that it was here that Lieutenants Edwards and Fowler, on their way to Chitral with ammunition and engineering supplies, had been waylaid by the forces of Sher Afzul. They had been fired upon from well concealed *sangers** and bombarded from above with boulders, rocks and stones. Then the road wound up a long spur before dropping back down to the river to the village of Reshun. We passed the former British post and the adjacent polo-ground, where, in 1895, during the lull in the fighting, the enemy had asked for peace negotiations, followed a while later by a request to hold a polo-game! The British officers, invited to attend the match and the subsequent dancing, were then seized by Sher Afzul's men and kept bound hand and foot overnight before being force marched to Chitral. En route they met up with some of Umra Khan's men who took them into their custody. In Chitral they were allowed to communicate with the British in the besieged garrison—done to let those inside the fort know what had happened to the British detachment in the hope of depressing the spirit of the defence. The two captives, however, were well treated by both Sher Afzul and Umra Khan and were later released unhurt by the latter.

As we travelled on, it seemed as if the very cliffs and rocks were alive with memories of the past. Not far from the small hamlet of Koragh, we started down towards a narrow twisting gorge. Both sides lay in deep

---

*Moslem holiday. Two months and ten days after Ramadan, (in Pakistan, the d becomes z) the festival of Eid-ul-Azha is held by Moslems to commemorate the sacrifice of Ismail, the Prophet, by his father, Prophet Ibrahim. On this occasion goats or sheep are sacrificed in the name of God and the meat is used for preparing food which is served to family members, guests and the poor. The day before, the annual Moslem pilgrimage to Haj takes place at the holy shrine of Ka'aba in the city of Mecca in Saudi Arabia.

Sangers—hideaways in the rocks.

shadow. This was the notorious defile where Captain Ross and Lieutenant Jones with a small party, en route to give assistance to Lieutenants Edwards and Fowler, had also been ambushed. They, too, were fired upon from the *sangers* on both sides of the river and pelted with rocks and stones from above. The subsequent battle resulted in the death of Captain Ross and a number of his men. Gazing on the darkened recesses of those high rocky cliffs, I was struck again by the courage of those nineteenth-century British soldiers, who had fought in this harsh barren region.

Now the road continued to climb until eventually we dropped into the valley of Booni. In this part of Upper Chitral, the earth is red as are the mud-brick farmhouses set in the fertile green fields and shady orchards. Just beyond the village, we had a blow-out. While the driver, helped by some of the passengers, changed the wheel, I stood gazing up ahead to where a suspension bridge crossed over the river. I knew that once on the other side, the way was barely negotiable by jeeps, for the narrow track leading to Kosht resembled little more than an uneven rocky path more suitable for mules than a four-wheeled vehicle.

Now it was mid-summer. Then it had been autumn and the valley of Kosht had been aglow with the colours of the red and yellow maple trees, the yellow of the poplars and the copper of the plane trees; together, they had competed with the snow-crested peaks and the green of the fertile slopes for an admiring glance from one who saw the beauty, but did not have to suffer the harsh winter to follow. It had been nearly sunset when we had driven into the village, that time of day when the encircling mountains had turned red, pink and mauve, their peaks rising as far as the eye could see, so very different from the rolling, serried ranges near Bumburet and the Lowarai. Here I had felt shut in, truly dwarfed by those mighty, jagged peaks.

Behind me, I could hear the Chitralis changing the wheel and laughing among themselves, as I continued to reminisce about the valley of Kosht where I shall not easily forget being offered roast sparrows for dinner, nor the moonlit trek to the tourist officer's house farther up the mountainside, the frogs jumping across our path and the gleam of an oil lamp in the window of a lonely homestead; nor the uncanny silence that had engulfed the whole valley, interrupted only occasionally by the sudden mournful howl of a dog.

A shout to my rear announced that the jeep was serviceable once more. Laughing and chatting, the Chitralis clambered into the back of the jeep as I and another passenger got in the front. A few hundred yards further on, we ploughed our way through a deep slough of water that oozed out into thick red mud at the sides. I tried to put from my mind

In the valley of Kosht, children play among the mud bricks.

that one reason why the jeeps had a tendency to slip over a cliff edge was because the brakes failed.

Soon the road became a narrow track, climbing up around hairpin bends and through wide mountain torrents. At the foot of one particularly precipitous ascent, the jeep stopped and the driver told all those in the back to get out. To me he turned and said in English: 'Very dangerous,' then closed his eyes and started to recite the first sura of the Koran before putting the jeep into gear. The road was scarcely wider than the width of the vehicle. On every turn, he had to reverse right to the brink of the precipice. Beside me, the passenger who had taken over the Koranic chant still mumbled on, while the others scrambled up the mountainside on foot. Arriving at the top before us, they waited, laughing gaily as though they were on some festive picnic. Nothing ever seemed to dampen their spirits.

Shortly afterwards, our way was blocked by a landslide which had swept away most of the road. Well over a thousand feet below, the river wound through the bottom of a narrow gorge. The men packed large stones along the edge of the cliff and we all moved forward along the track to watch the driver negotiate his way over the landslide, his wheels but an inch from the edge of the cliff. Nervously I took photographs, afraid of distracting him, but for him it was all part of the day's work.

We reached Mastuj, a large fertile valley surrounded by high mountains, at about five in the evening. The jeep stopped in the small, almost deserted bazaar, where, pocketing my seventy rupees, the driver summoned an old man and a young boy who were passing to help me with my baggage and lead me to the fort of Prince Sikander. The prince was a friend of Haider Ali Shah, the owner of the Mountain Inn in Chitral. I protested, but the old man, without a word, shouldered my rucksack and started marching along a narrow track that wound between stretches of grassland, before disappearing among a grove of tall trees. The young boy cast me such a hurt look when I lifted my heavy camera-bag that I handed him my water-bottle and flask, bringing a happy grin to his face. The track was rough and stony, and I was very glad that I did not have my rucksack to carry, after all. Riding boots with wooden soles and heels are not made for walking.

The trees thinned out, and, situated on a knoll above a wide plain, stretching to a lake and to the mountains in the distance, there rose the dung-coloured walls of the old fort. We passed beneath one of the towers, beyond the main gate, past a well and around to an apple orchard at the back. Having spent some time on the North-West Frontier, I had become blasé about forts. Whereas I once viewed every new fort I came upon with fascination, noting all its individualistic features, I now went

62

On the way to Mastuj we had to negotiate a landslide.

by them almost as casually as one would pass a supermarket in an English town. Few forts can dazzle the eye after one has beheld the huge rambling walls of Akbar's great fortress on the banks of the Indus at Attock. Now, however, as I delved into my pocket to give the old man and the boy a small gratuity, I felt keenly the brooding presence of those high walls.

Prince Sikander's retainers appeared and led me to a table placed beneath a tall apple tree where I met the prince himself. I had seen him a number of times in Chitral playing polo, which he played with much verve and daring. Now, as he strode briskly across the grass to greet me, I thought again what a handsome young man he was with his blue eyes and fair hair. These together with his name Sikander, meaning Alexander, gave further credence to the legend that the inhabitants of Chitral date back to the time of Alexander's invasion. While we drank tea, we discussed my plans for crossing the Shandur Pass. Haider Ali Shah had already informed him of my plans and had enlisted his help in finding me a horse and guide.

It was not long before one of the servants returned, accompanied by a short wizened old man who, on meeting me, smiled but eyed me shrewdly. Luck was with me. For a hundred rupees a day (just over three pounds), including food and lodgings for him and his horse, he would guide me over the pass. For an extra thirty rupees he would carry my rucksack. As I quickly agreed to all this, Murad continued to weigh me up. Like Sikander, he was fair and had blue eyes, but there the resemblance ended. Murad was in his sixties with a thin face, hollow cheeks, a hook nose, pointed chin, and thinning grey hair coming down over his receding forehead in a widow's peak. From time to time he gave an embarrassed smile when spoken to by Sikander, who asked me if I would be willing to do the same as the locals and do two stages the first day for the same price. I readily agreed. Ignorance is indeed bliss.

It was a pleasantly warm evening and when Prince Sikander suggested dining outside, I was happy to consent, having already savoured the guest-quarters which led off the orchard. The dusty sitting-room, with its faded, upholstered chairs, tiny window and the curtained-off bedroom, containing only a single high bed and a small table, were airless and very dark, and I was glad to return to the open air.

Dinner, which consisted of curry and thick tasty bread containing goats' cheese, was an agreeable meal taken up mainly with discussion of the Russian-Afghanistan conflict. As night fell, I became even more aware of the oppressive nature of those high walls, barely a hundred feet away. When a servant came bearing a lamp, only the face of my companion and the table between us were visible. Before retiring for the night, Sikander presented me with his visitors' book to sign. Flicking through the earlier pages, I was interested to see that it dated back to before the Second World War.

All night I left the lantern burning but sleep would not come. The air of decay, with the tiny windows of the sitting-room permanently sealed against the weather, was stifling. It was a shame, I reflected, that these royal establishments were allowed to fall into disrepair, although, from the outside, Sikander's fort appeared in a better state of repair than the old Mehtar's fort in Chitral. There, I had had the privilege of visiting the women's *zenana* where I had been entertained kindly and generously, but all the while I had been conscious of that same sense of decay.

I awakened at dawn and washed using a bucket and a tin bath filled with ice-cold water that had been placed in a small room containing a flushless Asian toilet. Although I had found the quarters airless and claustrophobic, I was extremely grateful for Prince Sikander's hospitality and he had proved to be a genial and interesting host. Out in the sunlight, I was greeted by a view of the lake shrouded in mist. The valley lay tranquil in its early morning beauty, yet somehow remote and mysterious.

While I breakfasted on bread, goats' butter and tea, Murad arrived, leading Tooruh, a black pony with two white spots on his forehead. Murad forced a smile and made it plain that I should have been ready and waiting to leave. Gulping down the remainder of my tea, I quickly collected my gear, with the aid of one of Prince Sikander's retainers, and set about trying to organize how best to carry it for the three-day journey ahead. The rucksack, although bigger, I knew was easier to carry than the heavy camera-bag, but Murad was not convinced, and after repeated attempts to tie the rucksack on to the back of the saddle, leaving me no room whatsoever, he gave up and instead tied on the bag containing films, spare camera and various odds and ends. With Prince Sikander's retainers openly laughing, and much to my embarrassment and to Murad's obvious bad temper, I led the pony to a large rock in order to mount. There, standing precariously on the edge, I hauled myself with difficulty into what was left of the saddle and slung my small hunter's pouch, containing my favourite camera, across my chest. Murad, who I had by now realized had little relish for the task ahead of him, hoisted my pack onto his back and grabbed Tooruh's reins. I just had time to snatch my water-bottle and flask from the servants, and retrieve Tooruh's reins, before Murad set off. My trek across the Shandur Pass had begun.

Over the Shandur

We went through a grove of trees and then we were out in the open, travelling along stony paths through ground crusted over with saltpetre. Every so often, fast-flowing streams cut across our path. Tooruh forded them without difficulty, while Murad, in spite of his age, jumped from rock to rock with apparent ease. When we reached the jeep track, running below a steep cliff, Murad informed me by way of gestures, Urdu and the odd word of English, that he wanted to return to his home to fetch a forgotten jacket, and that I should continue on slowly. It was early and the air still chilly, but the sun's rays promised a day of extreme heat. I was glad when Murad disappeared over a rise to be left with just Tooruh and my thoughts for company.

For about an hour I rode along without sight or sound of another living soul. The track dropped down into a narrow valley with rocky mountains rising steeply on either side. In front of me lay craggy peaks topped with snow. The mountains here had an even greater majestic sweep and more grandeur about them than in the Kalash valleys. My thoughts went back to when I was a child. Then I had hungered for wild desolate places, but had known only the Cornish coast. When I had grown older, the Alps of southern France had bewitched me, and later still I had become drawn to and enchanted by deserts. Now it was the rugged mountains of the Frontier and the Northern Areas, where barrenness and beauty lay side by side, that intoxicated me. Here the mountains made the Alps seem somehow insignificant—now that I had been captivated by the wildernesses of Pakistan, the beauty of lesser mountain ranges could only act as balm upon inner yearnings; they could never again satisfy.

My peaceful poetic mood came to an abrupt end when I was all but garrotted by a downed telegraph line. A lone horseman appeared from nowhere and trotted past. 'Peace be upon you,' he gaily called. As I returned his salutation I noticed in the distance, Murad walking towards me. Without a word he threw his jacket over the front of the saddle and my happy mood was momentarily dampened. His crusty personality and

66

Murad holds Tooruh for the author at the beginning of their trek over the Shandur.

scowling face did not endear him to me, and we travelled on in silence.

After only two hours in the saddle, I was in agony. It was years since I had sat on a horse and the last time, in northern California, I had only ridden for an hour, and then over flat, easy ground. My legs now were suffering from cramp, due to lack of circulation, and one stirrup being longer than the other did not help matters. After considerable arguing, Murad let down the shorter stirrup and tied it with a piece of string—one of the many useful items I always carry with me.

We began to climb. Below us, by the river, I could see mud-brick houses amidst fields of ripening wheat, some already harvested, and others of bright green corn. We climbed higher. Now there were no mountain streams. The water-bottle I had filled at the fort was already empty and the flask, topped up the previous day by the Chitralis from a stream and unchecked by me because of my hasty departure, was unfit to drink. Instead of being crystal clear, as was usual, it was full of all manner of foreign bodies. As Murad had forgotten to tell me to refill it at the last stream, we now went thirsty.

On we climbed, ever higher. The track wound around the mountain-side which rose sheer on our left, while huge sandstone boulders to our right sloped inwards, forming a sort of tunnel open to the sky. The sun blazed down, burning my face, and I was parched with thirst. I felt totally exposed. The sun's rays bounced off the tops of the sandstone cliffs and beamed down upon me mercilessly as though we were under a magnifying glass. The track levelled out over shale and shingle and I had to keep a tight rein on Tooruh, lest he stumble on that uneven and treacherous ground. When at last the trail began to drop to the cool valley below, I relished the shade offered by the groves of tall conifers and lines of poplar trees, and was overjoyed when we came to water! We stopped beside the first stream we reached, where, with difficulty, I tried to dismount. Not only did the cumbersome bag on the back of my saddle make it awkward, but my legs had lost all feeling. Murad must have felt sorry for me because not only did he help me down, but, to my surprise, he unscrewed the top of my flask and handed me back the cup filled with clear cool water, tasting sweeter than any vintage wine. To my even greater surprise, when I returned the cup, Murad actually smiled—and before I had a chance to recover from this, he offered me an apple too.

He led the way off the jeep track, down through some rough grassland, towards a small mud-brick house. We had arrived at the hamlet of Harchin—a distance of some twenty kilometres. I had been in the saddle for five hours—one day's stage. It was already noon, and although I had agreed to do the two stages in one, I prayed Murad would change his mind and stop there for the night.

68

Murad again helped me to dismount as a young man came forward to welcome us. When my feet hit the ground, I stumbled and would have fallen if he had not sprung forward and caught me. While he massaged my aching knees and numb legs, Murad unsaddled Tooruh with barely a glance in my direction; obviously our truce was at an end. Rising to my feet, I hobbled over to the horse to offer him a piece of apple, but Tooruh was as unfriendly as his master and would accept neither apple nor sugar. Murad, perhaps thinking Tooruh did not conform to Moslem etiquette when it came to giving and receiving, tried to force-feed Tooruh with the sugar, in spite of my protestations.

While I sat on the wooden porch, waiting for the forthcoming tea, Murad brought my pack and bag and laid them out on a *charpoy*. Relief! Obviously he had decided that, after all, one day's stage was enough for the greenhorn. Fortified by the tea and the thick tasty bread, I leaned back in my chair while Murad dozed in front of me. The young man disappeared inside and returned moments later, proudly decked out in his soldier's uniform. As I fumbled to focus my lens, Murad roused himself, and, to my dismay, began resaddling Tooruh. I watched in silence as he tied on my bag. It was one o'clock—the very hottest part of the day. He had to be kidding! I couldn't do another twenty kilometres! The soldier, whom I had temporarily forgotten, pulled impatiently at my sleeve. In my general anxiety I took his photograph but completely forgot to take down his name and postal address. Hot and dusty, and with still aching limbs, I climbed back into the saddle. Pride alone prevented me from begging for mercy. After only one five-hour stage, my trek had taken on the feeling of an endurance test.

For a while, we followed a meandering stream and rode beneath a line of poplar trees. In spite of my fatigue, I was enthralled by the grand sweep of the mountains surrounding me, but when we came out of the shade and began to climb again, the heat hit me and Murad's figure, with my blue rucksack on his back, began to waver before my eyes. I could no longer focus properly. The heat shimmered around him. He became unreal, a mirage. Again, my throat was parched with thirst. Again, my legs had lost all feeling. My buttocks were sore and the bag pushed painfully into the small of my back. The right stirrup slipped and I cried out. Impatiently, Murad turned around. Five minutes' break and we were off again.

After an eternally long afternoon, the sun dipped in the sky and we began a long descent towards cultivated fields. At last we were nearing a village. Every time Tooruh scented another horse, he quickened his pace. Now he wanted to hurry. Perhaps we were nearing the end of our day's journey, I thought hopefully. Some donkeys, loaded with *joshi* (local animal fodder), came towards us along the narrow mountain path. To my right, the edge of the cliff fell in a sheer drop of several hundred feet. I remembered Surgeon-Major Robertson's description of these mountain tracks: 'Good nerves are necessary to ride along them in comfort...' Even as they came to mind, I spotted a jeep behind the straggling donkey train. No way was there room for us to pass each other. Murad obviously thought the same, for he stopped and waited for me to catch up, and, as the jeep and donkeys were already on the nearside, he pulled me over to the very edge of the precipice to give the others maximum space. Great, I thought, if Tooruh shies I'll be over that cliff and nothing will save me. If it hadn't been so difficult to do, I would have dismounted. I held my breath as the jeep approached, and held onto the English saddle tightly, wishing it were an American Western type with the handy pommel. As the jeep passed, Tooruh shied and then reared: Mercifully, his hooves landed well away from the edge, and I remained glued to the saddle. Relieved, I breathed freely once more.

Moments later, we caught sight of the village and left the jeep track to make our way down the perilously steep, rocky incline that would take us there. The descent was uncomfortable because since the bag left me no room to lean back and brace myself in the stirrups, I had to grip Tooruh's flanks tightly with my knees. By the time I reached the rock-strewn, overgrown path at the bottom, Murad was away in front, walking beside a rider with a foal. When Tooruh saw the foal he broke into a fast trot. As I tried to rein him in, my shins crashed against the boulders to the side of the path, briars ripped at my shirt and jeans and scratched my arms and face. In spite of my nervousness, though, I was caught by the poetry of the moment—the foal, hearing Tooruh, stopped and started to dance on spindly legs, his golden coat glistening in the bright sunlight. When we were only a few yards away, Tooruh pawed the ground and reared. I held on and shouted at the men to help. When order was restored it was with relief that for the second time that day, I saw Murad smile and point to a mud-brick house about half-a-mile distant and declare: 'Dak Bungalow!'

Thank heavens, we had arrived! As we drew closer, it became obvious that the rest-house was in ruins, but I had only one thought in mind. Not waiting for Murad to assist me, I practically fell out of the saddle, sprawled full length on the ground and plunged my burning face into the ice-cold and fast-running stream.

The people in the house opposite came to our rescue and offered us food and shelter for the night. The woman, in her late thirties, had once been beautiful, but a hard life had etched fine lines upon her face. Only the large brown eyes still burned bright, belying the weariness of the rest of her features.

70

While we drank tea on the verandah, the woman chokingly related some distressing story to Murad. By the time she had finished, tears were slipping down her cheeks. I gestured enquiringly to Murad who shrugged his shoulders and mimed that the woman's daughter was unwell. Delving into my pack, I took out my first-aid kit, and, while Murad removed his *chaplis*, exposing red-raw blister on his toes, I followed the woman into a small walled garden. The daughter must have heard us for she came towards us, her garments open to the waist. She clutched my hand and thrust it between her breasts and moved it down to her stomach. She and her mother looked at me questioningly. Maybe menstrual cramps, worms, food poisoning? I really had no way of knowing. Helplessly, I fell back on the modern-day remedy of Paracetamol, hoping that it might at least prove psychologically beneficial and, unlike aspirin, not irritate the stomach

Returning to the verandah, where Murad was still nursing his sore toes, I ministered to his blisters. Perhaps out of gratitude or sudden compassion, Murad turned to me and offered to massage my legs. Until travelling on the Frontier, I had never known the blessed relief that simple massage can bring to aching limbs.

All evening, I was aware of the woman watching me, and I felt sad and helpless that I could not do more for her ailing daughter. At one stage, I impulsively took out two hundred rupees and offered them so that she might be able to take her daughter to Chitral to seek medical help. At first she appeared bewildered and then she laughed. To my astonishment she smilingly refused. In retrospect, it would have been an arduous journey for both women, and, in Chitral, they would probably have had no place to stay. But at that moment, tired and exhausted, I was not motivated by reason, and I regarded the woman enquiringly. Her eyes met mine. In that instant, I knew that if I had handed her another five hundred, her answer would have been the same, and I marvelled at her pride.

The next morning, after a breakfast of tea, bread and eggs, we prepared to leave. As the woman shook hands with me and our eyes met for the last time, I felt the rapport between us. I knew I should never forget her, nor that she had charged me only ten rupees for our food and shelter.

Seven o'clock the next morning, as we made our way along a shallow stream bed on the floor of the valley, I felt intoxicated by the bright, early morning sunlight as it shone through the trees and sparkled on the water around Tooruh's hooves, but as the terrain became more rugged, and the path steeper, I had to concentrate on every step. About a mile or so from Solaspur, Murad ignored a small boy's warning (it wasn't only me, he

71

didn't seem too kindly disposed to any strangers) and lost the way. Instead of back-tracking, he turned to the mountain slope we had been skirting and started zig-zagging straight up it. Not even in Westerns had I seen a horse go up such a steep gradient for so long a distance, and, to my surprise, Tooruh took the climb with enthusiasm. I leaned well forward in the saddle, for I knew that if I lost my balance we should go hurtling down the mountainside. This time the accursed bag in my back was a godsend, and we reached the jeep track without incident.

Ignoring Murad's directives to use the switch he had given me, I allowed Tooruh, who was breathing heavily, to stop whenever he wanted to. Although unfriendly, he was a game little horse and showed no trace of meanness. We entered a narrow, twisting defile and met several people with donkeys, loaded with *joshi*, coming down from the Shandur Top. The pass opened up, and, as we topped a rise, before us lay flat meadowland. We had reached the Shandur Top. I'd made it! I paused to drink in my surroundings of luna-type cliffs and ridges, lofty jagged peaks edged with snow and a dark blue lake. Some young shepherds, leaving their herds of goats and yaks grazing on the banks of the lake, came to meet us. They were an oddly assorted bunch and were dressed in jackets and sweaters several sizes too big for them. But all, without exception, were smiling cheerfully and obviously intrigued to see a Westerner in such a remote place. When we reached the small polo-ground (at 12,400 feet it is reputed to be the highest in the world), where Chitral and Gilgit sometimes engage in a tournament, I dismounted. In that romantic setting, I could easily imagine the teams of horsemen thundering across the grass in the late afternoon sunshine to the sound of drums and the crowd shouting encouragement. The Chitralis play polo with scant attention to rules, but with such skill that it is rare indeed that either horse or rider suffers even a slight injury.

The Shandur Top was peaceful and magnificent, wild and desolate. The only sign of civilization was more fallen telegraph lines. My thoughts turned again to Colonel Kelly and his native troops who had crossed the Shandur en route to relieve Chitral. They had done it in the depths of winter with two field guns on their backs which they had stubbornly refused to leave behind; I shuddered at the thought of their ordeal—my journey was a picnic in comparison.

We travelled on. It was one o'clock. I kept trying to catch Murad's eye, as he walked alongside me on the now wide, sandy track. Surely our day's stage must be nearly over? As we approached the shepherds' encampment, I could see the stone and wooden tops of their simple dwellings. The rest of the houses were below ground, built there partly for warmth and partly because there was a lack of suitable wood for building materials. As I dismounted, a couple of women, followed by a horde of small children, approached me. They were unveiled and wore maroon, patterned pill-box hats. Their matching *shalwar-khameez* were of heavier material than normal, again presumably for additional warmth.

While the life-giving tea was brewing, the women and children clustered around me. The men stood laughing on the periphery of the group, or squatted upon the grass, obviously entertained by this sudden intrusion into their lives. Then a woman 'asked' for a pill for a headache. Someone else held up a hand with an infected cut. I brought out my first-aid kit and store of mild drugs. The crowd swelled. Where they all came from, I could not imagine, unless those underground houses were part of a vast underground village. I glanced around me. Deep lines were etched onto the weather-beaten faces; a hundred hands with layers of grime were thrust before my eyes; fingers pointed to heads and bellies. I began dressing minor wounds and doling out pills, until it suddenly dawned on me that the same people, taking advantage of my obvious confusion, were accepting pills for head, stomach and throat.

Murad, whose mood was blacker than usual, began shouting at me. He was obviously working himself into a real tizzy. Regretfully, as I should have loved to stay longer and seen inside their houses, I smiled at the grubby, wide-eyed children pulling at my shirt sleeves, and closed the blade of my penknife on my thigh, an inch away from a child's ear. Some bandaids fell into a pile of manure at my feet. A young boy picked them up and carefully placed them back in my first-aid box. It was time to abandon my attempts at playing doctor, and, with Murad ranting and raving, we left the amused shepherds and travelled on in the heat.

Riding ahead, I soon left Murad and his bad humour behind me to revel in the wild desolation of the desert that now stretched before me and the mountains ahead looking like sandhills, their undulating sensuous curves reminiscent of a woman's body.

The valley narrowed and once more we began following a stream as we dropped down from the top of the Shandur. After a while, bushes and other vegetation appeared and the valley opened up. I reined in and a group of women and teenage boys, herding cattle, called out to us cheerily. One handed me an apple. The stream to our right now became a river, with the sparse vegetation giving way to long grass, bushes, trees and a bull. A bull? I shook myself awake. No, I hadn't been mistaken. Emerging from a thicket some way ahead, nostrils flaring, was a bull loping excitedly towards us. Murad did not falter in his step and neither did Tooruh. I held a tighter rein and watched incredulously as the animal, gaining speed, passed us without so much as a look. I turned in the saddle and then realized that, in comparison to the herd of cows behind us, we were really of little attraction.

We turned a bend and it was with joy that I saw cultivated fields, farmsteads, a small bridge across the river, and men on horseback taking home their cattle. I ardently hoped it would be Teru, our destination.

A handsome man came over to greet us. 'Hello, my Sister. From where you come?' After exchanging a few words of greeting and telling us he would meet us later at his home in the next hamlet, he dropped back. When we got there, Murad led me into the courtyard beside a mud-brick house and, with something approaching a smile, indicated I should dismount.

'Teru?' I asked.

'No, Baset,' Murad replied, and pointed into the distance. 'Teru!'

As I groaned inwardly, I noticed two riders appear on the track. One was a woman who was sitting side-saddle on a grey-white horse, wearing a scarlet pill-box hat, a white cloak, and a white veil over the lower part of her face. In the late afternoon light, she could have ridden out of the pages of *The Arabian Nights*.

While we drank tea, I noticed that some of the women used the same cone-shaped baskets as the Kalash, and, like the women at the shepherds' encampment (they were also unveiled*), wore the same brooch-like pieces of jewelry on their shoulders as well as similar ear-rings and bangles. Was it possible the Kalash may have ventured this far over the mountains from Upper Chitral? Or had they perhaps come from the opposite direction, from Nepal, as some anthropologists have claimed, citing the similarity in the carvings of wooden figures as evidence.

The body's recuperative powers are marvellous, and, refreshed by the tea, I climbed back into the saddle with comparative ease. The young man who had greeted me near the bridge and supervised the making and pouring of the tea (my sweeteners had been an instant success among the household), now walked with us out of the courtyard to the track. As Murad marched on ahead, I leaned down in the saddle and grasped him by the hand. I gazed into his deep brown eyes and was struck again by the strange intensity which seems to surround these brief, chance encounters.

He smiled warmly. 'God go with you, oh my Sister!'

As I waved goodbye and 'rode off into the sunset', I pondered his use of the word 'sister'. Only in the Kalash valleys had I heard this salutation

---

*They may have belonged to the Ismaili sect, followers of the Aga Khan, who are less strict than the Sunni and Shia Moslems.

used. Was this further evidence of the Kalash having once inhabited this region?

On either side of me rose sloping treeless mountains with farmhouses nestling in the hollows. Children, herdsboys, travellers and a man with a team of bullocks passed me by. The golden valley stretched before me, bathed in an ethereal light. At last it narrowed and the stony path began to climb very steeply. Poor Tooruh, had I not been wearing those wretched riding-boots, I should have dismounted and continued on foot.

When my camera bag fell off, Murad clumsily tied it back on, and, for the first time since we had left Mastuj, seemed worried about Tooruh. Another hundred yards and the bag slipped again. 'You jeep, Teru!' he muttered through clenched teeth. I said nothing, thinking it an excellent idea for all concerned. Murad stalked off, leaving me with both bag and stirrup slipping yet again, while Tooruh blew hard up the steep incline.

When I finally reached Teru I came upon Murad sitting on a rock with my rucksack beside him. Not only did the small village appear deserted, but Murad looked tired and disconsolate. He pointed to a very closed and deserted building. 'Resthouse closed. No *chai*. No *chapik* (food). No *chowkidar*.'*

It was now seven. I had been in the saddle nearly twelve hours and night was falling. For Murad, it had been worse for he had been walking on blistered feet. Only Tooruh seemed unconcerned, as he contentedly chewed on some grass by the side of the track. I looked at Murad stubbornly. '*Chai?*' From where I expected the poor man to suddenly produce it, I don't know, but my mind was beyond quiet reason.

Murad nodded desperately with an almost a human look on his face. I realized I should pity him. He was old and needed the money. It was not his fault the resthouse was closed, but, uncharitably and unreasonably, I began in my mind, to berate Prince Sikander for enlisting an ageing and very unwilling guide who was obviously unfamiliar with the route. Thankfully, though, Tooruh had proved to be a quiet and reliable horse. I could have done considerably worse.

Murad dragged himself to his feet, and, after consulting several strangers, we eventually ended up at a *dukan** where we were given tea and stale *chappatis*.*

I watched as Murad laid out my ground-sheet on the narrow and roofless verandah. No *charpoy*, no roof, and just one small quilt from the *dukan* and my very thin space sheet between us. Murad generously gave me the quilt, and his jacket for my head, leaving himself with only

Chowkidar—night watchman.
Chappatis—flat unleavened bread.
Dukan—a small store.

Tooruh's saddle-blanket and the saddle for a pillow. Grateful for this simple human kindness, I bedded down for the night with my space sheet pulled tightly around me and the quilt up over my chin, and tried to forget I was cold. Again, I wished I had brought my sleeping-bag left behind in the interests of weight. Disconsolately, I stared at the clouds scurrying across the face of the almost full moon. I woke from a half sleep to find a wind blowing and drops of rain falling on us. I pulled the ground sheet from beneath Murad's sleeping form and covered us both. The rain storm passed us by, but the wind continued to blow dust on us the rest of the night.

At the first glimmer of light, Murad saddled Tooruh, while I staggered to my feet and made for a nearby stream.

Before leaving us the night before, the *dukan* owner had informed us a jeep would be leaving for Gilgit at six. I had also been offered the option of another horse. To continue on horseback appealed to my romantic spirit, but I had no idea of the length of the journey, nor if the resthouse at Panda might also be closed.* I had crossed the Shandur Pass and had done three stages in two days. I had achieved my objective of making the crossing on horseback. What sense was there in subjecting myself to further punishment when I could get a jeep all the way to Gilgit? For once in my life I would be sensible. Now, as I washed the dirt and grime from my face in the cold light of dawn, I smugly reflected on my cool wisdom. Three nights without sleep can do strange things to the brain and does nothing for one's memory. Whenever I have done 'the sensible thing' I have invariably regretted it, but, now, as I hobbled along beside Murad, I was relieved that my 'ordeal' was over and glad that I should be riding to Gilgit in the 'comfort' of a jeep. Depositing me at another *dukan*, which served as a service station, Murad took his leave of me. We parted with a simple handshake, and, without a backward glance, he rode off into the sunrise. Still gagging from the salt-laced tea, I obtained a fresh pot with just milk, to which I added one of my sweeteners, and patiently waited for the jeep.

Twelve hours later, with only one tea-break I arrived in Gilgit—a dusty bazaar town and once a staging post on the old Silk Road. I was dehydrated, suffering from heat exhaustion, my face was blistered by the sun and my legs were black and blue. 'The next time I undertake such a trip, I'll go on foot,' I thought as I collapsed on a bed in a cheap hotel in the bazaar.

Some things remain the same even if circumstances change and time moves on—true friendships, deep, abiding love, the thrill of exploring a

---

*Many resthouses have now been refurbished.

land one has learnt to love. Journeys in such a place, undertaken at different times, diffuse in the mind and are as one. And so it is for me travelling in this vast mountain region—events overlap, intermingle and flow together in ever decreasing circles until, ultimately, they flow towards a distant goal.

Even as I tried to shut out the sounds of the bazaar and recover from my trek, I was planning my next trip.

The words of a German friend I had met in Chitral came to mind: 'Why not go back to Islamabad via the Babusar Pass? It lies in the shadow of Nanga Parbat. I hear it is wild and beautiful. Of course, you would have to go to Chilas first. "They" say it is situated in a hell hole—a real devil's anvil—and that the people are very wild. I have heard it's best to go from north to south. It's easier. Think about it!'

I was thinking about it, and ultimately the dream would turn into reality, but not quite in the way I had anticipated.

The Road to Naran

I doubt anyone would have called Ambika beautiful—her cheeks were too fat and her nose too small—but attractive she most certainly was. Her warm brown eyes, ringed with kohl, held a velvet softness; her small, even, white teeth gleamed brightly from beneath full, painted red lips, and her long, black hair flowed gracefully down her back, as she walked regally towards her car. Beneath the lamplight, I could see sweat glistening on her dusky skin against her orange sari. The fragrance of her jasmine scent engulfed me as I climbed in beside her. As she switched on the engine, this middle-aged Bengali widow started on her favourite topic—men.

While we drove back from Islamabad to 'Pindi beneath a full moon, past the deserted race track and past wavering palm trees silhouetted against the night sky, she switched from lambasting the opposite sex to telling me ribald stories that would have made a sailor blush and then turned to singing the latest Indian love songs, interspersed now and then with an Islamic love poem. As we drove up in front of the hotel of which she was housekeeper, and where I had a room, she promised me that she would give me a letter of introduction to a friend of hers in Abbottobad.

A few days later, she deposited me at the 'wagon'*-stop for Abbotto-bad. On her advice, I had booked the two front seats next to the driver, so that I might travel in comfort. As soon as the wagon left the outskirts of Rawalpindi behind, I rolled down my window and settled back to enjoy the ride.

My immediate goal was to cross the Babusar Pass to Chilas and Gilgit en route for Hunza and the Khunjerab Pass—two more passes! On my previous trip I had not had time to cross the Babusar, as I had wanted to reach the Kalash valleys in time for the autumn festival. Now again I was filled with that marvellous feeling, not experienced since journeying across the Shandur, of not knowing for sure where I should be spending the night, what I should eat and whom I should meet—the thrill of the unknown. The letter Ambika had given me nestled in the inside pocket of my waistcoat.

At first the land was flat and dull reaching to foothills on the distant horizon. The road ran over the gentle Margella Pass, past the statue of Lord Nicholson, one of Britain's famous frontier administrators (his bequest of vast tracts of land to his orderly, in appreciation of services, have brought that gentleman's descendants immense wealth) and on through the bustling bazaar of Taxilla, situated some miles from the ancient city of the same name which was conquered by Alexander the Great in 327 B.C., and which later became a great Buddhist centre under King Asoka. Soft, sand-coloured loess cliffs bordered the road, and I caught a glimpse of cliff dwellings as we flashed past. Then the land continued flat, mostly arable with a few industrial plants and factory chimneys dotted here and there.

The sky began to darken. No-one spoke. There was no cassette blaring out Pakistani music. In the plains of Pakistan, travellers always seemed more subdued, with none of the devil-may-care, fun-loving attitude shown by the mountain men on my jeep rides north of the Lowarai. The man beside me drove with the usual speed of the plains' driver, which meant I was always putting my foot on 'the brake' every time an animal or cyclist wandered into the middle of the road.

The sky grew even darker, the driver drove even faster, his hand on the horn as we blazed through towns and village bazaars, evoking memories of riding an ambulance when I was taking my EMT course in New York.* We crossed over a bridge straddling a river and suddenly we were in the North-West Frontier Province. The land became rockier, the distant hills began closing in. There was a smell of rain in the air, and as the road began to climb the storm broke.

For a while the driver slowed down through the lashing rain, but as soon as the sun came out and the mauve and black clouds moved on, we picked up speed again. I saw villages where houses clung to the banks of the river, white and grey minarets standing out against lush green trees, water buffalo wading through muddy water, and I was reminded of pictures painted in the days of the Raj.

Nearing a small village, we passed two men, the Asian equivalent to our buskers, each leading a brown bear with a collar of rosettes and accompanied by a crowd of small children. In the distance a rainbow arched above the green hills. The road climbed further and the town of Abbottobad, named after the last British Deputy Commissioner, was before us, nestling in a valley.

---

*A popular form of transport in Pakistan is the Volkswagen bus, familiarly known as the 'wagon'.
*Emergency Medical Technician—one step before becoming a para-medic.

There was a smell of pines and woodsmoke as we drove through an avenue of trees. To be back in the hills after the heat and dust of the plains was bliss, as it was to be away from the crazy traffic and exhaust fumes of the cities, the torpid heat, the merciless sun and the tongas.

As we drove through the attractive hill station of Abbottobad, now the home of Pakistan's military academy—the equivalent of Sandhurst and West Point—I took out the envelope Ambika had given me. As she had thrust it into my hand, she had emphatically told me to make use of it, as her friend, a school teacher, would be most happy to meet me. I showed the envelope with its Persian script to a man sitting behind me, and, within moments, there was a heated discussion between my previously silent companions as to the whereabouts of the address. Here was a stranger to their country in need of assistance, and, in true Pakistani fashion, they were all eager to help me. I was transferred with my baggage to a small Suzuki pick-up truck and taken through the town. Rows of trees sped past as we rode into the Cantonment, past regimental offices and barracks, past the tall memorial erected to Pakistan's wars with India, and, finally, into the drive of a large house on the edge of some fields adjacent to a school.

My fears about disrupting the household were soon dispersed, for it became obvious that my arrival had provided Aliya, who was having marital problems with her estranged husband, with a welcome diversion, especially as she was on leave from school. My intention of staying just one night had to be abandoned. For three days I enjoyed this good woman's hospitality and the companionship of her two daughters and her in-laws.

One morning, sitting comfortably in a Western style sitting-room, augmented by oriental antique furniture, I sat listening with interest to Aliya. Frustrated by the antics of her husband, who was presently co-habiting with his second wife in another residence, she let the conversation flow.

'How I miss Kashmir. You see my grandmother was English, part of the Raj you could say. She fell in love with this handsome Kashmiri, who was a brilliant scholar and lawyer. He was also very esoteric and had studied all the great religions. My grandmother converted to Islam of her own free will. She used to hold her own courts inside the home for all the local women. She was very much loved and she became famous in Kashmir. For my grandfather it was an enormous risk, for if it were found out it would have meant death for him at the hands of the British. He would have been arrested under some pretext like Harry Kumar in

---

Jewel In The Crown—part of the *Raj Quartet* by Paul Scott.

80

Jewel in the Crown.* I'm afraid the Merricks were the norm and not the exception.'

I went on listening attentively.

'When my grandmother died, her twin sister married my grandfather for the sake of the children. One of these sons, my father, was imprisoned at Partition and was sent in a 'plane load of exiles into what is now Pakistan. Partition was a terrible mistake. You know, I don't think it was only Mountbatten that should be blamed. There are those who think it was really the work of foreign powers done to de-stabilize the region, and Partition was a way to ensure India would not be a force to reckon with, vis-à-vis the two sides of Pakistan with India in the middle. A British and American power game. Now the Russians are infiltrating all over Pakistan with their Afghan Khad spies. Peshawar could become another Beirut. Some of these refugees make huge profits, receiving shipments from Afghanistan and not paying Pakistan levies. Shipped out of Karachi, goods disappear internally. (I had heard a similar story in Karachi.) India is thick with Russia, and Pakistan is being squeezed in all directions. American aid is pouring in along with all the armaments. Why should the United States pour in such massive aid, something to the tune of four billion dollars, I believe, unless to counter Russia? The Great Game is alive and well. The pot is boiling beneath.' Again Aliya paused. She looked at me intently, as she went to pour us more tea.

'It's a pity you can't read Urdu. My father has written a book on China. He did an official tour of the country a couple of years ago. Would you believe, that vast subterranean cities have been built in China, way beneath the ground, with hotels, restaurants and transport systems? All prepared to withstand ten years below ground in the event of a nuclear attack?'

Shades of *The Lost World of Agharti*,* I thought, remembering a book I had read about Atlantis and lost continents. I also remembered hearing about UFOs coming out of the earth in Central Asia. I continued to listen, all the while twirling a fading necklace of jasmine which Aliya had bought me the evening before.

Later that same day, I sat with her father-in-law in the sitting-room, while Aliya consulted with her lawyer in the study. He leaned back in his chair and shook his head sadly.

'You see, my son has managed things badly. I, also, have two wives, the younger one, my second, you have met. She is the mother of my young son and daughter. My first wife, who is considerably older, did not give me children, but she is still a respected member of my household,

---

**The Lost World of Agharti* by Alec Maclellan.

and she and my second wife get on fine. They are close friends. But it is not easy. One has to be a diplomat to prevent jealousy and ill feeling. Each wife must be treated the same, or at least as much as is humanly possible. Perhaps my training in labour relations and settling disputes has given me an edge over my son. But this trouble between him and Aliya will blow over. It has happened before.'

As I was an honoured guest and it was a weekend, it was felt I should be taken out to see the surrounding countryside. The Galies, as they are called, which lie between Abbottobad and Murree, were pleasant, attractive hill resorts with wave upon wave of green moss-covered ridges rising into pine-clad summits. They did little, however, for my craving for wild places, although the narrow twisting mountain roads lent a little excitement, especially when the brakes failed one day and on another we got caught in the mist.

One night, as I lay in bed, a storm lashed the town of Abbottobad. I got up and stood gazing out of the window, spellbound. It reminded me of the London blitz. Only in Dharamsala, nestling at the foot of the Great Himalaya, have I ever seen such a remarkable show of sheet and fork lightning which continually lit up the whole sky. The surrounding hills stood silhouetted against an orange back-drop, while the thunder kept up a steady barrage like a battery of guns. The next day, I was told it was the beginning of the 'baby' monsoons. Aliya was sceptical about my crossing the Babusar on foot, either it would still be snowbound or I would be caught in the monsoons. It would perhaps be wiser for me to return to 'Pindi and take the Karakoram Highway (KKH) all the way to Gilgit. This idea did not appeal to me as I had no desire to do that long and infamous bus ride and hated going back on my tracks.

On the fourth day after my arrival in Abbottobad, Aliya's father-in-law and his young wife drove me to the wagon-stop for Mansehra. Owing to my overweight rucksack, he kindly drove me right into the wagon station. The station was a chaotic mass of people, cars and bikes. After he had had his bumper almost ripped off, and had rescued me from being nearly hit by a car, he found me a seat in a wagon and left me to begin the next leg of my journey.

Ever since I had climbed with Saifullah to the shepherds' encampment, at a height of 14,500 feet, in the Kalash valley of Rumbur, my love of mountains had taken on a greater intensity. During both my childhood and adult years, I had read many books about men pitting their strength against the mighty Karakorams and the Great Himalaya. Crossing the Babusar at a height of 13,600 feet could hardly be ranked with climbing the world's greatest mountains, but with a broken rib and heavy rucksack, and weighed down with Aliya's dire warnings of landslides, avalanches and glaciers, not to mention my German friend's remark that it was easier to go from north to south (I was going in the opposite direction), it was with some trepidation I began the journey.

The road to Mansehra ran through gently undulating green and brown hills but the terrain grew rockier the nearer we got to Mansehra, a small bazaar town where I had to change wagons. This time I had a seat in the rear with some Pakistani students who smiled in welcome.

Slowly, the wagon began to climb the narrow hairpin bends to the top of a hill before descending again to the Kunhar valley. Adobe and stone farmsteads with their nearby cup-cake haystacks heralded the arrival of the small town of Balakot. It was a pretty little place and not unlike Chitral, with the Kunhar river snaking through its centre, its wooden swinging bridge, erected in 1895, and its old bazaar straddling the hillside. The new and busy main bazaar was wide and dusty and open to trucks and buses, as well as wagons, Suzukis and jeeps.

Here I broke my journey and spent the night in the local P.T.D.C. motel, where the tourist officer imparted the news that the Babusar had seen the worst winter for over twenty years and that the road to Naran, at the head of the Kaghan Valley, had only opened a day or so before. Apparently, few jeeps were prepared to make the journey yet.

I enjoyed my visit to the old bazaar. Its smell of cow dung, cedar, wood-smoke, spices and the aroma of a thick, red and very sweet fruit drink, made a pleasant accompaniment to the visual delight of entering the little serendipity stores, which must surely be a stock-taker's nightmare. Hundreds of different commodities lined the dusty shelves. Boot polish sat next to tins of sardines, cans of insect spray lay next to boxes of tea, hair oil nestled in between bottles of Indian ink and plastic shoes; old faded boxes of Chanel No 5 lay atop aluminium pots leaning on rolls of Chinese toilet paper, while insect-stained packets of custard powder were squashed between padlocks, pocket torches, fountain pens, Chinese porcelain spoons, bars of scented soap and umbrellas in plastic cases.

On the other side of the bridge, in the new bazaar, I took note of some of the signs hanging jauntily from the roofs of the tiny wooden stores: 'Paris Hairdresser', 'Shangri-La Shopping Centre'; 'Diamond Cloth Centre'. Beside the latter was a wagon with the words 'Body Sockser' painted on its side. In front of the National Savings Centre, amidst the mud and dust, someone had lovingly erected a picket fence around a ten-foot-square plot of land and planted a patch of tall yellow sunflowers.

That evening the tourist officer volunteered to search out a jeep to take me to Naran. It would leave the next morning at 6.30 and would pick me up on the way, as the road ran past the motel.

I rose early and sat waiting; 6.30 came and went as did 7.30 and 8.30. I had forgotten that both jeeps and wagons never leave until they are full to overflowing. At ten o'clock, with the help of the *chowkidar*, I duly set off for the bazaar to see what was going on. En route, we passed some children crowding around a travelling salesman who was demonstrating a toy Father Christmas. I wondered if either the salesman or the obviously fascinated Moslem onlookers, realized what the red-coated toy represented.

Arriving at the jeep station, I found that no jeeps were going to Naran and was pointed instead in the direction of a wagon that was slowly filling up with passengers. Although dubious about riding in one of these vehicles which did not have four-wheel drive, on a road which I had been told was only just suitable for jeeps, I paid my fare and got in.

While I sat waiting for the wagon to fill up, I looked about me at the people. It was good to be back on the Frontier, I thought. In front of me two men embraced. One was blue-eyed with traces of fair hair peeping from beneath his mountain Chitrali hat. The other, a mere youth, carrying a rifle and sporting a bandolier, had strong, even features below a green turban. Here the men walked tall, and even the male youths had a bearing and presence about them which inspired respect. I doubted that the growing heroin addiction, now on the increase on the Frontier, found favour in the rural areas where the family unit was still strong.

When I was working for a civil rights group in Harlem, back in the sixties, I was told by a social worker that it was the members of organized crime who had introduced drugs into Harlem. Looking around for a potential market, they had quite rightly assessed that a people who were deprived and jobless and living in urban squalor, would be ripe for anything which would appear to soothe the spirit and make them forget their problems. I doubted that the drug runners on the Frontier would find this fertile territory.

The last people to come aboard were the students from the Punjab that I had met the previous day. They greeted me with smiles as they climbed in behind me.

At first the bus drove through terrain similar to that of the day before, as it twisted around the mountains and passed farmsteads and terraced fields. Passing one paddy-field in the making, I observed a group of naked boys splashing one another in the muddy water. The road wound around twisting hairpin bends, some 2,000 feet above the river. If I had been nervous the day before, it was nothing to the way I felt now. The driver had a nasty habit of sounding his horn about ten seconds too late, with the result that, on several corners, we had to swerve to miss an oncoming jeep, wagon, bus or truck. Another hazard was the nomads

84

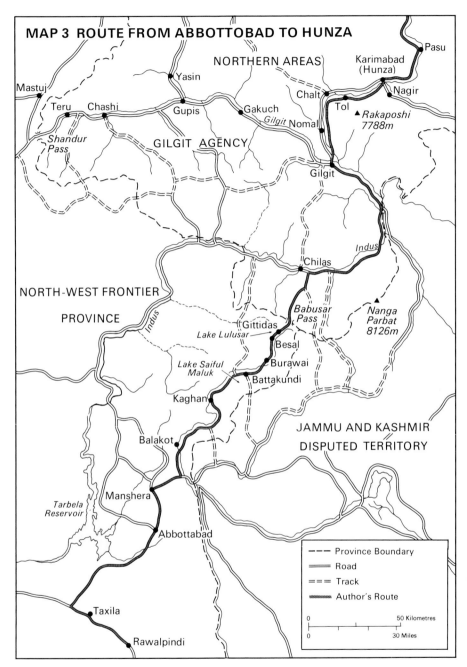

MAP 3 ROUTE FROM ABBOTTOBAD TO HUNZA

NORTHERN AREAS

Mastuj

Yasin

Pasu

Karimabad
(Hunza)

Chalt

Nagir

Teru Chashi

Gupis

Gakuch

Tol

Rakaposhi
7788m

Gilgit Nomal

Shandur
Pass

GILGIT AGENCY

Gilgit

Indus

Chilas

NORTH-WEST FRONTIER

Indus

Babusar
Pass

Nanga
Parbat
8126m

PROVINCE

Gittidas

Lake Lulusar

Besal

Lake Saiful
Maluk

Burawai

Battakundi

Kaghan

JAMMU AND KASHMIR

Balakot

DISPUTED TERRITORY

Tarbela
Reservoir

Manshera

Abbottabad

- - - - Province Boundary
——— Road
= = = Track
━━━ Author's Route

0   50 Kilometres

Taxila

0   30 Miles

Rawalpindi

taking their livestock up to the summer pastures just below the Babusar:
bullocks, cattle, sheep, goats, horses, dogs and puppies. The last, on
ropes and chains, thankfully kept well to the edge when we passed, but
on one particularly dangerous curve, the driver had to swerve to avoid an

oncoming jeep on the inside and a dog on the outside. There was only one way open to the driver—straight ahead over the cliff. By some miracle, he managed to turn the steering-wheel hard over to the right at the last minute, and the front wheel on my side just skated along the crumbling edge. I glanced back at the students behind me. They grimaced and we all intoned '*Il humdu'illah*'! (Thanks be to God).

At the village of Kaghan, we stopped for tea. Tea-houses or *chai-khanas* are an institution in Pakistan, where, if friends of mine in Karachi are to be believed, all the tea is 'doctored'. Whether this is true, I have no idea. What I do know is that Pakistani tea, especially on the Frontier, gives one pep and energy, and that jeep and wagon-drivers always drive faster after a *chai* stop.

The majority of the tea-houses* are open affairs on ground level while others can only be reached by a flight of very high stone steps, made all the more difficult by being narrow and twisting. The one in Kaghan was of the latter variety, and one of the students, seeing me view the steps with consternation, shouldered my camera bag and when we got to the top, kindly paid for my tea. It is seldom indeed that the rare lone foreigner, riding in public vehicles in these mountain areas, would ever be allowed to pay either for tea or food. The Moslem belief in hospitality is practised in its widest sense in Pakistan.

Back in the wagon, the students took care of my camera bag so I might sit in greater comfort, for now the metalled road had ended. From now on, we would be travelling on a mere track in rough terrain. Above us the mountains became taller and snow appeared on the slopes above the pines and cedars as we still followed a wild, turbulent river. I felt light-hearted, for I was back in the real mountains and the drive ahead promised to be exciting. It was not long before we came to a glacier. It was the first glacier I had ever seen albeit a small one—nothing more than a thick snowy river of ice which blocked our path. The icy surface was not suitable for a vehicle without four-wheel drive and snow tyres, so we all got out to make it easier for the driver. While Azhar, one of the students and I took photographs, the driver, with the help of the others, put grass and rocks on the snow and pushed the wagon across. This was an act that was to be repeated many times before we finally reached our destination.

As we drove into Naran, I revelled in the sight of the ever-higher mountains, their sides streaked with snow. At the wagon-stop, a teenage boy, dressed in the traditional *shalwar-khameez*, but wearing a blue

---

*Tea-houses also provide meals and generally have a few *charpoys* on which the traveller may rest or stay overnight. *Chai*-shops and *chai*-stalls usually serve only tea, with perhaps cake or some other small snack.

baseball cap pressed tightly down over his forehead, helped the students with their baggage and volunteered to carry my rucksack to a nearby tea-house, where we decided to rest while one of us investigated the hotels.

Over tea, Arlem, who spoke a little English, told us he was eighteen and that he lived alone with his widowed mother. In the summer, he guided Pakistani tourists to Saiful Maluk, a lake famed for its natural beauty.

After the boys had ensconced themselves in tents in a tourist camp, and I had found quarters in the local resthouse, I agreed to trek with Arlem and the students to the lake the following day.

Although the Kaghan Valley is a tourist resort, few foreigners, other than those based in Islamabad, know of its beauty. I was enchanted as much with the legend of the lake as with the scenery...

> A prince from Delhi, named Saiful Maluk, had heard stories of a beautiful fairy queen who lived on the edge of a lake at the foot of Malika Parbat (Queen of the Mountain) in the shadow of Nanga Parbat. He left his home to journey there in search of her, but during the months it took him to reach the lake, it came to him in a vision, that he would have to wait twelve years before he could see his Fairy Queen. He was a patient man, and one day he was rewarded by seeing the Queen and her attendants bathing in the dammed up lake. Stealthily, he crept up and stole the Queen's clothes. Modesty prevented the Queen from leaving the water, and only when she consented to marry him did Prince Saiful Maluk return her clothes. When their Queen left in the company of the Prince, her attendants fled weeping into the mountains and were heard by the Demon King. Jealously, as he had been once scorned by the Queen, he chased the lovers over the mountains, but they were too fleet of foot. In fury he burnt down the dam, unleashing a torrent of water which destroyed everything in its wake. The waters, however, passed by the lovers, and Saiful Maluk lived to take home his new bride...

When we arrived back at the students' tent in Naran, we discussed my problem of hiring a guide-cum-porter for crossing the Babusar. As we talked, Arlem sat listening quietly, swinging his legs. While he was an obvious candidate he had never crossed the Babusar and appeared frail; he had had jaundice ten months before. As two of the boys were suffering from altitude sickness and I, too, had a headache, the conversation ended with my asking Arlem to find me a suitable guide. He looked most upset, and, standing up, virtually on his toes as if to make himself appear taller, said 'Please take me. I be very good guide. I can carry two times your rucksack. I am strong, very strong.'

I glanced at the boys. They shrugged their shoulders. Azhar looked dubiously at Arlem and then at me: 'He *is* honest. He *is* reliable. And he *is* keen to go.'

I said nothing and stared at Arlem. There was a pleading look in those sombre eyes. His dark skin still seemed to have a yellowish tinge to it, but he looked determined.

'Okay, Arlem, you be my guide.'

The sigh that went around the tent was almost audible. A broad smile spread across Arlem's youthful features. Had I realized then what I was letting myself in for, no doubt I should have made a different choice, but Arlem's loyalty and strength of character were perhaps, the prime factors which resulted in my crossing the Babusar in one piece. Had I chosen another guide, it is more than possible I might have perished on the slopes of that austere mountain top, but, as I left the tent that sunny afternoon with Arlem by my side, I felt carefree and happy, I was on my way. In a few days I should be in Gilgit, back in the high mountains. Adventure awaited me and I was ready to embrace it.

I Travel with the Nomads

The day of my great adventure dawned clear and sunny. Arlem arrived a few minutes after our pre-arranged time, carrying the second-hand yellow baseball jacket I had bought him the previous day in the bazaar. It amazed me how, perhaps due to lack of money, these mountain men invariably travelled with only the clothes on their backs and no possessions. My baggage, however, now distributed into two rucksacks, was more than enough for the two of us. Although I try to travel light, I was carrying summer and winter clothes, a few small gifts for the Kalash, three boxes of medicines for me and anyone else who needed them, maps and reference books, cameras and films, a bulky but warm sleeping-bag and odds and ends of camping equipment.

Thus laden, we set off for the jeep station. The road was open up to Battakundi, a small village some ten kilometers distant, but we should have to walk from there. In the early morning light, I was struck by the varying shades of green around me—the emerald turf, chartreuse river and bottle-green ridges of pine. The road was incredibly rough, but the driver skilfully ploughed on, through rushing streams, over beds of rocks and across the ever-present rivers of glacial ice.

Two hours later, we arrived in Battakundi, from where Arlem and I set off along the rocky but easily visible path. For about ten kilometres, we continued steadily, though found it necessary to rest frequently. Although I had been first to weaken, it soon became painfully obvious that Arlem, in spite of his continual protestations of 'no problem', was finding my heavier rucksack a problem.

A kindly middle-aged man, driving a small herd up to the summer pastures, came to our rescue. He was a 'townie' from 'Pindi who enjoyed the countryside and revelled in the fresh, clean air of the mountains. Gallantly, he offered to take my rucksack on his horse and I accepted gladly. Arlem manfully refused even to exchange rucksacks. The farther we went, the more herds we came upon moving north or resting by the side of the track.

In the heat of the day, our fellow traveller came to a halt at a water-hole, in order to rest himself and his animals, and bade us to continue. He would bring my rucksack and catch us up at the next village before nightfall. We travelled on, stopping only to quench our thirst and give Arlem a chance to rest his aching shoulders.

As the shadows began to lengthen, I found myself anxiously glancing back. In that rucksack were all my rolls of film and my spare camera. No, it was safe, I assured myself. In all my travels in Pakistan and other Moslem countries, I had left baggage and valuables with complete strangers on more occasions than I could possibly remember. The loss of my camera in Dir was another matter altogether.

The scenic beauty of the morning had now been replaced by a more desolate terrain. The trees had disappeared, except for a few scrawny pines, and it became very rocky and dusty as we followed a narrow valley just above the river. The sun was blisteringly hot, and as we approached the village of Burawai, we met a cyclist coming towards us, pushing his bike. I immediately recognized the young German I had met in 'Pindi. He had travelled overland and had spent a week as a 'guest' of the Iranian authorities for having been caught photographing a bridge. Undaunted by this, he was going to carry out his dream of cycling across the Khunjerab. He recognized me, but there was no smile on his face, the Babusar had defeated him. He had gone too quickly and had become a victim of altitude sickness, and he was now having to return to Islamabad.

The approach to Burawai was made over a quaint wooden bridge straddling the river. All around us were nomads herding their livestock for the journey to the summer pastures below the Babusar. We deposited ourselves at the nearest tea-house, and, while I ordered tea and attended to various cuts, bruises and infections of the local people, Arlem went in search of the *chowkidar* who ran the resthouse. The old man looked at me suspiciously. When I handed him a letter, written in English from the Government Tourism Division in Islamabad, giving me permission to stay in government resthouses, I knew he would not understand the words, but I trusted the official stamp at the bottom would suffice. Had I known beforehand what it would be like I would have opted for a sooty *charpoy* in the tea-house.

The room itself was reasonably large with two bedsteads, a very faded armchair, a broken table and a couple of rickety wooden chairs, and on the floor was an old rug, but it was the bathroom which made me blanch. The floor was covered with scurrying black beetles. Every time I took a step, I could hear a sickening sound, but there were so many it was impossible to avoid them. There was no toilet and to go to the loo, I

The tea-house at Burawai.

should have to go down by the river. I looked helplessly around the dark interior for somewhere to hang my towel, but the pegs above my head were covered in stalactites of bird droppings. At least the *chowkidar* had brought me some warm water, but, when the back door swung open on its rusty hinges to let some welcome light into the room, I saw that the enamel bowl I was just about to use was thick with grime.

After a quick wash and visit to the river, I returned to find Arlem stretched full length on one of the beds, and the *chowkidar* in earnest conversation with a dozen or so of the local inhabitants who were sitting on or around my belongings. Grabbing my camera-bag, I went out into the sunlight. Arlem followed, and as we approached the tea-house someone called out to us.

'Hi, there!'

I looked around to find a Westerner dressed in *shalwar-khameez* and wearing a Chitrali hat, coming towards me with proffered hand. He had a pleasant smiling face with light brown hair, green eyes, and a tidy, short-cropped beard and sideburns. Richard hailed from Australia, and I took to him immediately. Over tea he showed me a sketch he had just finished. It was obvious he was very talented. As we chatted, the man with my rucksack appeared, and soon the tea-house was crowded as we discussed how best I should progress farther. The man from 'Pindi suggested that we should join up with the nomads. This idea appealed to me enormously, as it did to Arlem since it meant we could probably use one of the nomads' horses to carry a rucksack. While we talked, I noticed a gleam in Richard's eyes. He had come to Burawai just for a short outing to do some sketching, but as he listened to our plans I could see he was interested in joining us.

As the conversation drifted from plans of crossing the Babusar to ourselves, Richard and I began revealing our personal history to one another, as well as 'talking' to the gathering crowd. Richard, who was an architect and interior designer by trade, was afflicted by wanderlust. Born in the Isle of Man, he had started travelling at the age of two, when his father, an electrical engineer, went to work in the tin mines of Malaya. In 1957, the family moved to Perth, Australia. At thirty-eight— he looked considerably younger—Richard was still travelling, and, aside from living and working in his native Australia, the United States and Europe, doing various jobs such as bank clerk, baker, seaman on a yacht, waiter etc, he had also lived in Sri Lanka studying Buddhism. It soon became evident, without either of us actually discussing it, that Richard would be accompanying me the following day. Simply put, he thought it might be fun to do some sketching a little farther north, and he was interested in studying the nomads.

For years I had dreamed of travelling with nomads. It didn't matter where—Africa, Arabia, Iran, Pakistan, anywhere that man still roamed free. Unfortunately, today, what wars and famine have left undone, border restrictions have finished. Also, I had always been fascinated by trade routes, and the old caravan trail, across the Babusar to Chilas and beyond, to Hunza and Turkestan, was one of the oldest in the world.

Before we left Burawai the next morning, Richard and I looked through the visitors' book in the resthouse. The entries read:

> 1955 'Service indifferent. Lamp out of order and there was also no curtains.'
>
> 1956 'Building needs urgent repairs.'
>
> 1964 'How distant and yet how near. We would wish to stay here and meditate provided the resthouse was furnished with better amenities.'
>
> 1967 'It would be appreciated if a flush system were installed.'
>
> 1969 'What heaven on earth, but what hell one goes through to reach it. Push on folks if you wish to go on to eternity.'
>
> 1969 'Even this place has no consolation for a disheartened person.'

I wondered who the guest of 1969 had been; his name and profession were illegible. I sympathized with the army captain who had wanted the flush system installed, and I agreed with the writer of 1956, who had suggested the building was in need of urgent repairs. As there were very few entries in the book (some years there might be only one), I wondered if in thirty years *any* repairs had been made.

While Richard returned to the tea-house to collect his things, and Arlem went in search of the leader of the nomad caravan, I sat on the tumbledown porch of the inspection bungalow. We had been told it was an eleven-mile hike to the next small village, and while I was looking forward to it, I was anxious about the blisters on my heels and toes, and Arlem's aching shoulders; I prayed we could hire a pack-horse.

With my journal on my knees, I gazed out at the small valley to the point where it disappeared around the side of a mountain; even as a child, I had always wanted to know what lay around a bend in the road. In the foreground were a number of small stone huts with flat cedar roofs covered with mud and grass, while beyond them horses and cattle grazed and the smoke from the nomads' camp fires wafted into the clear air. It was restful to sit there, before the start of a new day. This was also a favourite time of mine in the big cities—that time before the population has started on its busy rounds and only the few are about—the milkman, road-sweepers, newspaper sellers—the only time the cities ever seem to pause. Now, alone for a few minutes before the journey got underway, I breathed in deeply and felt entirely relaxed and happy.

The morning was well advanced, when Arlem, Richard and I joined the nomads for the last day of their trek to the high pastures. For thirty rupees, the leader of the caravan had agreed to take my baggage. Both Richard and I were greatly impressed with Yakoob. Of medium height and dressed in dark blue pantaloons and *kurta* with a rust and orange-coloured waistcoat and orange turban, he cut a romantic figure as he strode along. Dark sideburns, moustache and heavy beard together with his flashing dark eyes gave him the look of a brigand. From Arlem, we learned that he and his people were semi-nomadic and came from Kohistan, living in and around Balakot during the winter and returning every summer to pastures below the Babusar. In appearance, they looked very different from the nomads I had met at Balakot. There, the black-turbanned men and dour slovenly women had held my attention, on account of their extraordinarily long, hooked noses. Yakoob and his people were more aristocratic. They had finer features and they walked with pride.

The track we followed, which I had seen from the bungalow porch, soon began to wind its way along the river, which flowed into one of the greenest lakes I have ever seen. Arlem was also impressed, and asked me to take his photograph beside the lake. Again, I was struck by the many

93

shades of green around us varying from light pastel to very dark.

Soon after leaving the lake, we crossed over another part of the river by way of a small wooden bridge. On the other side, Yakoob paused and taking pity on Richard volunteered to take the lighter of his two canvas bags. The heavier one, filled with his collection of rocks, he had to continue carrying himself.

Now the track began climbing, winding round and round the mountainside. The sun shimmered on the river below, silver one moment, golden the next, where it widened, becoming a vivid green. I noticed how the pines and cedars seemed to grow along the ridges and curves of the mountains in straight lines, as if planted by man.

As Richard fell back to talk to a small boy and a number of giggling girls, I turned my attention to the women. I wondered if some of them were originally nomads from Afghanistan. Although their clothes were dusty and drab, the red and brown backgrounds of their *shalwar-khameez* looked similar to those worn by some *powendas* or gypsies I had seen near Peshawar.* I also noted that these women wore the long Afghan ear-rings which I had seen on the Frontier. Children too small to walk were carried in pouches on their mothers' backs tied by a band across the women's foreheads. All around me, the herdsmen were calling out to their livestock, goading them on further. Small hump-backed cattle, large, sad-eyed water-buffalo, goats, foals, calves and pack-horses moved along the trail in a long line. It was the pack-horses that held my gaze the longest, however, as, besides carrying the customary household effects, such as aluminium pots and blankets, some had, on their saddles, a small 'tent' made out of sticks and blankets beneath which rested the odd chicken or puppy.

Occasionally, a terraced field or a small stone and cedar hut showed signs of life, but otherwise the land became more austere the higher we climbed. Now I found it wise to walk on the inside, away from the precipice since a collision with a water-buffalo could otherwise send me hurtling down to the river below. As we progressed further the path flattened out and not long after the sun had reached its zenith, we came upon the first of two bridgeless rivers. I looked aghast at the fast-moving water plunging over sharp, pointed rocks. We watched nervously as Yakoob supervised the crossing of his people and the herds. Youths with

---

*Generally, the nomads using this old caravan trail are from Kohistan (the land of mountains) in the north. I have been told that the Gujars, a nomadic people, originally from Nuristan in Afghanistan, who wander from the Afghan border in the west, to the plains of the Punjab in the south, also use it to take their flocks and herds up to the high pastures. Although I believe Yakoob and his people were from the former group, there may well have been Gujars travelling with them, as they are reputed to be the only ones to keep buffalo.

94

calves and baby goats in their arms struggled across the water up to their knees. Small boys herded the large animals across, while men carried or took the arms of their wives. When all were safely across, Yakoob turned to us and motioned for us to proceed.

'Okay, Richard, you go first,' I said as I reached for my camera. Rather unkindly, I thought, he glared at me, but saying nothing he picked up the legs of his *shalwar*, and with his bag slung over his shoulder and his scarf wrapped around his head, he stepped gingerly into the water.

Once on the other side, he got his own back when he stood smugly watching my undignified crossing. With my boots slung around my neck, Yakoob holding one hand and Arlem the other, I slipped and staggered as the two men struggled to stop me falling into the icy water.

As I sat down to put on my socks and boots, Richard pointed to a small stone building in the distance. I turned: 'You don't suppose?'

'It's not possible, dearie.'

We quickened our pace. Could it be? Surely not? Yes it was! We'd found a *chai*-shop!

In the blackened interior of the hut, we drank cup after sooty cup of the piping hot, sugary, energy-giving thirst-quenching brew. The break gave us time to talk to some of the local inhabitants who had joined us. Who were we? Where were we going? And that all-important question—WHY? These questions are familiar to the traveller in remote areas and in the developing countries. Travel for its own sake is incomprehensible to the majority of people in the world, for to them it is a luxury. Here in the hills and mountains of Pakistan, people only travel for a specific reason. The traveller is fortunate indeed to be able to travel the world exploring, enjoying new experiences, meeting new people. Never does this come home to me more strongly than when I am in a plane or train rushing past men and women toiling in the fields—to be born, to live and to die in one place, never to know what is over the horizon seems inconceivable. To this day, there are believed to be villagers in the more remote Hunza valleys who still believe the world is small and is bounded by the great Central Asian peaks.

We came across Yakoob and the rest of the caravan not far from the *chai*-shop where they had made camp for the afternoon rest. As I came up, he pointed to his tooth as he had done on a previous rest-stop. Then, he had refused any medical aid, but now he had either decided that I was to be trusted, or he was in so much pain it overcame his misgivings. I gave him some Paracetamol which I knew would help relieve his discomfort.

When we moved off again I glanced at Arlem. Without the burden of the rucksack, he was proving to be a good walker and was in fine spirits.

His ready smile and easy-going manner appealed to both Richard and me, and we made a compatible threesome as we pressed on in the afternoon heat. The valley provided us with no shelter from the sun, but we continued on, our rest-stops becoming more frequent.

With Yakoob and the caravan far behind us, we now found ourselves left to our own devices in terrain which was becoming increasingly more hostile. After crossing several small glaciers, not easy without crampons, our way was barred by a very wild and turbulent river plunging down a slope from the snout of a wide glacier above. We had two choices—either climb up much higher and cross over the glacier, or go down river in the hope it might be more shallow and therefore easier to cross. The climb up the mountain and across the glacier appeared to be the more formidable of the two choices, and I found both Arlem and Richard in agreement. The river, however, posed a problem. Nowhere did it seem negotiable. Even though it could not have been more than a foot deep, it was plunging down the mountain slope at an enormous speed and its entire width, about a hundred feet across, was strewn with boulders and sharp rocks.

With Arlem muttering 'no problem' and Richard smiling cheerfully (they were both wearing *chaplis*), I once more divested myself of my hiking-boots and took each of the men by the hand. When I put my right foot into the water, I screamed. Although I was expecting it to be cold, my toes actually burned in this glacial flow. I looked up to see that the sun was low in the sky; this was no time to be faint-hearted. I plunged in, determined not to stop until I reached the other side, but it was a painful business. Not only was the water icy, but the pebbles and sharp rocks were like needles beneath my feet.

Sitting safely on the far bank, for a moment I could hardly speak. My feet were on fire and bleeding at the heels. Richard, who needed no explanation, baled up handfuls of water and bathed my feet. Strangely enough, the cold water brought instant relief, and I smiled gratefully at him. Arlem, who had been looking on anxiously, relaxed once more.

Not many miles on we came upon an encampment of stone huts inhabited by a group of nomads. The women boiled us some milk, laid down blankets for us to sit on, and, observing my fatigue, set to work to give me a massage. My arms, legs, shoulders, back and thighs were pummelled and stroked, while over my head, they delightedly discussed the arrival of the three strangers. Their pleasure matched our own, and, in the only way we could, we paid them back for their kindness by giving first-aid to a young child with a bad facial injury. We should have liked to stay longer, but we had to catch up with the others and reach the village of Besal before nightfall.

The tea-house at Besal where Richard and I stayed the night.

In Besal, which boasted only a few houses, one *dukan* and a small circular tea-house that was built of stone with a canvas roof, we made friends with four young Pakistanis travelling on motor-bikes en route for the Khunjerab. Together, we took up quarters in the tea-house, which was exceptionally clean and had fresh white bedding laid out in a semi-circle around the hearth, located near the entrance. It was just what I needed.

Yakoob arrived with the rucksacks and gave only a faint smile when I gave him the thirty rupees with an extra five plus ten cigarettes. As he and many like him could not afford to smoke regularly, I did not feel that my gesture was in any way lowering his life expectancy. It is perhaps unfortunate that the West has seduced the world into buying cigarettes, but for those who cannot afford this doubtful luxury, the odd cigarette is a precious commodity and is regarded as an expected gratuity to either smoke or barter. In Hunza, where the people are more affluent and more enlightened, the inhabitants recently burned their complete stock of cigarettes in a bonfire, declaring they would never smoke again.

As Yakoob pocketed what I had given him, his eyes still held the same wary, sceptical gleam that I had come to expect. Whether it was because I was a foreigner or because I was a woman, I did not know, but, in spite of his attitude, he was a man I trusted instinctively.

Through Arlem and the *dukan* owner, I asked him if he would help us next day which he agreed to do.

Together, Richard, Arlem and myself dined with the motor-bike riders on curried mutton and *chappatis*, all the while swapping tales of our travel experiences and entertaining the owner and the cook. It was not long though before fatigue took over, and we bedded down for the night. Turning round, my back against the lamplight, I mistook the sleeping form of one of the young Pakistanis, who had retired early, for a bag of potatoes, and sat upon him. This led to shrieks, much teasing and laughter, before, squashed between Arlem and the wall, I finally lay down for the night. To the sound of snores, muffled giggles and sonorous voices, I dozed off, hoping there were no black beetles or worse lodged in the stones of the wall, barely an inch from my face.

Over the Babusar

One of the most difficult aspects of travel in northern Pakistan is the unreliability of departure times, and so it was with frustration that I waited for Yakoob. The night before, I had been told by the owner of the *dukan* not to stay in Gittidas because the people were no good. Although I appreciated the warning, I took it with a pinch of salt, since the mountain valleys in northern Pakistan are much like Greek islands where the inhabitants of one tightly-knit community mistrust those of another. But now with the warnings repeated again this morning, not only by the *dukan* owner but by some of the other locals, Richard and I thought perhaps we should press on all the way to Babusar—a village on the other side of the pass, some twenty miles distant and most of them uphill.

The sun was already high in the sky, and in Yakoob's absence, I found myself worrying about who or what was going to carry my rucksacks for the day.

The bright idea of a donkey for seventy rupees was suggested, but, just as I was about to agree, I was told, as an afterthought, that if we should come to a river, the donkey would not cross. I glanced at Arlem and Richard. Richard was busy sketching the tea-house, quite content to let me see to the planning and negotiating (unlike Yakoob, Richard was not sceptical about the role of women) while Arlem stood frowning, rubbing his sandalled foot in the dust, waiting for a decision. Hiding my irritation, I asked him to go and look for Yakoob. It did not occur to me that my request was unreasonable and neither apparently did it seem to Arlem, for he grinned and said: '*Tikay*, no problem.'

An hour or so later after the students had left, I arrived back from a trip to the river to find Richard still contentedly sketching, and Arlem squatting dejectedly by my rucksack.

'Yakoob leave early,' he announced.

Before I could reply, the owner of the *dukan*, standing in the doorway just a few feet away, beckoned me over. There, sitting cross-legged on a raised platform, sat Yakoob, twirling his goading stick. How Arlem, or for that matter anyone else, could possibly have missed him, I shall never know.

Yakoob greeted me with what I took to be a grin of amusement as I smiled at him in very obvious relief. For one hundred and fifty rupees I could ride one of his horses up to the top of the pass and put my packs on another; or, for just seventy, I could have the services of a pack-horse, again only to the top. He could go no farther as he had to return to his people. I thought for a moment. It was not only a question of finance (though I was on a very limited budget), but as memories of my horse ride across the Shandur came vividly to mind, I opted just to hire the pack-horse.

Richard and I got together our bits and pieces, packed up some boiled eggs, *chappatis* and dried fruit and settled with the owner of the tea-house, while Arlem was given the task of filling the water-bottle and milk-churn. As with my decision to take a pack-horse, putting Arlem in charge of our supply of drinking water was one I should live to regret. Yakoob grabbed both rucksacks, and, without so much as a grimace or sigh, hoisted them easily onto his shoulders and set off at a fast pace through the tiny settlement to a distant patch of ground where his horses were grazing.

As we came to a halt, Yakoob motioned for us to continue. We walked on through what at first was rather barren terrain, following the river. To our left, the mountainside seemed to whisper a ghostly sound as if sand were gently falling, but the rocky slope gave no hint of movement. A bright green lake appeared around the bend. Again, Arlem posed for a photograph. In my life, I have been lucky enough to see many beautiful natural landscapes, but never have I seen anything to match the beauty of the countryside we trekked through on our crossing of the Babusar.

Shortly before noon, we reached Lake Lulusar, seemingly even greener and the most beautiful spot we had yet encountered. We found ourselves standing on a carpet of wild flowers—yellow poppies and dandelions, white daises and peonies, dark and light blue forget-me-nots, gentians, columbines, irises, blue and purple violets and pink mallows. Behind us lay those inviting snow-clad summits and below us on the edge of the lake yawned great holes in a glacier, while tiny ice floes dotted the edge of the very still water. A white butterfly hovered in front of me before alighting on a yellow poppy. I stood for a moment absolutely enraptured. The spell affected us all and even Yakoob stopped to let me take his photograph. Moving on, Richard and I had great fun trying to count and name the flowers. The lake narrowed and where it became a river once more, we stopped to cross. I was just about to sit down and unlace my hiking boots, when Yakoob said 'No' and pointed to the pack-horse. I looked at him in disbelief. Besides there being no room, the combined weight of myself and the rucksacks would surely bring the mare to her knees, and the yearling brought along for the benefit of both mother and offspring was out of the question. Yakoob gave a mischievous smile and beckoned me forward. I protested, but, catching me just as I turned to look for a rock to mount from, he suddenly flung two strong arms around me in a bear hug and scooped me up onto the neck of the poor mare. My loss of dignity made me glare at both Yakoob and my amused companions, as he literally threw my legs across the mare's neck and bade me hold onto the pack ropes behind me—no easy feat. The mare gingerly took the first step into the water, and then, with Yakoob holding tightly onto the halter, she lunged across and no doubt would have unseated me if Yakoob had not steadied me in time.

Once on the other side, we criss-crossed numerous tributaries. Way ahead, we could see the trail winding ever upwards to the Babusar Top. It not only looked an awfully long way but also very high. My step faltered. It was already one-thirty in the afternoon. Now snow-capped peaks beyond the Babusar appeared. I knew that way ahead, somewhere to the east of the Babusar, lay Nanga Parbat, 'The Naked Mountain', and the beginning of the Great Himalaya and to the north-east, the mighty Karakorams. My anxiety was tempered with exhilaration.

The trail led over spongy turf that was laced with streams and dotted with stones and rocks. Yakoob strode ahead searching for a place to find the river again. He ventured to the water's edge, abandoned the idea of crossing and continued on. Another time he waded out and came back; the river seemed unfordable. We were still searching for a way across when in the distance we saw a small wooden bridge close to a few dwellings of stone and mud. While the three of us crossed over, Yakoob drove the horses into the river for a drink. On the opposite shore, shepherds came to meet us. Their children, ragged and with cheerful, dirty-smeared faces, stood behind the men, at first hesistant and then increasingly bold, as we smiled and sank down thankfully upon the soft grass.

Yakoob turned to us and told Arlem in a matter of fact voice, that the shepherds had neither tea nor sugar—only milk. My disappointment was offset by my suddenly remembering some Earl Grey tea bags in my pack, that had been given to me by friends in Karachi. As for the sugar, that was no problem, as I had sweeteners. It was two-thirty in the afternoon and apart from being thirsty, everyone was ravenous. The boiled eggs and chappatis we had brought with us soon appeased our hunger.

When the hot brew arrived, the children were fascinated by the tea bags (lovingly kept to one side of the bowl for further use by the shepherds), and I gave them the paper coverings which seemed to be of equal interest. Yakoob, ever wary, at first refused to take sweeteners in his tea, but suddenly changed his mind when his cup was half empty, and put in four before I could stay his hand.

While Yakoob loaded up the pack-horse, I sent Arlem off to fill the water-bottle and milk-churn. On our last rest-stop, I had been angry to find that Arlem had tipped away the contents of the milk-churn as Yakoob had told him there was plenty of water along the route. Although the water in the mountain areas in Pakistan is deliciously cool and clear and often full of nutritious minerals, care has to be taken not to drink below a settlement or from a river where cattle may have crossed— this last indiscretion can lead to the catching of jardia, a particularly unpleasant form of intestinal bacterium. I now made him take advantage of the lovely clear spring water that was nearby.

When Arlem returned, I found that the milk-churn was only half full. I appreciated that the more water there was in it, the heavier it would be, but to travel on up to the pass where there either might not be any water or if there was it might be muddy, would hardly be wise, so I sent him reluctantly back to the spring.

It was three o'clock when we resumed our journey. We were on the outer edge of the village of Gittidas. Several of the shepherds, their children scampering before us, led us down the now rocky grasslands to the maze of low stone buildings that resembled an ancient Indian site I had once visited in Arizona. The people of Gittidas came out to meet us and all seemed friendly, belying the words of the *dukan* owner and the residents of Besal. I wondered if it would be wise to call a halt, but I had only hired Yakoob for the day, and if I let him go, how would I transport my baggage up to the pass the following day? I asked someone how long it would take to the top. Two hours. Then it was only four miles down the other side to the village of Babusar. With luck, I thought (but forgetting we would be climbing all the way to the top), we should reach there by seven. It would be wise then to press on.

Leaving Gittidas behind, we crossed a difficult ice bridge over another part of the river, only to be confronted by a high cliff blocking our way to the top. Earlier, we had spotted the dust sent up by the motor-bikes on the ascent to the Babusar; since they should by then have been a long way in front of us, these obstacles had obviously delayed them for several hours. Having ridden up as steep a gradient on my trek across the Shandur, I knew that Yakoob and the horses would make it okay, but I was less confident of my own ability. The trail was steep and very rocky and already I was beginning to tire.

Arlem, gallantly shouldering my heavier milk-churn while I carried the bottle, turned to me as if guessing my fears and said brightly: 'No problem.' So hand in hand, we climbed up the mountainside. Every now and then I had to stop. The youths from the village who were accompanying us gave me encouraging smiles as Arlem resolutely pulled me up the cliff. How Yakoob managed I did not know, but as we neared the top, there he was marching ahead, seemingly effortlessly.

Richard called a conference. Earlier he had come to me saying that Yakoob was worried as to whether I understood that he could only take us up to the top of the pass and not on to the village of Babusar, some miles below on the other side. Over lunch I had told Yakoob (through Arlem) that I understood but that if he changed his mind, I should be glad to hire him to go on farther. He had declined so now I thought that Richard's decision to go on ahead, as far as Yakoob would take us (and the rucksacks), was a wise one. Richard, who had by now emptied most of the rocks from his canvas bag, soon pulled ahead, leaving me with Arlem. The villagers waved goodbye and once more we were on our own.

The next three hours (two hours was the estimated time for lithe young men and the likes of Yakoob) was a mixture of exhilaration and torture.

The torture began before the exhilaration and it was not long before I had to stop every hundred yards or so to take a breather. Arlem also drew away, leaving me to enjoy that great wilderness alone. Behind and to my right the white peaks grew in stature as I climbed higher, while to my left was the unfriendly rocky ridge of the mountain (which barred our way to the village of Babusar), beneath which, except for some stone huts no bigger than a large dog kennel, there was no shelter from the sun which had been blazing down all day. I was now nearing exhaustion: my hands were covered in red blotches, my legs ached and my knees trembled; my lips were sore, and blisters on my heels and toes made walking agony.

Every so often Arlem would sit on a rock and wait for me to catch up. Thankfully, he did not pass any comment but just smiled encouragingly before moving on, sometimes disappearing round a bend. In those moments, I was reminded of how, as a child, I would escape from my parents at the sea-shore and hide myself behind some rocks so that I might commune with nature alone. I turned to the wide expanse that was opening up before me with every painful step. The higher I climbed, the greater became the panorama—stretching into the distance was a great mass of white rock, of glaciers and cliffs and crested ridges until they rose up to be lost in a swirling misty cloud. I paused for a moment, desiring to embrace the whole world about me. Here, in the shadow of Nanga Parbat (26,600 ft), I beheld the beginning of the greatest mountain massif in the world, reaching on interminably across the vast subcontinent. The sight to me seemed so magnificent, I was filled with wonder and a feeling of awe. Perhaps it is only through strain and physical pain that such grandeur can be truly savoured.

I was in awe, too, of the history of the 'Naked Mountain', or as some climbers have called it, 'Killer Mountain'. Somewhere out there, in that beautiful mass of snow and ice, over thirty climbers had lost their lives. This knowledge, together with my exhaustion, induced in me a feeling of vulnerability. At that moment I was acutely aware of the intrinsic loneliness of man and of his frailty. Here he was insignificant—at the mercy of the landscape. Although not a believer in the accepted sense, at that moment I prayed that I might have the strength to be able to carry on up that never-ending trail that always seemed to stretch round one more bend.

Rounding such a bend, I came upon Arlem sitting on a rock. He looked as tired as I felt, but when I reached out for the milk-churn, he looked embarrassed. 'Oh, Arlem! No!' I glared at the boy as I spoke through dry lips, my speech sounding strange to my ears. My own bottle was empty, too, but as he was carrying the bigger container, there should have been some left. I needed a drink desperately.

About two hours or so after we had left Gittidas, Yakoob came riding the mare back towards me and leading the yearling. He handed me a note from Richard which said that he had asked Yakoob if he would be willing to carry on and that the answer has still been in the negative. I folded the note and looked wistfully at Yakoob, who steadily and wordlessly returned my gaze. I tried one more time. I was acutely aware that I was in a perilous position (it was nearly five o'clock and we still had glaciers and four miles of unknown terrain to cover before dark), and that I had inadvertently placed both Arlem and Richard in danger as well as myself. No doubt I should have taken up Yakoob's offer of riding on horseback instead of trekking on foot, but there was no point in regretting a past decision. I swallowed my pride and asked Yakoob once more. Gravely he said no, he could not, he had to return to his people. I smiled and pulled out a hundred rupee note to cover his fee, plus a gratuity, and handed it to him. As he took it from me, he seemed to hesitate, looking at me uncomfortably. I realized at that moment that he had no wish to leave us there; it was just a question of priorities and his people came first. Yakoob was, as I had surmised, a thoroughly responsible and reliable man. He had kept his part of the bargain. It was not his fault if some fool Westerner had wanted to trek over the pass on foot and had reached the point of exhaustion. Then with a handshake and without a backward glance, he went out of my life as casually as he

104

had come into it.

It was nearly half an hour later that I saw a figure waving from a ridge in front of me. Arlem pointed and exclaimed in relief: 'Richard!'

Encouraged at last, I struggled on, stopping now at fifty-second intervals. At ten minutes past six, I staggered across the uneven, slate-filled rocky ground, dotted with pools and rivulets of water, of the Babusar Top, to where Richard was seated on a cairn, placidly sketching. I wondered if anything would ever disturb this seemingly unflappable young man as he looked up and said cheerfully: 'Well dearie, how are you? Welcome to the Babusar Top!'

Beyond speech, I nodded and, staggering a few more steps, reached the edge of the giant bowl of 'ice cream cones' that lay before me in the last rays of the afternoon sun. A cold wind whipped through my shirt sleeves, but for once in my life, the cold did not bother me. The austere beauty and the feeling of achievement in doing what I had set out to do held me riveted to the spot, until a particularly strong gust brought me back to the reality of our situation. We still had four miles to cover, and the sun would soon be setting; we were without clean water and we had some difficult terrain ahead of us.

'Don't you want to put on a sweater or jacket?' asked Richard kindly.

It was strange. Arlem was wearing his yellow baseball jacket and Richard had draped a blanket around his shoulders, but the biting wind, whipping against my body, felt cool and refreshing. I desperately needed water.

We started down a slate-filled incline that lead to the first of the large glaciers. Richard went on ahead tentatively carrying my blue rucksack, while Arlem, burdened once more with the big green one, took my hand. The glacier was steep and slippery; it was like trying to walk down the inside of a basin. Looking worried for the first time, Richard went on ahead. Ever so slowly, we slithered and sunk to our knees in the snow and ice. Once I sprawled headlong and it was all Arlem could do to pull me to my feet. When at last we came to the end, I drank thirstily from one of the numerous streams that were pouring down from the glacier and Arlem filled both the containers.

After we had rested and I'd shared a couple of stale health food bars, we moved off, hoping the going would get easier. It didn't. Instead we found ourselves in a wasteland of boggy ground. Arlem, now in the lead, took a wrong step and sank to his knees in the quagmire. The sun had set, twilight was upon us, and in the distance, directly in our path, was another glacier. In my journal, filled in the next day, I wrote that at that point 'I was a little worried'. That was an understatement. I wondered if Arlem, who was looking decidedly anxious, and Richard, now once again appearing unperturbed, were aware of our plight. The Babusar Top was 13,600 feet high. Night was almost upon us, and we were a long way from the village.

Across the glacier, through more rock-strewn bogland we went, until we found a track which was also partly a river of melted snow. As both Arlem and Richard were wearing *chaplis*, the water was cold against their feet, but this time I was luckier, for my strong hiking-boots kept out the water. When we reached the tree line, night was closing in fast. Walking in single file, it was hard to see the person in front. To make matters worse, I was having difficulty in breathing. In retrospect, I realize I must have been hyperventilating, because I was growing increasingly nervous over my inability to articulate. Although I stopped frequently to take a sip of water, my mouth and lips were parched, and I found it impossible to frame a word. I would struggle to pronounce the name of Arlem or Richard, only to be rewarded with a strange inarticulate croak. It was at this juncture, I heard Arlem say for the first time: 'We have big problem!'

When Arlem asked for a flash-light, I held off, knowing a beam from a torch, with three people in line, could throw shadows for someone and lead to an accident, but when the watery trail gave way to a precipitous jeep track I gave in. One false step and we could plunge over the edge. I brought out my torch, and, walking three abreast, with our arms linked, we marched on, the beam from the torch growing fainter and fainter. There was one awful moment, when, fishing for batteries in the rucksacks, we were plunged into total darkness. To be in the middle of a cold mountain forest at night, without a light of any kind, is an eerie, not to say frightening, experience. With the torch working once more and now armed with staves, we continued along the jeep track. Every so often, I had to pull Arlem to me, as he drifted dangerously near the edge. Suddenly, in the distance, we heard a dog bark. Then we saw the chassis of a jeep appear in the beam of light cast by the torch, but that was all it was, a broken-down chassis. Far to our right in the void, there was an occasional flicker of a lamp. We went on encouraged. Surely we could not be far from habitation.

The wind was now blowing very cold, but I was still delighting in the coolness, worried only by my now complete inability to speak. My breathing was becoming more laboured, especially when I tried to open my mouth in order to say something to my companions. No matter how often I took a sip of water, it made no difference. I could sense, too, that Richard and Arlem were worried.

'What you need is some electrolite powder,' Richard said, when I tried to speak. 'I think you must be suffering from dehydration.'

A little way on the trees began to thin out, the path no longer hugged the mountainside, and, thankfully, there was no longer a precipice to haunt our footsteps. But as our spirits rose they were dashed again when we saw our way was barred. Wherever we flashed the torch, the beam of light lit up a narrow river. Richard and I looked at one another. It would be foolish to attempt to cross it in the dark.

I pointed to a nearby grassy slope. Richard nodded, and, with Arlem muttering 'Big problem', we set about making camp. It was strange, I reflected later, that it didn't matter I was beyond talking, for Richard and I worked as one mind. Together we built a fire, while Arlem, of his own volition, helped us to collect firewood.

My milk-churn, hated by Arlem and loved by me, proved a valuable asset. Once we had a fire blazing, we were able to have a drink of hot water, and then Richard doled out some electrolite powder (the same as ORS powders), which put back the salts into our bodies. As Richard had rightly guessed, I was dehydrated. Almost immediately, I was able to speak again, only to become aware that I was freezing. I pulled on some extra clothing and managed to find stale biscuits and some raisins in my pack which helped to ease the pains in our stomachs. While I sorted out my gear, Richard soaked dates and coconut pieces for the morning. Mentally, I congratulated him for his forethought in bringing them along from Naran.

Fortunately, we had dropped down far enough to have escaped the cold winds of the glacier basins—and being camped among some pines, we were reasonably sheltered. The weather was kind to us. I gave Arlem my insulated waistcoat and survival bag and placed him nearest the fire. With Richard's plastic sheeting and blanket beneath us, and my sleeping-bag opened up as a covering, Richard and I bedded down next to him.

We awakened at dawn. Within twenty feet of our camp was a small wooden bridge. We all stared at it and then looked at one another and fell about laughing. It was in cheerful mood that we relit the fire and had our frugal breakfast of hot water, electrolite powder, dates, raisins and coconut.

As we were breaking camp, a herd of goats came into view on the other side of the river, followed by some children. It was obvious we were not far from our goal. Although we had been only feet away from the bridge, it was just as well we had not ventured farther, for the track had again become one with the river. Even in daylight, it was ankle-breaking terrain, made all the more difficult by high walls on either side and great boulders and rocks strewn all the way along.

We were soon passing through a narrow valley hemmed in by rugged ridges of straggling pines. Every so often, we caught a glimpse of small cedar-built cabins. People appeared, then a polo ground, and then we were walking through a deserted bazaar of closed *dukans*. At last we had arrived in Babusar, the first village on the other side of the pass. We had made it! And, as Richard spoke of the difficult terrain we had passed through and commented that glaciers were no places for horses, I not only offered up a prayer of thanks, but felt supremely grateful that Yakoob had proved such a strong, wise and noble guide.

Arlem—Tourist Guide

The second most difficult aspect of travel in Pakistan is obtaining privacy. Small hotels, tea-houses, inspection bungalows, government resthouses, in fact anywhere one might lay one's head, are likely to be invaded by the local male populace if a Westerner arrives in their midst. It is not only a question of curiosity, but in the countries east of Athens, as I had found out to my cost, people do not have the Western mania for space and privacy—it is a luxury that many people in the developing countries cannot afford. In some languages, the word privacy does not even exist.

When the three of us staggered down the grassy incline to the old and dilapidated resthouse, we were followed by half the male population of Babusar. The *chowkidar*, as is usual, was elderly, eager to use his few words of English, suspicious of who we might be but at the same time keen to earn a few rupees. My letter with the official stamp soon dispelled his fears and he set about making us welcome. His long white beard and big whiskers framed a kindly face with twinkling brown eyes, and I immediately warmed to the old man. With much chatter and chuckling, he showed us into a large comfortable room with two bedsteads, a coffee table and chairs that were strong and stable, and, to our joy, he said we could light a fire in the open grate.

As we unpacked amidst the crowd of spectators, the *chowkidar* went off to search for food in the bazaar. Eventually, we sat down to our first meal in something like twenty hours: the freshly boiled eggs, *chappatis*, and sugary milkless tea did much to restore our depleted energy. Our audience, who had at first seemed unfriendly, began to relax as Arlem related to them the tale of our trek across the Babusar; he made a good liaison officer—the young looked up to him with admiration, while the elderly looked on with affection, wise to his inexperience. Once the inhabitants of Babusar had decided that we were okay people, and our breakfast, under their concentrated gaze, had been finished, I was called upon to take up my camera and bring out my first-aid kit.

The morning passed quickly and in the late afternoon and early evening, jeep drivers came and went and haggled with Arlem over the price and departure time of a jeep for the following morning. We settled for one at eight o'clock. All day, our room was never empty of people, but I had grown so used to this phenomenon, it was only rarely that this bothered me unduly.

Always worried about Arlem's comfort and well-being, I was delighted when the *chowkidar* gave us leave to use the sitting-room, so that the three of us could sleep in comfort. Arlem, as my guide and bearer, always manfully saw to it I came first, Richard second and himself last. We went to sleep listening to the wind rustling the leaves outside and smelling the aroma of resin from the smoking pine cones in the grate.

Early next morning, I took a lone walk through the deserted bazaar and out past the polo-ground. I wanted one more glimpse of that mountain top and glistening white glacier. The valley was still in gloom, but the sun shone directly on the Babusar Top, and it looked cool and remote in the early morning light. It had an almost mystical pull. I gazed at it in much the same way one looks upon a lover. I was bound to that mountain for life; wherever I go, that cold windy spot will remain forever with me. I felt then I could understand what drew climbers to mountains and why they yearned to return again and again.

The third difficulty in travelling in Pakistan is that one always rides in or on vehicles that are literally bulging at the seams. Once in Swat, I rode inside a wagon (officially seating twelve) with twenty-nine other passengers, with a further ten crammed into the luggage rack on top. In one small village, I saw thirty-odd school children hanging onto the back of a bus in the form of a Christmas tree. In the towns and cities, I had become accustomed to seeing two and sometimes three on a bicycle, and I had often noticed three or four on a scooter or motor-bike. On one occasion in Lahore, I had observed in disbelief six on a motor-bike complete with a mother and baby, the woman's *chowdar* draped over the rear wheel. During my first visit to the Frontier, I had found myself at a late hour (due to a shortage of transport) in a jeep with sixteen Mujahideen, armed with rifles, crammed into the rear, two squeezed between me and the driver and one on the bonnet. Every time the driver changed gear, usually on a steep gradient or dangerous curve, the headlights had dimmed, leaving us suspended above a deep black void, our lives in the balance.

This time, however, we were luckier for few people would be travelling from Babusar down to the sweltering bowl of Chilas and we were, so we thought, assured of a comfortable ride. When we boarded the jeep, it came as no surprise to find that our driver was not one of those with whom we had haggled the day before, but a complete stranger.

110

The ride when it began proved to be one of the most terrifying of my travels even though it was perhaps not more than a couple of miles long. The track was steep and wound down the mountainside in treacherous hairpin bends, on the edges of which lay large stones and rocks submerged in several inches of water. At every corner, we went to the very edge of the precipice overlooking the valley below. Once, the front fender pushed over a rock which made a larger one move forward, before settling back in its old position. Another inch or so and the front wheels of the jeep would have been suspended in mid-air. It was a moment when my blood really did run cold and sweat begin to break out on my forehead. I found myself clenching my fists, my heart was thumping madly, and there was an empty feeling in the pit of my stomach. Behind me, Richard looked pale. Arlem's face was in shadow, as he had the peak of his baseball cap pulled right down, but the rigidity of his body told its own story.

When the jeep finally came to a stop it was at a large glacier. When the locals jumped out though, it wasn't to help get us across, but to carve out great lumps of ice with their shovels and pickaxes, which the driver, through Arlem, cheerfully explained would be packed in the jeep and taken down with us to Chilas. Calmly Richard drew out his sketch pad while I smiled at the jeep driver and took my camera from the bag. Two hours later, after one of the men had fallen down a crevice, Richard had drawn a couple of sketches and I had used up a roll of film, we resumed our journey, with Arlem and Richard now sitting on a tarpaulin covering several tons of ice. Of all the jeeps I've ridden in, that one, as regards actual weight, was probably the most heavily laden.

The road was again very treacherous, water-logged and filled sometimes with boulders and at others with large muddy pools. The youths with the pickaxes and shovels had now departed, but a man carrying a rifle now 'rode shotgun' next to the driver, not to look out for bandits but to help clear the way ahead. His companion joined Arlem and Richard in the back and all went smoothly until one of the tyres burst.

There were to be many more stops for landslides, for putting back the accelerator pin and for disembarking to lessen the danger of the jeep going over the edge or becoming bogged down. But I think it was the last stop that was probably the most hazardous. The road had narrowed to the width of the vehicle. On one side was a rocky cliff, on the other, a wild raging river with the bank, on the edge of the jeep track, washed away. On that occasion, while the rest of us were sent on ahead, three of the men stood on the front bumper, near to the cliff so that the driver, after repeated attempts, could inch his vehicle safely across.

Still the track was going downhill and still it was narrow. The mountain ridge to our right was occasionally split by a gap, giving us a fleeting glimpse of ice and snow; perhaps the western flank of Nanga Parbet, I wasn't sure. Soon the colour of the river turned to a muddy grey and the few terraced fields of corn on the other side heralded the end of habitation. The mountainside became barren as first the trees disappeared and then the grass, to be replaced by arid sandy soil and stones like fire-burnt cinders. We had entered that savage and soulless land that lies between Nanga Parbet and the town of Chilas. The mountainsides now became grey sandstone and granite cliffs. Amidst the bleak and grassless sandy gravel of the valley floor, there rose huge, towering blocks of black, brown and burnt umber, while smaller ones, worn down by erosion and time, littered the desert at their feet. Not for the first time in northern Pakistan, although here it was on a vaster scale and infinitely more stark and savage, I felt, looking at the scene all around, that at some point in the distant past, 'someone' had picked up a mountain, taken it to an enormous height, and had then dropped it, with the result that huge pieces of rock, lying beside one another, were a perfect jig-saw fit, while the terrain around them would be filled with slivers and shavings spewed in all directions: black, orange, burnt-umber offal spread out across the land burning bright in the harsh unrelenting sun. It was a cruel, remorseless place where not a flicker of life could be seen.

As we drove deeper into that fearful landscape, away from the shelter of cliff and mountainside, and into the constant red-hot sun, I became aware of the steady drip from the ice behind me. No wonder the citizens of Chilas would pay the jeep driver to hack away at the glaciers. I wondered what it must have been like in the days before motorized transport, when caravans trekked across the 'devil's anvil'. I had heard this term applied to other regions of the world, but no desert area I have seen could match this in its unrelenting hostility. The oasis of Chilas must have been welcomed with hysterical jubilation in the days of the Silk Road, when the town was an important staging post.

For us, Chilas represented the end of an adventure; for our jeep driver it meant getting his precious cargo to his customers. For many of them, it was the only means of preserving food and cooling soft drinks, for although electricity has come to Chilas, appliances such as refrigerators are only for the few. I did not envy the inhabitants, I thought, as we drove into the dusty bazaar.

It was lunch time and the sunburnt lanes were thronged with people; since the opening of the Khunjerab, Chilashas has regained her status as a staging-post on the route to China. As the jeep pulled up in the crowded main bazaar right outside an hotel, we got out and walked straight into what was obviously a dining-room, but which somehow

112

reminded me of a saloon in a Western movie. Alpine views of Pakistan were painted on the rough mud walls and the large room was filled with dirty red-topped formica tables and brown-backed plastic chairs. Loud music barely hid the noise of fifty or so patrons, and the food they were eating looked anything but appetizing.

Put off by what we had seen, we reversed out again and once more found ourselves in the heat of the bazaar, glad to be away from that unsettling atmosphere.

The next place we ventured into was, at first sight, little better than the previous one, except that here we were shown through the dining-room and out onto a small verandah overlooking a valley filled with orchards. As we squeezed in among a crowd of diners at a large table, Richard and I, having both worked in restaurants, looked around us with great interest. The *pièce de résistance* was the tall tree growing out of the verandah into which a spiral staircase had been hewn. This led to a small kitchen in which *chappatis* were being made. Beside the tree trunk was a tap where the patrons could wash their hands. Opposite us was the cook-house. In the doorway stood the cook, dressed in a brown *shalwar* and a once white, but now grey Pakistani vest, both of which were stained with sweat and grease and blackened with soot from the fire. He was obviously hot and tired, and, as he brushed away the sweat from his brow with the back of his hand, he regarded us with friendly curiosity. I liked his face, and I hoped the food would be good, but before we could eat, we asked that the table should be cleaned. We were not the only people to ask, and some of the locals even went so far as to bang the dirty plates and cups on the table-top in order to catch the attention of the cook's helpers—an old man and a small boy.

Now the banging was joined by shouts and yells from the frustrated customers, made all the more angry at seeing us, the foreigners, treated with what to them appeared rank discourtesy. One of the men next to us shouted at the boy, who truculently came towards us, brandishing a dirty towel with which he swiped at the crumbs, and a number of dead flies drowned in pools of water and gravy on the table-top.

Surprisingly, the food, when it came, was one of the most tasty dishes of *dhal* and rice I have ever eaten, and it was followed by the delicious cardamom flavoured green tea that I had become accustomed to on the Frontier and in the Northern Areas. The cook, who had bowed with pleasure when we had complimented him on the meal, rounded it off by sending a young man to show us the way to the resthouse. As he led us through the bazaar and across some waste ground to a wide street where new housing and shops, deserted in the afternoon heat, were struggling to rise out of the desert, the light wind blew sand into our faces and made

113

an old petrol sign creak in the breeze, reminding me of a windy night in Khartoum some years ago. There is something about desert towns that produce a languid attitude, a feeling of inertia, bringing to mind memories of starry nights and sleepy afternoons.

To my surprise, the government resthouse in Chilas, located off the new main road, was a grand affair and extremely comfortable, and, at fifty rupees a night, no dearer than any other resthouse. Carpets on the floor elicited 'Ohs' from all of us, and hot water in the bathroom was a bonus that none of us had dared to dream of.

Just before sunset, we ventured into the bazaar to purchase some oddments and to get my small alarm-clock mended. The shopkeepers proved to be friendly and helpful. The young watchmender looked at me with a grin and when he said '*ne tik tok*' (not very good) and I replied 'Tick-tock *ne tik tok*,' he repeated it to his companion and they both collapsed with laughter. 'Tick-tock *ne tik tok*' I kept hearing as we walked away, having not been charged for the work. From one shop to another we went, with interested and helpful spectators all the way. Once we stopped and entered a *chai*-shop where the numerous electrical wires stapled onto the walls formed a variety of symmetrical patterns, including the word 'Wel Come'. It was a work of art and held our attention for the time it took us to down two cups of tea.

When we returned to the same restaurant for dinner, it was quieter, but the food was just as good. Some police officers at the same table struck up a conversation with us and lectured Arlem on how to become a good tourist guide. They appeared to know all about us. Once again the bush-telegraph of the bazaars had worked with surprising speed and accuracy. Giving us side-long glances of amusement, they suggested to him that when he took another party across, he should notify people ahead. Arlem, twitching with pleasure at being called a tourist guide, and, at the same time, abashed at being gently reprimanded, looked down at his plate with teenage embarrassment.

On our way back to the resthouse, I advised Arlem to check again the time and departure point of his bus for the morrow. I felt very sad at the thought of our imminent parting. He was a likeable lad and we had been through a lot together in our short acquaintance. His inexperience was something he would lose (or had already lost, Richard ventured to say), and he would grow out of his difficulty in carrying heavy packs. So long as he remembered to carry a plentiful supply of drinking water, I felt sure he would serve a fellow traveller well.

Later, I sat on the porch of the resthouse enjoying the warm desert air, inhaling the strange intoxicating smell of fresh cow-dung plastered walls and intermittently watching huge flying beetles alight on the table next to me. All around me, the cicadas were chirping. As I busily wrote out some references for Arlem on the back of my calling cards, he sat beside me, swinging his leg, looking like a small boy waiting for his teacher to hand him his term report. Earlier, in the lazy afternoon, after our hectic lunch hour, I had seen him stretched out on the mattress that had been put down for him in the other room. He had been lying on his side in the foetal position, his cap on the floor beside his shaven head, and his lean thin dark-skinned body appearing frail and vulnerable.

As I glanced up at the star-studded sky, and listened to the wind rattling the doors, I was painfully aware that I held this young man's fate in my hands. I assured the would-be traveller he was eager to please, that he would find them porters for their baggage, and that he was honest and reliable. I knew that when he left me, he was bound for Manshera, where he had an interview for a temporary job, so I also wrote him a letter of reference.

With this, the reference cards, his fee, bus fare, a tip, the few things I had given him towards his career as a tourist guide, plus some vitamins and liver tablets, he seemed very happy when he bedded down for the night.

Dawn the next day saw us waiting for a non-existent bus at a non-existent bus stop. Arlem had assured me his bus went from this place at five o'clock. Controlling my annoyance, I asked a number of early risers the whereabouts of the bus going south. I was pointed in all directions. Arlem, wearing his small-boy look, asked a fellow teenager, smiled in relief and happily pointed back in the direction we had come. Now the sun had appeared and was threatening to push the mercury to new heights. I glanced at Arlem doubtfully and started walking. We passed the resthouse. Arlem kept walking straight on. I suddenly stopped. Before us was nothing but desert and those towering huge rocks of burnt umber.

'Arlem! *Where* is the bus-station?' I demanded.

Arlem pointed straight into the desert.

'How far? Arlem!'

Arlem shrugged. 'Two kilometres?'

That was enough for me. I literally ordered him to stop, and we headed back for the old bazaar. Outside the restaurant where our jeep had stopped the day before, we found out that the bus leaving for the south would depart from there at eight o'clock. It was a bashful Arlem I embraced in that ancient bazaar, watched by a crowd of amused and interested spectators.

When I arrived back in England several months later, there was a letter awaiting me. On the envelope, in the lower right hand corner and twice on the back was written: 'Letter writer, Mohammed Arlem, tourist guide.' The letter was written in both English and Urdu.* The English read as follows:

'My dear Maureen P Lines,
   Assalam Alykum,
   I am quite well and I hope you will be the same. You know I speak little English I write a letter to Urdu. I thankfull to you and your good lession.
   May you live long.
   I remember you much.
   Please mistak excuse me.
   Your loving tourist guide.
   Mohammed Arlem, tourist guide.'

Then followed his address, in turn to be followed with again.
'Your loving tourist guide, Mohammad Arlem, tourist guide.'

---

*According to linguist, Eugene H. Glassman, Urdu came into recognized use in the reign of the Moghul emperor, Akbar, during the latter half of the sixteenth century and was the language of his multilingual army—a sort of 'common denominator' which had evolved from many languages (e.g. Arabic, Hindi Persian, Pashto, Turkish, Sanskrit) in order to enable them to communicate with each other. It then became the official language of his empire and was written in the Persian form of the Arabic script.

The Road to Hunza

The bus finally left at nine o'clock that morning, and as Richard and I left the sandy, windswept streets of Chilas and its oasis of fruit trees behind, we drove, it seemed, into the very 'fires of hell'. The intense heat was devastating and apart from our discomfort, I worried about the precious films stashed away in my rucksack on the roof of the wagon, directly in the rays of the blazing sun.

From my privileged seat in the front of the bus, I enjoyed an unrestricted view across the desert. Not even the wastes of the Nubian desert could compare with the desolation of the luna-type terrain around us. We were back in that intimidating land that stretches from the western flanks of Nanga Parbet to Chilas and beyond, where the huge black grey, brown and burnt umber rocks tower above the desert floor. Not a speck of green could be seen—no trees, no shrubs, not a blade of grass. The sun blazed down remorselessly, burning the back of my hand which lay on the edge of the open window. After a while, my eyelids began to droop, my mind to wander; I had to fight to stay awake.

Through the welcome shade of the Indus Gorge, where awesome grey sandstone cliffs rise above an equally grey river, we occasionally came across small clusters of houses perched on narrow mud strips, their fields stubbornly defying the elements. Compressed tightly between the cliffs, the Indus, having drained the glaciers all the way from its source in Tibet and gathered en route, the tributaries Shyok, Shigar and Gilgit, was now all powerful in its headlong voyage to the plains. No wonder then that this savage land was referred to as an 'abomination of desolation' by a British general.

As we continued to follow that thundering ribbon of grey, I was again forcibly struck by the thought that we were following an old caravan trail. According to Chinese sources, this path through the mountains, linking the Punjab plains with the Tarim Basin in China, was referred to as the 'suspended crossing', and was once used for diplomatic missions before becoming a route for Buddhist pilgrims and trading caravans. Near

Chilas, and in Hunza, there are a number of rock carvings and inscriptions, some of which are purported to be shrines for travellers to leave offerings beside, before or after crossing the river. Many of the shrines are believed to date back to the first millennium AD, while others may have been sacrificial sites of pre-Buddhist times. During my previous visit, I had seen examples at Shatial Bridge near Ganesh in Hunza. Among the inscriptions were small carvings of goats, insects, astronaut-like figures and what, to my mind, resembled hieroglyphics.

In the time of Fa Hsien, the most famous of the Chinese Buddhist pilgrims, travellers through the gorge had had to break through walls and use ladders and rope bridges to facilitate their passage. Today, with the jeep, bus and road—the first road (a dirt track for jeeps) was completed in the late sixties—the modern traveller is spared these Herculean feats, but the terrain is no less fearful because of it. At any moment, a giant boulder or rockslide may come crashing down the cliffs, and landslides are not uncommon.

Any land helps form the character of its people and this is perhaps why I like those who live by the sea, or in deserts or mountains, for they tend to be strong, fearless, individualistic people with quite different priorities to those who live in the city. Of course, there is always the other side of the coin. Even to this day, the inhabitants of Gilgit will tell of a particularly barbaric ritual that was practised many centuries ago. In one tribe it used to be the task of the eldest son to carry his father, once he was too old to work, in a basket to the nearest precipice over the Indus and throw him off. Not surprisingly, legends surround this gruesome practice, and, according to Jean Fairley, in her book *Lion River*, there is one which tells of one old man who, as his son sadly carried him to the precipice, started to chuckle. He told his son he was remembering when he had thrown his own father over the precipice, and that the day would come when it would be the son's turn: 'The father's basket is for the son, too.' This apparently struck at the heart of the youth, who then hid his father in a cave. Not long after, when Alexander the Great arrived, seeking directions to the 'Waters of Life', he found that all the old men who could have told him its whereabouts had been killed. The youth, hearing of this, consulted his father, obtained the information and imparted it to Alexander. The old man was finally produced in answer to Alexander's queries and the practice stopped, for Alexander made it clear to the people that wisdom and knowledge could only be found in the old.

As we approached Gilgit, I thought back over her colourful history. In 1877, Gilgit became the most northerly political agency of the British Indian Government. It was established to protect the tribes against the

Maharajah of Kashmir (who then had control over the whole region) and to monitor the activities of the Russians, who were slowly taking over central Asia and hovering on the borders of Afghanistan. In 1880, it was deemed too vulnerable in the face of a large uprising of tribesmen along the Indus, and, in the following year, was closed down.

The next decade, however, saw skulduggery in the Gilgit-Hunza region equal to that which was to take place in Chitral. In 1886, Safda Ali (who claimed to be descended from Alexander the Great and a fairy*) of the Hindu-Kush, connived in the death of his father, seized the throne of Hunza and murdered three of his brothers—two by strangulation, the third thrown over a cliff. For years the people of Nagar and Hunza had terrorized the caravans travelling between Kashmir and Turkestan, and, in 1888, Safda Ali entered into an unholy alliance with the Rajah of Nagar (the people of Hunza were Ismailis* while the Nagars were Shiahs and the two states were traditional enemies), and their combined forces advanced on Gilgit. Trouble was averted by negotiations, but the British felt it prudent to send a mission to Gilgit, led by Algernon Durand and accompanied by Surgeon-Major Robertson (later to find fame for holding out in the siege of Chitral in 1895). On the recommendation of Durand the Agency was re-established.

In 1889, the chiefs of Hunza and Nagar undertook to stop their raiding of caravans bound for Turkestan, but the treaty was soon broken, and Safda Ali, who preferred the Russians to the British, informed Captain Younghusband, who was then surveying the northern passes and negotiating with the Russians, that unless he was given a large subsidy, he would resume his caravan raids. The following year he kept his promise.

In 1891, Uzar Khan seized the throne of Nagar from his father and murdered two of his half-brothers because he resented their friendship with the British. News reached Gilgit that the two chiefs planned to advance down the valley, and a company of two hundred Kashmiri *sepoys* were quickly deployed to Chalt. Trouble was again averted, but the Russians were now looming large on the horizon. They had violated Afghan territory and Wakhan, had reached the Darkot Pass in Upper Chitral, and were poised to seize the Pamirs.

In December 1891, the battle for Nilt took place. It was another story

---

*Fairies—supernatural beings.
*The Ismailis are an offshoot of the Shiah sect of Islam and follow the Aga Khan, who is descended from Ismail, the eldest son of the sixth Shiah Imam. They are less strict than both the Sunnis and Shiahs, and have a reputation for being progressive and industrious. Throughout the Northern Areas, there are clinics established by the Ismailis, and, carved on rocks between Gilgit and the Shandur, there are inscriptions praising the Aga Khan.

of derring-do, of hand-to-hand fighting, more logistical engineering feats, acts of bravery in the face of impossible odds, the scaling of a thousand foot cliff under cover of darkness—a battle which left Durand wounded, Safda Ali and Uzar Khan fleeing to Yarkhand, and the Russians left with the hoped-for route into India closed.

In 1893, the tribes around Chilas rose up against the British, and it was only because of the superiority of British logistics and weapons, plus their own inter-tribal conflicts, that they were defeated. In 1895, it was from Gilgit that Colonel Kelly marched to relieve Chitral.

The confluence of the Indus and Gilgit rivers was passed to our right and the road continued, now alongside the Gilgit, beneath grey granite and sandstone cliffs. Gradually, the wasteland gave way to orchards and soon we were entering the Gilgit valley. Gilgit, an important staging-post, hemmed in by dark mountains, their craggy summits still topped by snow, was much as I remembered it from my previous visit. I disliked its hot, dusty, sprawling bazaar; it was noisy and had a tawdriness about it. The opening of the Khunjerab had made it even more bustling, and I felt as alienated there as I do in a big city. It is only its history and trading associations that I find appealing. Within minutes, I was hankering for the mountains again. Along with the people of Hunza, the inhabitants of Gilgit proudly maintain they are descended from the soldiers of Alexander the Great's army. Just outside the town, there is a large Buddhist cliff sculpture proving its importance long before the people were converted to Islam in the thirteenth century.

Perhaps its most romantic appeal lies in its having been a cross-roads on the Silk Road, as well as once being a caravan stop for a flow of trade from Srinigar in the west. The road over the Shandur to Gilgit is believed to be the one taken by Marco Polo, and those who believe Christ survived the cross and died in Kashmir maintain this was the road he took after passing through Iran and Afghanistan. With Partition* in 1947, and the coming down of the 'Bamboo Curtain' shortly after, Gilgit was left in a vacuum; but now, with the opening of the Khunjerab, it has again become an important staging-post.

---

*At Partition, in 1947, control of the 'Gilgit Agency' was handed back to Kashmir, and, in the October, the Maharajah of Kashmir acceded to India. The Moslem inhabitants now found themselves under Hindu rule and having to abide by Hindu laws, such as being unable to slaughter cows, which were one of their chief sources of protein during the winter months. Also, the Kashmiri authorities favoured their own people, when it came to filling administrative posts. A small uprising in Gilgit led to the relatively bloodless accession to Pakistan of all the states of the Gilgit Agency. In November, the Pakistan flag was raised. The following year, during the fighting for Kashmir, Gilgit was bombed by the Indian air force.

It was with some difficulty, because of my baggage, that we obtained transport to the Tourist Cottages, a little way out of town. None of the crowded Suzukis would take us, but a local, seeing our problem, flagged down a car for us, and within minutes our thirteen-year-old driver screeched to a halt on the dusty drive of the tumbledown, privately-owned mecca for those travelling rough and with limited means.

Richard and I stayed in Gilgit as long as it took to find him medical aid for the abscess on his tooth, to make some necessary purchases and to change money. Aside from enjoying mango milkshakes, and thick home-made yoghurt, it was the changing of money which provided us with our most entertaining moments in the few tiring days we spent there.

The bank opened at eight o'clock, and at a few minutes past we walked through the doors and were immediately ushered into the manager's office. After politely answering all the usual questions and drinking the customary *chai*, the manager, a short dapper little man, finally asked us what we wanted to change. When we told him he bent his head to the ledger upon his desk and started writing some figures. After a few minutes of this, when the sound of the clock was becoming increasingly audible, I turned and glanced at Richard, who grimaced and shrugged his shoulders. A few minutes more, and the manager raised his head, smiled and lifted the receiver of the rather ancient looking 'phone on the desk. When he replaced it, after a brief conversation, I cleared my throat and asked if the bank was really open. Again, he smiled and assured me the bank was indeed open and went back to his ledger. On the dot of nine, without another word from the manager, an elderly man entered and ushered us into the bank proper. This was a small dusty room with a mud floor containing a bench for the use of customers. Everywhere, piled up on the two antiquated wooden desks, chairs, window sills and on top of a tall metal cabinet, were hundreds of old and tatty ledgers. On the front of the metal cabinet was a sticker declaring it to be a strong room and the last person out to lock the doors.

After handing in our travellers' cheques and passports, we were politely asked to wait. More time passed. Then the front door swung open and a solemn procession entered. An old man was in the lead, and, with funeral-like steps, he marched solemnly forward, carrying a number of heavy ledgers in his arms, as did the man behind him. Bringing up the rear was a boy carrying a cardboard box filled with bundles of notes. A clerk sitting at one of the desks, not a man whose appearance inspired confidence, lurched to his feet, unlocked the metal cabinet and yanked open the doors, with the inevitable result that the ledgers piled haphazardly on the top tumbled to the floor. I tried to smother a giggle, and not to catch Richard's eye but without success. Another clerk, still at his desk and seemingly unperturbed by the cascade which had narrowly missed his head, looked at me steadily and asked: 'Why does Madam laugh?' Moments later, clutching my Pakistani currency, I rolled out into the bazaar and howled with laughter.

It was without regret that we journeyed on to the high, clear mountains of Hunza, a short run by wagon which belies the route's dangerous past. Crossing over the Gilgit River, we rumbled on along the dusty valley, to the confluence of the Hunza and Gilgit rivers, and turned north into the beginning of the Hunza valley. Here the valley was quite wide, but the surging river was wilder than the Gilgit and no greenery lined its shore. The farther north we went, the narrower grew the valley, until past the green oasis of Normal, we entered a ravine which cuts through the Kailas Range. The cliffs loomed overhead, three times as high as the Grand Canyon.

Above the village of Chalt in Nagar, the ancient caravan trail can still be seen on the left bank of the river. I had thought of following it, but now, due to the landslips and rockfalls, it would be too hazardous. What remains visible to the naked eye leaves one wondering how those ancient caravaners could possibly have travelled such a narrow and precarious trail. Aside from the cliffs being unstable, due to explosives used in the building of the KKH,* the rock here is reputed to contain pyrite, which, when mixed with rain water, makes sulphuric acid which eats into the rock. That this is an area of landslides was made apparent by the warning notices along the route—not designed to calm the faint-hearted— although other signs saying 'Relax' or 'Have a safe journey' brought smiles to our faces. At one particularly dangerous place, we saw two men running towards us, waving their arms; moments earlier, some boulders had narrowly missed a car. We continued on cautiously, with the driver glancing uneasily at the rocks above, while his companion, riding 'shotgun', ran ahead to move any obstacles and to give us the all-clear.

In the old days, before the coming of motorized transport and metalled roads, entry to the Hunza Valley was even more perilous. Near a place called Gwech, on the border of Nagar, the cliffs form a sheer drop to the river, and here, a stranger could only pass with the aid of one of the inhabitants, who would descend the cliffs to drive wooden pegs into the rocks. The traveller moved forward by clinging on to ropes attached to the pegs. The only alternative route meant crossing the river over a rope bridge. With such natural defences, plus high mountains and green valleys, it is easy to see how James Hilton may well have used Hunza as his model for *Lost Horizon*.

The terraced fields of Hunza came into view, and I enjoyed, through Richard, reliving my first sight of the great mountain of Rakoposhi in its

122

full glory, towering above the twin ancient kingdoms. Famed for the longevity of is citizens, Hunza has often been referred to as a veritable Shangri-La, even by people unfamiliar with James Hilton's famous novel. Except in the burning heat of a summer's afternoon, it is one of the most comfortable and relaxing places in the subcontinent.

The whole mountain region of northern Pakistan has seen many an invader come in over the passes, besides the army of Alexander the Great. At one time, according to the archaeological explorer Aurel Stein, the area became a focal point for two warring factions. In the seventh century AD, the Chinese defeated the kingdom of the Western Turks, and, in so doing incurred the wrath of both the Arabs, who were pushing eastwards spreading Islam, and the Tibetans, who were laying claim to the city states of the Tarim Basin. In order to drive a wedge between these two allies, a Chinese army of three thousand crossed the Darkot Pass into Yasin.

The inhabitants of Hunza, who speak Burushaski, an ancient language believed by some scholars to be pre-Aryan, are friendly, hospitable and progressive. They are strong physically and generally fair of face; an industrious people known for their expertise in the engineering of irrigation channels and as tillers of the soil.

Unlike so many people in the world, they have handled the invasion of tourism with grace and intelligence. Since my first visit, a few more tourist hotels had opened up, along with some new small stores, but the prices were still modest, and, except for the occasional child who had fallen victim to some tourist's misguided generosity, we were rarely accosted. The people of Hunza are proud and courteous and treat the tourist accordingly. It is hard to imagine their recent ancestors were those who plundered the caravans en route to China. Now, along with farming those terraced fields, tourism has given them a steady income.

Two days later, Richard departed for Islamabad, to retrieve baggage and money left with a friend. I was sorry to see him go. I knew I was going to miss him. Our attempt, the day before, to climb the Ultar Glacier (the main source of Hunza's water supply) had ended at the beginning of the grey end of the snout; neither of us, after five hours' strenuous climbing, in the burning heat, had the desire to carry on. The sight of the avalanche as we approached, however, had been spectacular and had made it an interesting and exciting outing.

Now, alone for the first time since my evening in Balakot, I decided to spend a leisurely day. In the quiet of the afternoon, I sat on the verandah of the small hotel, enjoying the scenery and catching up on my mail.

I again read Saifullah's letter which had been waiting for me at the Poste Restante in Gilgit. I was thankful he and my Kalash 'mother' were

well. Many of his letters during the past five years had not reached me, no doubt because of my flitting to and fro between New York and England.

For a moment, my mind travelled back over the past. In the sixties I had had a very successful house-painting business in New York, before taking off for North Africa and Beirut. A brief career as a Gothic novelist and a year in Greece had followed. In the seventies, I had again taken up residence in Britain and, eventually, had gone back to decorating. In 1981, after my sojourn in the Kalash valleys, I had been determined not only to return there, but to return as a qualified emergency worker. In order to do this, I had decided to go back to America, but my intention of earning money as a New York ambulance driver was cut short when I all but collapsed with health problems.

Now, hopefully, a book on Pakistan would not only fill the always depleted coffers but would pave the way for a book on the Kalash, who, like most ethnic groups suddenly exposed to tourism and the onslaught of the twentieth century, wish to make public their problems in the hope that their way of life might be saved.

I looked up from my writing and reflected that falling in love with countries was not unlike love affairs.

Spread out below me were the terraced fields of Nagar and Hunza. Between the rows of poplar trees, the rooftops of the houses were orange and brown from the ripening fruit. Higher up the valley, the rays of the sun shone on the green and blue woodwork of the larger houses while their Mediterranean white-washed walls reflected the bright sunlight. Towards evening, women, dressed in gaily coloured *shalwar-khameez* and bright pill-box hats, climbed the paths, bearing large baskets filled with grasses, while the men carried huge sheaves across their backs. On the other side of the river rose Rakoposhi, its many spurs lost in the clouds; at 25,550 feet, it is one of the highest mountains in the world. At sunrise and sunset on a clear day, the mountain top glows a soft diffused pink. To my right was a dark ridge, its pinnacles silhouetted against the bright sky, half hidden by clouds. The Ultar Glacier looked down upon the Mir's deserted solitary palace, which sat upon the hillside above the village of Baltir, the capital of Hunza.

Sword dancing in Hunza.

Over the Khunjerab

The road from Ganesh, below Karimabad, followed the Hunza River through a deep rocky gorge. Every so often we glimpsed a welcome patch of green as we passed a few trees or narrow, terraced fields nestling beneath the cliffs. It always astounds visitors to the region how, in these northern areas of Pakistan, the local inhabitants manage to scratch a livelihood from such hostile land. Their water channels, fed by the snows and the great glaciers, are a remarkable feat of engineering.

As the gorge opened up into a valley, the wagon came to a stop in Gulmit, and I was deposited on the steps of a small hotel. In the sweltering mid-day heat, I gazed upon a valley bleached almost grey and white by the glare of the ultra-violet rays, while above, the jagged saw-tooth pinnacles of Karun Pir, splattered with a little snow, rose into a grey-blue sky. After two hours of waiting, I was lucky enough to get a ride on the bus from Gilgit. Shortly after leaving the village, the road-way ran into the river. Although the road from Babusar had been water-logged, and had, in some stretches, become part of the river, this stretch was nothing but water and only a line of red flags appeared to prevent the driver from drowning us all. It was the first time I had ever driven through a vast sheet of water in a vehicle that was not amphibious. My fellow passengers, all Pakistanis, dressed in rumpled and travel-stained clothes and sporting several days' growth of beard, seemed to derive as much amusement and enjoyment from the experience as myself.

Beyond the wide valley of Pasu, where the lofty serrated peaks almost hypnotized me with their grandeur, the KKH continues on through a narrow ravine. Legend has it that this cleft was once barred by a door with a lock and key. Having seen the massive doors and gates of forts in Rajasthan, with their enormous locks and keys, several hundred years old, I could understand how the legend originated. Now, however, it is the historic feat of the Chinese and Pakistan army engineers that is awe-inspiring.

The planning and execution of the 774-mile-long highway took nearly twenty years, over 8,000 tons of explosives, and 80,000 tons of cement,

126

with machinery having to be flown in by helicopter. Estimates of the number of lives lost among the combined 20,000 Pakistani and Chinese workers vary: figures as high as 2,500 have been mentioned, but no-one really knows.

There is something romantic about frontiers, but the same cannot be said of modern-day border check-points. They are an impediment to the free flow of travel, and the towns which spring up around them are invariably overcrowded and full of unsavoury characters. Sust was no exception to this. Set on the banks of the river, beneath the towering Karakorams, it was an attractive place scenically, but the growing tent-city had that border-town atmosphere of tawdriness. Luckily, I met up with the local Police Chief who offered me accommodation at the police post.

The next morning I was shown down to the tent-city to buy my ticket for the Chinese border, where, I had been told by other travellers in Gilgit, I should then have to change to a Chinese bus.

It was a bright sunlit morning, and the huge tent which served as a mosque, with its bright oriental carpets, and devotees dressed in long, white, ankle-length *kurtas* (looking more like the North African *d'jella-ba*) and white prayer hats, was in sharp contrast to the one housing the ticket-seller for the bus to Pirali. Here the canvas was greenish-grey, with the words 'GRATEFULLY RECEIVED AS A GIFT FROM THE EUROPEAN COMMUNITY FOR AFGHAN REFUGEES' printed on it. If the smiling, pleasant-faced individual who sold me my ticket was an Afghan refugee, he hadn't been slow in utilizing this gift for what was undoubtedly a useful purpose. Going through the Pakistani customs was smooth, with the usual smiling, polite customs officials (surely one of the few countries where they are). I watched with interest as one of them, standing next to the immigration officer stamping passports, was using part of the table as an ironing board to press his *shalwar-khameez*. All around me were Pakistanis (many from the bus I had travelled in the day before) with huge bales of 'moonlight' material.* I had been tempted to bring a few pounds of this sparkling and highly prized commodity to sell in China myself, to help pay for the journey, but now having two broken ribs (the second had been broken in a bathroom in Gilgit), I felt it was essential I keep my baggage to an absolute minimum. I knew that it was perfectly legal to take in a few pounds, but the quantity that was going to be shipped over that day appeared to be enough to keep several Chinese factories going.

---

*Material that glitters, often with silver or gold threads running through it. On their return, the merchants bring back porcelain and hard-wearing cloth.

When I hauled myself up into the empty bus (again no easy feat, for the steps are always a long way off the ground), I had to thread my way through a mass of newspapers, fruit-peelings, sweet wrappers, empty bottles, crusts of bread and plastic bags, to climb over the engine cover in order to reach the front seat. As I made myself comfortable, I spied a Land-Rover parked a few feet away, with a small group of Westerners milling about it. One of them caught my eye and came over. 'Are you going to Kashgar?' she asked.

'Yes,' I replied, noting her expensive but dirt and sweat-stained blouse and tired face. 'Why?' I ventured.

'Well, my advice to you, is don't!'

'Why not?' I asked.

'You won't believe this,' she said, 'but the bus we travelled in, on the Chinese side, had no seats!'

I guess my face must have registered the right expression for she carried on. It had been an 'absolutely terrible experience'. They had just stayed one night in Kashgar and then, 'by some miracle', had got tickets for the weekly bus back to the border. Here their luck ran out. The driver did not have a passport and the Chinese authorities wouldn't let them proceed, forcing them to wait a whole day on the border, nearly 16,000 feet above sea level, without food or facilities. Their ordeal only ended when a man from Kashgar happened to turn up with a Land-Rover which he let them hire for the journey back.

As she and her companions moved away, I began to have misgivings. Unable to find out any information before I left England from either the Chinese Embassy or tourist office in London, I had hastened to the Chinese Embassy on reaching Islamabad, where I had met Mali-Wan, a fifty-six-year-old American woman dressed in an Indian black *kurta* pyjama-suit who had travelled extensively in China, Tibet, Thailand, Burma and India; she had been a mine of information of the sort no tourist office supplies. It was she who told me that the most important word I should learn in Chinese was '*Maeo*'—'No!' And that under no circumstances was I ever to believe this nor should I believe anything I was told in the affirmative—scepticism should be my watch-word. The best way to tell if a Chinese official was important, she had said, was to look at his breast pockets since rank depended upon the number of pens in them. If the official boasted four, then I should be wary, for I was up against the top rank of officialdom.

But of the information I had just been given, the point that concerned me most was food, or rather my lack of it. I had taken it for granted that Chinese bus drivers, like Pakistani jeep and bus drivers, wished to eat and drink and would stop frequently for us. I was to learn, however, that nothing can be taken for granted in China, and that, in spite of my preconceived ideas, nothing in China is logical.

While I waited for the bus to fill up, I settled back to watch the goings on around me. Besides the congestion at the nearby immigration and customs post, I noticed a number of men and women carrying their belongings on their heads. I have always been amazed by the amount one person can carry in that fashion, and I mused that if we were brought up to do the same in the West, there might be less middle-aged and elderly people with rounded backs and stooping shoulders. My gaze then alighted upon a fellow Westerner on the other side of the road. He was wearing, above a very white face, a brightly coloured turban, a very long white shirt with low neckline and large balloon sleeves, a bright red *dhoti** and hiking boots below hairy calves. As I sat marvelling at his appearance which commanded the stares of all who passed by, I was glad that my attire, the male form of the Pakistani *shalwar-khameez*, which I had had especially tailored for me in Gilgit, was a conservative sandy colour. For trekking, I find this apparel to be the most comfortable, and the attractive women's variety is ideal for cities, being cool and smart at the same time.

Although I had been told that the bus left at nine, it was nearly eleven o'clock before the driver finally took his seat. Just as he switched on the engine, a squabble broke out between a Chinese man, accompanied by his Pakistani wife and child,* and a young Pakistani immediately behind me. I had already lost a number of valuable seat inches beside me, and I saw that unless I fought for it, my space would be eroded still further. I counted fifty-eight passengers crammed in the bus and there was no room to move. People sat on baggage, in the aisle and, in some cases, on one another. The upshot of the altercation was that the Chinese man squashed himself next to me, forcing me to raise my legs and drape them beside the driver's right elbow.

The driver sounded his horn and to a chorus of shouts and cheers from the passengers, the bus moved off, only to brake suddenly a few yards along the road. Someone had been left behind. While the driver sighed and waited patiently for the hapless passenger to catch up, the 'conductor' got out, climbed through the driver's door and squeezed next to him—right where my legs were. This left only one place for my legs to go—straight through the driver's window! The other passengers thought this very funny and in spite of my contortions, I joined in the laughter.

Out of Sust the road led through a narrow rocky gorge, and after many

Dhoti—loin cloth generally worn by Hindu males.
*With the coming down of the 'Bamboo Curtain' at the end of the forties, a number of traders from Kashgar were stranded in Gilgit where they subsequently took up residence.

hours we made our final official *chai* stop and passport check on the Pakistani side. Badly needing to stretch my legs, I got out and reconnoitred the *chai-khana* where, happily, I was able to buy a packet of biscuits, while the Punjabis resorted to their favourite pastime of playing cards. Fitting us all back into the bus though was as chaotic as before, and again I found the only place for my legs was out of the window.

Slowly we chugged our way round and round the mountainside and up towards the Khunjerab. Now the sun had disappeared and there was a greyish cast to the sky. A cool wind blew in through the window. To the south lay the Karakorams (named after a pass meaning 'black stones')* and the Great Himalaya—'the abode of snow', while to the east were the Kunlun Mountains (Mountains of Darkness), and, to the north and north-west, the Pamirs, named Bam-i-Dunja or 'Roof of the World' by the Arabs, home of the nomadic Kirghiz and the Marco Polo sheep. There was no magnificent and awe-inspiring view, but I felt an over-riding sense of history and geography. There I was at the very heart of that vast mountain complex of Central Asia; it was a thrilling moment.

The rocky cliffs disappeared, to be replaced by squat, snow-covered mountain tops, as we drove onto a wide plateau that was empty and remote. Moments later, we stopped at our first Chinese check-point. Although there was no sun, the younger border-guards were wearing expensive-looking sun-glasses, while others wore what looked like card dealers' eye shades and the green Mao uniforms and caps. Then, with one of the guards squatting on the engine cover, we rode across 'no man's land'. The straight road ran between lines of telegraph poles, across the desolate Khunjerab, punctuated only by a few deserted homesteads. Now the terrain was high desert and the mountains were hidden by huge sandhills. Back in 'Pindi and Gilgit, I had heard stories that the Chinese and Pakistani authorities were going to build a 'friendship city' here. The idea seemed a good one, if somewhat impractical at a height of nearly 16,000 feet; the only sign of life, between the first checkpoint and the customs and immigration, was one solitary, tethered camel. Just before we came to a halt at the barrier, I noticed a stone had been erected to the first overland crossing by bicycle, finished the day before by a party of Pakistani students. I wondered if the students I had met with Richard in Besal had made it safely across on their motor-bikes.

The barrier was raised, the bus came to a stop, and the driver and his companion jumped out. One of the border-guards came running up and he and the bus driver swept into each other's arms and embraced. It was a long ecstatic greeting and caught the attention of another border-guard,

---

*Also sometimes called the Mustagh Range (Ice Mountains).

as well as my fellow passengers, who after sending black looks in the direction of his colleague suddenly started doing some physical jerks. It all seemed very informal.

When we disembarked, it was three o'clock, and it was only five past when I heard '*Maeo!*' for the first time! I had just tentatively taken aim with my camera and the shout came from a disgruntled border-guard. He didn't seem to mind though when I focused my lens away from him and his colleagues standing by the barrier.

It took five hours for us all to go through customs, and that was with myself and two Swiss men helping our fellow passengers fill in their immigration forms—which we did not only for altruistic reasons, but because we knew that only when all the forms were completed would we have a chance of proceeding with our journey. Although my head was thumping painfully from staying so long at the high altitude,* I noticed that when I asked each individual to name his occupation, each said he was a businessman; but when I asked 'Reason for visit?', all of them, their loads of material not withstanding, replied tourist. No doubt in Islamabad, along with every other traveller, they had asked for a tourist visa which in the modern world is often the only way to legally enter another country. They were pleasant, good-humoured men, and for most it was their first trip to Kashgar; they were generally young and were as excited as I was at the prospect of travelling to China.

The Chinese customs' men, working in a long cold hall, were pleasant and helpful, and I moved on to the end of the room, where two men, in plain jackets and trousers, sat behind a table, exchanging money. Beside me were three men I had seen at Sust—an unkempt and unprepossessing trio. One of them dropped a wad of American Express travellers' cheques down on the table. The spot where the signature should have been was occupied by a large ink thumb mark. The chief banker took one look and threw them aside with disgust. Another of the men, seeing this, pocketed his own wad of travellers' cheques and brought out a pile of hundred-dollar bills.

With my own modest fifty dollars' worth of FEC (Chinese government money), I went out into the cold mountain air with one thought uppermost in my mind—to find something to eat. Having already discovered that the 'restaurant' was padlocked, I headed straight for a crowd of passengers standing in front of the kiosk which sold biscuits, fruit drinks and sweets. Except for a few biscuits and a *parrata** for breakfast, I hadn't eaten anything since the evening before. My

*Visitors coming straight from Gilgit (elevation 4,770 ft) expose themselves to considerable risk. Staying for a short while in the Hunza valley (elevation 8,000 ft) helps to cut down the risk of altitude sickness.

companions greeted me with sullen looks and mumblings. The kiosk, which had been open for business when we had had no currency, was now closed. A cup of boiled water (the equivalent of the Pakistani offering of *chai*) handed to me by a friendly customs official, helped to make my thumping head more bearable, and I returned to where the other passengers were now gathered near two lightweight and ram-shackle Chinese buses.

It was eight-thirty when we were finally allowed to board. Two buses had been deemed necessary as they were smaller than the heavy Pakistani vehicles and we now had additional passengers—the three wealthy merchants with the thumb-marked travellers' cheques, who must have come by jeep to the border, and four students who had just cycled over the Pass en route to Kashgar, already commemorated on a small monument. Their adventure had come to an untimely end the day before when two of them had crashed into one another on the rough track (the KKH had ended at the border). With only superficial injuries, they were now completing their trip by public transport.

On boarding the bus, our baggage was taken unceremoniously from us and thrown up onto the roof of a separate truck. Luckily, I had been warned of this and had kept my sleeping-bag and washkit in a day-pack which I wedged between the broken rungs of the luggage rack above my head. A moment later a plump merchant sat down beside me. At least we had seats and it was a luxury to have no-one sitting in the aisle. It was only when the bus moved off into the twilight that I realized the springs had gone, but my sleeping-bag made a good cushion and relieved the feeling of being squashed by my neighbour. Through the grimy window, the landscape seemed to be nothing but sandhills. Beneath a dusty moon, I caught a glimpse of a narrow, slow-moving ribbon of river before it was hidden by a long avenue of poplar trees. We were on a dirt road and it was shake, rattle and roll all the way. Every so often, there would be a sudden lurch as the bus went over a bump or sloughed through a rocky stream. Every time this happened, the Pakistanis let out a shout of protest.

A tree-lined avenue led into Tashkurghan, the only town of any size between the border and Kashgar, and the place where we were to stay the night. Except for a few lights, there was no sign of life anywhere. Even when we suddenly pulled off the road and came to a halt in front of a huge stone arch, it took a number of long hoots on the driver's horn before the massive iron gate swung open. As we drove into the centre of a large compound I was able to see by the light of the bus's headlamps,

---

Parrata—fried chappatis.

that this official hotel for foreigners was made up of several buildings. One looked reasonably modern and it was into this we were herded. The reception room contained a number of armchairs of varying degrees of faded elegance, while brightly embroidered head-rests gave the room a splash of colour, but the towels draped over the arms to protect them only created a sense of dishevelment as not one was correctly placed and had either fallen onto the seats of the chairs or onto the floor.

The young night-clerk did not appear to relish our arrival any more than did the woman attendants summoned to show us to our rooms. The chef and dining-room attendants were likewise disgruntled at the lateness of the hour, but eight of us were grateful to share between us one small plate of fried beef and snow peas, a small dish of cold cabbage, some very stale bread and some salty black tea. At the end of the meal, we even won a smile from one of the staff. In that cold, uninviting place at that late hour, I thought it was a brave face the young attractive woman was putting on. In her brightly coloured head-scarf, tailored suit jacket over a Western-style blouse and skirt, she provided the only real warmth in that large cold dining-room. With its high ceiling, blue formica tables, their white trays on top and red plastic chairs; only the dark red curtains eased the coldness. Stretched across one end of the room were Christmas-type decorations commemorating a 'Chinese/Pakistan children's long march team'. I wondered how long they had been there. When I returned ten days later, they were still in place.

Like my companions, I was disconcerted by our welcome. Again, I suddenly found myself filled with misgivings. Those travellers' tales I had heard in Gilgit and in Sust, could they be true? Not generally one to be influenced by other people's tales of woe, I gave myself a proverbial shake. Tomorrow would be another day.

With the two Swiss, I was led into an old L-shaped building and along a long dank corridor where the paint on the dilapidated woodwork was peeling and where water dripped down the cracked white-washed walls. We were shown into an elongated dormitory that was furnished with six beds and a broken-down wooden table bearing only a thermos of hot water. It was cold and sparse, but we were all tired and glad to lie down even if sleep was hard to come by.

Generally, my first twenty-four hours in a new country are filled with elation and childish wonder. Since a small girl, I had dreamed of travelling to Turkestan and later that had included all of China. Now here I was actually in China. That first morning I awoke with only a measure of excitement—intense curiosity was the over-riding emotion.

A huge thermos at the end of the corridor at the entrance to the courtyard provided water for morning ablutions which were conducted in the courtyard. The latrines which were nothing more than boards set over a trench were not a place to linger in, and as I came out into the welcome relief of the sun's first rays, there came the sound of what I could only figure were 'instructions' on a loud-speaker. This was followed by a bugle call, which was not only haunting in its sound, but was beautiful for its unexpectedness and quite different from the martial music which had accompanied us across the border the day before.

A local woman and a teenage girl crossed the compound in front of me. They stopped and the mother straightened her daughter's jacket, saying something as she did so that brought a smile to both their faces. They continued in the direction of the arch. That brief interaction could have happened anywhere in the West or the East, where mothers take pride in their offspring. Again I was reminded of how people of different cultures are more alike than they are different.

After the hotel breakfast of roasted peanuts, the previous night's stale bread and black salty tea, I joined some of my companions to find out what had happened to the buses. The previous evening we had been directed that we must be ready for a very early departure. Most of the passengers wanted to go in search of food, but were afraid to wander off to a small bazaar, believed to be within walking distance, for fear of being left behind.

Now a group of us decided to go in search of the buses and the place where we had to get our passports stamped. My first impressions of China (although this was Turkestan, and not China proper, so far my dealings had been with the Chinese rather than the indigenous Moslem inhabitants) were at this point confused. Although the sunshine had brushed away the feelings of tiredness, the pangs of hunger were making me feel light-headed and I began to view everything as though I were some way off and looking into a picture-frame. This feeling became particularly strong when we passed through the gate of the compound and came upon a butcher's cart. While rank, fly-blown, hairy hides lay on the ground at the butcher's feet, large bloody and fatty hunks of meat covered the wooden surface of the cart. Averting my eyes from the bloody scene before me which threatened nausea as much from the sight of it as the unhygienic display (I seldom eat red meat), I fled to a nearby kiosk where I bought a packet of biscuits and rejoined the group still in search of the buses and checkpoint.

The avenue we were walking along was lined by poplar trees, and full of cyclists. Some cast interested looks in our direction. I stared back, noticing that some of the men wore blue cotton boiler-suits which I had seen in photographs taken of China decades ago. The women for the most part wore the traditional coloured headscarves, suit jackets and skirts, some with trousers beneath. We hadn't travelled far before word came back from those at the front of the group, that we were going the wrong way and we had to turn back; the police check-point was in the other direction. Although we had been told to be ready for a six o'clock departure, by the time we had had our passports stamped and then waited for the late arrival of the buses, it was nearly ten when we started out for Kashgar.

The lateness of our departure did not surprise me, but the Punjabi merchants, from the cities on the plains, unused to the vagaries of the jeeps and wagons of the mountain regions, appeared surprised that the Chinese buses did not adhere to a more disciplined schedule. They were not looking forward to the day's journey, and, I must confess, that by now, neither was I.

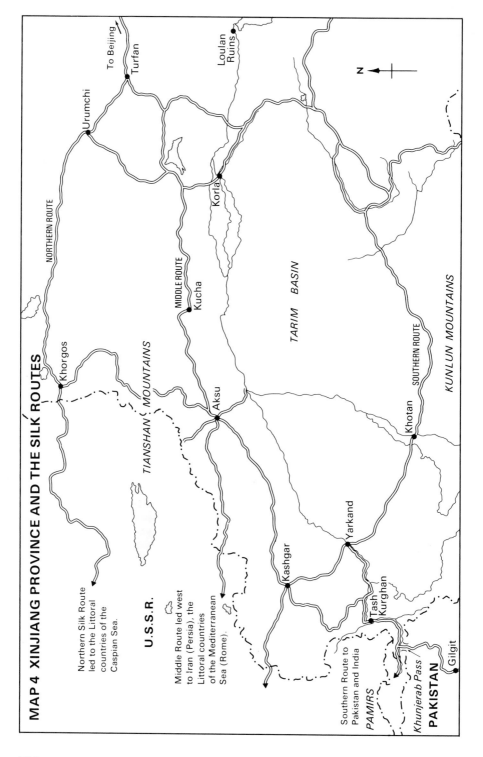

MAP 4 XINJIANG PROVINCE AND THE SILK ROUTES

To Beijing

Turfan

Loulan
Ruins

N

Urumchi

NORTHERN ROUTE

Korla

Northern Silk Route
led to the Littoral
countries of the
Caspian Sea.

Khorgos

MIDDLE ROUTE

Kucha

TARIM   BASIN

TIANSHAN MOUNTAINS

U.S.S.R.

Aksu

Middle Route led west
to Iran (Persia), the
Littoral countries
of the Mediterranean
Sea (Rome).

SOUTHERN ROUTE

KUNLUN MOUNTAINS

Khotan

Yarkand

Kashgar

Tash
Kurghan

Southern Route to
Pakistan and India

PAMIRS

Gilgit

Khunjerab Pass

PAKISTAN

The Road to Kashgar

After leaving the hotel in Tashkurghan, which I surmised had been on the town's outskirts, we drove on through a dusty valley and beside a narrow fast-flowing river. The dirt road we had been following ever since we had entered China was now worse than ever. We were bumping and lurching over the broken ground that was both pitted with muddy troughs and littered with stones and rocks: it was also washed by the occasional stream. The desert, cold and forbidding beneath a cloudy sky, stretched into the distance all around us with only the occasional welcoming belt of grassland and mud brick farmhouse to relieve the loneliness. They were usually long rambling ranch-style affairs, invariably half-hidden by high walls.

Sometimes I would see Turki* nomads riding their horses in the distance. Here and there small mud-brick mausoleums, in the shape of beehives, dotted the land. Sometimes, when bulldozers came into view (the Chinese were now building a road from Kashgar to link up with the KKH at the border), we would see a group of women shovelling sand and

---

*In the province of Sinkiang, or, as it is called in China, Xinjiang, the uplands are populated by Kirghiz and Kazaks, both Moslem nomadic peoples, and a small group called Tajiks. Those who live in and around the oases are mostly Turkis: all are of Turkish origin. Mongols and Chinese Moslems (Tungans) are also in evidence as are a few Han Chinese – mostly soldiers and officials. In the mid-tenth century, the Uighurs, who, according to Chinese tourist brochures, had emigrated to Sinkiang from the Orkhon River Valley, aligned with aboriginal Turkis in setting up a separatist regime known as the Karahanids Dynasty. According to a former British consular official in China, Sir Eric Teichman, the Uighurs, who form the bulk of the Turki population, were once called 'Chan-t'ou' or 'Turban-heads'. Then in 1935, after several years of upheaval which saw a Moslem uprising and a near civil war between the Chinese government and the Tungans (Chinese Moslems), the government, in an effort to conciliate the Turkis, now referred to them as Wei-we-erh—'Uighurs', a Turkish people who ruled Central Asia before the Mongols. According to Filippo de Filippi, the Turkestani are a mixture of tribes and races of the two main Asiatic families, the Turks and the Tartars, and speak a Turki dialect, Uighur.

The oasis town of Kashgar is situated in the south-west part of Xinjiang Uighur Autonomous Region.

137

gravel into pails, which they then bore across their shoulders on a yoke to waiting wooden handcarts. Sometimes the women would return our wave, but the men seldom did. I noticed with particular interest that one of the road surveyors, standing before an eye-piece mounted on a tripod, was a young woman. As the strip of green beside the river grew wider, so a cluster of *yurts** came into view and the sight of nomads mounted on donkeys and horses, dressed in their distinctive roundish black hats and long black coats, became more frequent.

At the next check-point there was no roadhouse or hotel to prolong our stay and so we moved on. Now the landscape was strewn with peculiar rocks which looked like giant fossils and something else beyond them which looked like petrified wood. The occasional horseman and, to my joy, a herd of double-humped camels were the only signs of life. When tufts of grass appeared, I caught sight of a road leading off to a settlement which was built like a wooden fort and was possibly an army post. A bus passed us going the other way filled with local people, mostly men. From their attire, they were most probably road-workers. It was for sure that they were not bound for the border, as I knew that travel abroad is not generally allowed.

I closed the window for it was becoming cold again. We appeared to be very high up, for, rounding a bend, there was spread out before us a wide valley, bounded on one side by snub-nosed mountains and huge glaciers. More *yurts* were visible in the distance, surrounded by herds of goats, although the grazing was very sparse. Now and again marmots darted up from their burrows. More beehive mausoleums appeared, and then I caught sight of my first herd of yaks, animals I had not seen since crossing the Shandur. We continued on until we came to a small lake, where the road ran past a tiny settlement. Peering at my map, the snow glaciers on my right appeared to belong to Mustagh Ata. Known as 'Ice Mountain Father',* this great 'ice dome', as Eric Shipton called it, defeated both him and explorers Sven Hedin and Sir Aurel Stein.

I gazed at the mountain with interest and at the stretch of water below that had to be Lake Karakol, famous for its deep blue colour, although today it was grey, reflecting the sky above. I was not moved by Mustagh Ata, and asked myself why so often we are not affected by what touches another's spirit; I have yet to see the Taj Mahal and I wonder, almost fearfully, what my reaction will be. So far the desolate Pamirs had not

---

Yurts—a circular felt tent with a wooden framework used by Nomads of Central Asia.

*According to Eric Shipton, former explorer and British Consul-General in Kashgar, when Sven Hedin inquired its name of a Kirghiz nomad, he received the courteous reply: 'It is called Muztagh, Father.'

touched my soul—was it because there was no sun, or was it that my mind was not rising above the hunger and discomfort? On his travels in the Hindu-Kush during the fifties, Fosco Maraini speaks with eloquence of the discomfort of travel.* Perhaps our reaction to everything is not necessarily instinctive but due to our state of mind at a given moment.

It was now early afternoon and we had been travelling for four long, uncomfortable hours. Some of the passengers in the rear of the bus were trying to play cards, but every time the vehicle lurched, which was often, the cards fell on the floor and they would have to start again. We continued on through a wide ravine of crumbling sandstone cliffs and by the river which was now mostly a bed of stones, until the barren earth gave way to tufts of grassland and a tethered horse or two, and the river widened and flowed again beneath a mass of white snow summits. The high glaciers of Mount Kongur, over 25,000 feet,* were lost in cloud and overall there was only a faint glimmer of sunlight.

When the bus finally made a welcome stop, it was on the banks of the river beside a small settlement. While some of the passengers moved off to a large compound nearby, I watched as others laid out prayer rugs on the turf beside the river. This greatly impressed two of the elderly inhabitants who were dressed in long black coats, incongruous dirty white sneakers, and hats that were of the Cossack style, but rounder and larger in circumference. When the merchants finished their prayers, the two men went up to them and shook hands.

As soon as the merchants put away their prayer rugs, they brought out some bags and squatted on the turf. Within moments, a number of women and children appeared from the nearby mud and stone houses to gather round. Curiously, I watched as out of the bags they produced some cheap Pakistani costume jewelry which they bartered for the jewelry the local women were wearing and which did not appear to be very different. This gave me an idea. The few articles I had brought along for gifts were stashed away with my other belongings in my large rucksack which I had left in Gilgit, but in the bottom of my camera-bag was an attractive beaded necklace given to me by Aliya's eldest daughter as a talisman. I fished it out and glanced around me. My gaze alighted on a woman with a pleasant smiling face, dressed in old corduroy slacks, over which she wore a skirt with a drab suit jacket, rubber boots and a bright head-scarf.

I dangled the object in front of her and her face lit up. Having gained her interest, I pointed to my mouth and rubbed my stomach. Before I

---

*Where Four Worlds Meet. Fosco Maraini (1959)
*Climbed in 1980 by Chris Bonington.

had even finished miming, she had grabbed my hand and was leading me to her house nearby. The woman's husband, sitting outside on the step dressed in regulation dark green uniform and Mao cap, looked at me doubtfully but after his wife spoke to him he smiled and got to his feet.

I was ushered inside into what was evidently a kitchen-cum-dining room. Most of the room consisted of a three-foot-high raised platform, encircled by a wood and bamboo wall, covered partially by a faded oriental rug, while the roof above was made of straw and mud. The platform or k'ang,* which was covered in reed mats, was for sitting on during the day while the open space before the door was dominated by a wood-burning stove, above which there was a small smoke-hole in the roof. A few essential utensils, such as a kettle, pans and cups, were the only other visible objects in the room. To my right was another larger room with an even larger k'ang, covered in a faded oriental rug.

On entering the house, the woman had put the kettle on to boil. Now she stood before me, fingering the necklace eagerly. Then, hesitantly, she put it around her neck and looked at her husband. The man smiled. It was evident that my necklace was a success.

The black milkless tea, made more palatable by my sweeteners, was served in a large bowl and was perhaps the most delectable I've ever enjoyed as was the piping hot bread, even if it had little taste. I munched through a third, broke off another third, which I pocketed, and handed back the rest in case I had been given the whole of their afternoon meal.

I was pressed to eat more, but I declined, and hearing the sound of the bus horn, got up and took my leave. I returned to the bus feeling considerably brighter, not only because of the food and drink, but because I had made my first contact with local people and it had been a very pleasant experience.

The road out of the settlement ran beneath some sandstone cliffs, until it climbed and we found ourselves on a meandering track along the top of the cliffs. The view was staggering. On my right were the glaciers of Kongur, while on my left huge grey sand dunes rose above a partially dried-up lake bed. On the edge of the mud flats were two yurts and a herd of goats. The terrain was a cross between a pale grey desert and an arctic landscape. We were so busy exclaiming to each other and admiring the view, that none of us noticed the blind corner ahead until the bus suddenly stopped and we were all thrown forward. We had crashed into an army truck travelling in the opposite direction.

The bus driver and the two Chinese soldiers leapt out of their vehicles and were soon locked in argument. The rest of us got out, too, when it

---

*K'ang—Chinese platform bed sometimes filling up half a room, where a family sleeps, sits and eats.

became obvious that this was going to be a long, drawn-out affair—the truck was heading a large convoy, and none of them could pass until our two vehicles had been unlocked and the dispute resolved.

Within minutes, and seemingly from nowhere, a crowd began to gather, presumably from the settlement we had just left (how they got wind of what had happened and had arrived here so fast was another mystery), joined by nomads from the *yurts*, and, to me, the greatest surprise of all, a small girl and boy on bicycles. Surely, it was not possible they could have cycled the cliff road from the settlement? A side-show developed when two Pakistanis started wrestling with one another, much to the delight of the Chinese soldiers as well as the other Pakistanis.

Eventually, the vehicles were separated by the brute force of one of the Swiss, and with the dispute finally settled by the Chinese major writing out an IOU for the equivalent of seventy-five dollars (according to the rumour running around the bus), we once more resumed our journey with everyone in good spirits. Not for the first time, I viewed my companions with affection. They were good-humoured men, and, although not hardened travellers, were proving to be resilient. They had left their wives, children and parents behind in the warmth of the Punjab, and here they were alone, in what was to them a strange and desolate country. The 'crash' had provided them with some relief.

The sandy terrain now gave way to a 'road' littered with mounds of earth, sand and rubble, that had obviously been left by the bulldozers. To the sound of 'ahs', 'ohs', and screams mingled with laughter, playing cards cascaded all over the bus, water-bottles slid down the aisle and bundles tumbled from the broken luggage racks as we were mercilessly driven over the deeply rutted ground.

Once more our journey was interrupted, this time by an ominous wrenching and grating sound from beneath the bus. We all got out, and with the rest of us peering beneath the bus, the driver crawled under the chassis and removed part of the lower insides of the vehicle, which were lying broken across a rock. With mounting interest, we watched as he threw the parts over the edge of a mound, brushed his hands and climbed back in the bus.

The road continued along a gorge, with high rocky escarpments, on a very narrow, twisting and dangerous track about fifty feet above the river. There had been a few spots of rain earlier and the grey skies now only accentuated the bleak terrain.

Towards evening we came upon some young teenage boys working on the road, shovelling sand into wooden handcarts; they returned our greeting and waved cheerfully. At the next check-point our passports weren't examined because the officer in charge was negotiating with the driver to take an injured woman to Kashgar, while his subordinates appeared more interested in propping up the check-point and watching two men carry her on board rather than actually doing anything. She was obviously in pain and it was with some difficulty they laid her in the aisle on top of two eiderdowns. Unlike the women at the settlement, she wore high moccasin-type boots beneath her skirt. One of the Swiss and a couple of the cycling students gave up their seats and perched on the baggage table behind the driver and amused the woman's two children (the girl a carbon copy of the women at the settlement and the boy in long pants and peaked cap) while I handed over my sleeping-bag for padding and offered my water-bottle. The woman's escorts, two strong, commanding-looking men, with Aryan features and dressed in black jackets and trousers with white shirts and high black boots and the now familiar Cossack-style hats, along with the children, appeared to be as much concerned with her modesty as with her pain; whenever she stirred and dislodged the narrow quilt that had been flung over her, they jumped up to replace it. Unable to find out what was wrong, but suspecting a broken hip, there was little I could do.

I spent the next part of the journey alternating between watching the woman and her companions and reflecting that my three-day journey from Hunza to Kashgar would have taken me considerably longer a few decades ago. Back in the early thirties, it took writers Peter Fleming and Ella Maillart about a month to travel on horseback from Kashgar to Gilgit,* whereas it was now possible to do the same journey by bus in a matter of days. Returning to musing upon the poor woman's plight led me to think of a statement made by Dervla Murphy, a travel-writer I enjoy. I really cannot agree with her when she says that much of the challenge and danger has gone out of travel. Whether a traveller or a local person, if you become ill or are injured in these remote places where facilities and professional medical care are not readily available, your life can be in danger; local people regularly die of diseases or illnesses brought on by injuries or climatic conditions. For travellers, local people and expeditions alike, it is a question of logistics; wherever terrain is harsh and communications are poor, even the best equipped and organized expedition can come to grief. Having said that, however, I agree with other travellers that the dangers of exploring remote areas are often highly exaggerated, the longevity of such adventurous souls as Ella Maillart, Freya Stark and Wilfred Thesiger bear witness to this. When I purchase travel insurance, I am as much concerned with delays, strikes,

---

*On their historic journey, they used the Mintaka Pass (then the usual crossing point) north-west of the Khunjerab and several hundred feet lower.

cancellations, and the loss or theft of baggage at airports, as I am with falling victim to an avalanche, flood or fire.

Stream of consciousness thinking now led me to dwell on the Silk Road itself. According to Sven Hedin, the name 'Silk Road' was not originally used in China, and was probably a phrase coined by Professor Baron Von Richthofen or in 1910 by Professor Albert Herrman, inspired by the knowledge that, for over 2,000 years, Chinese silk was carried along this road by traders.

Although the Silk Road has many routes branching off, the main artery, from Sian in eastern China via Anhsi, Kashgar, Samarkand and Seleucia, to Tyre in Lebanon, was approximately 6,000 miles in length. In former times, it was the longest trading route in the world and was both historically and culturally an important link connecting peoples and continents, though there were times when wars and severe climatic conditions disrupted the flow of trade, as reported by Marco Polo in the thirteenth century.

In this day and age, with the advance of modern technology and jet aircraft, it is impossible to think of a comparable link. Even if one still travels by the old methods, border check-points, visas and boundaries haunt a traveller's progress every step of the way, and, in some cases, prevent the continuation of the journey. The opening of the Khunjerab Pass has helped this situation and perhaps, one day, it will be possible to journey the entire route again. The more people travel, the less racism and xenophobia there will be in the world.

At last the bleak terrain changed and I became entranced by the silver-leafed trees and villages. The walled-in compounds intrigued me since they enclosed not only houses but also fields most of which were lying fallow. These separate enclosures puzzled me. Perhaps the walls served as a windbreak to shelter crops from dust and sandstorms. Again, I marvelled at how man can farm such desolate areas.

The symmetrical lines that graced the mud walls, possibly done with a trowel or a hoe, only heightened my interest. The sight of some white flowers growing wild, which looked not unlike orchids, further aroused my curiosity. Surely the climate was not suitable for such flowers? Questions, questions, and no-one to answer them.

The bus began picking up speed as we passed through two small settlements. Desert gave way to enormous cliffs, some streaked with veins of grey, while others were of varying shades of red, some as deep as oxblood. Below, the main artery of the river also ran red. The sun glimmered for a while giving the cliffs some brighter hues, and with the sudden splashes of green and patches of white flowers it became a landscape meant for an artist's brush.

Towards evening the road ran through an avenue of poplar trees, as it had done when coming into Tashkurghan. The red cliffs, which had gradually become beige, now disappeared, and on either side was a wide expanse of desert, relieved only by a ridge of hills in the far distance to the west. In the middle distance, there were some low sandhills, and close by, areas of cultivation, including a few paddy-fields. Here and there, between the trees, I caught sight of water-holes surrounded by more trees; these patches of green disappeared back into the desert, and the sand became littered with stones, reminding me of a Cornish beach at low tide. Far to the west, above the ridge of hills, a weak orange sun was beginning to set. More fields appeared, fertile patches with grazing cattle, a few homesteads, more water-holes surrounded by trees, mounds of hay, farm houses, a herd of goats, fields of wheat, more paddy-fields mingling with the desert. The road now in a straight line and fairly even. A man on a donkey. A horse-cart. A truck passing, carrying logs. Cyclists. Children. People sitting on door-steps. Donkey-carts. Turkestan.

The bus came to a stop in a ramshackle bazaar in a small town some two or three hours from Kashgar. Many of the open stores were nothing but large tents with tables and handcarts piled high with vegetables, while others held flat bread rolls with a hole in the middle, looking not unlike the American bagel; and, to the joy of everyone, there were slices of water-melon and what looked like honeydew melons as well. I had just enough time to grab a roll, a slice of melon and a cup of black tea before we were ushered back on the bus. I gave the injured woman the contents of my water-bottle to drink but much to my frustration, other than try to make her more comfortable, there was nothing else I could do.

Soon after our stop, we began driving along a metalled road. The glint of oil lamps from windows and those eternal poplar trees lining the road in the half light mesmerized me. Suddenly I had a strange feeling of familiarity, a sense of 'coming home' and memories of an avenue of poplar trees in France, just outside Paris, and childhood memories of a relative's painting of an avenue of trees, came flooding back déjà vu. What did it all mean? Were these memories of a past life in Kashgar? Had I once travelled the Silk Road? Was this why I always felt so in tune with the East? Had I travelled this very road in another lifetime?

I settled back in my seat eager to arrive in Kashgar.

At the first sign of street lights, a cheer went up all round. We had finally arrived. I glanced at my watch to find it was nine o'clock. Thoughts of dinner and a hotel room were now uppermost in my mind. I had obtained the names of three places from travellers in Gilgit; the cheap run-down Chini Bagh (once the British Consulate), the Shin Bin

144

Gon (the new Kashgar Guest-House) and Seman's Hotel, once the Russian Consulate.

It always feels strange coming into a city at night for the first time, and my first impressions of Kashgar are confused and simply that, impressions: a brightly lit circle where a number of people were strolling and cycling (it was here we dropped off the injured woman and her family); brightly lit bazaars and some not so well illuminated; small modern apartment blocks; donkey-carts and horse-carts. When we pulled into the bus station, everyone cheerfully tumbled out, relieved and happy the journey was over. But the smiles were soon to disappear. The word quickly went round—no baggage until the following morning at eight o'clock. The truck carrying it all had stopped elsewhere for the night; at least I had my sleeping bag and wash things.

Declining the offer of the Pakistanis to join them at the Chini Bagh, I headed into the bazaar towards a donkey-cart. It was almost empty of its supply of animal fodder and manned, it turned out, by a husband and wife complete with small daughter. Repeating Shin Bin Gon several times, I sat perched on one side, with my legs dangling over the edge and the girl beside me. The man and woman took turns in driving the donkey, continually debating which way to go. They were a young couple and friendly, with the woman in an old suit jacket and skirt worn over booted trousers, with the inevitable coloured scarf adorning her head and the man in blue boiler trousers, jacket and cloth cap. It was a long bumpy ride (which did nothing for my aching ribs), through dusty lanes, some sheltered by poplars, then out into the open beside a stagnant pool. I felt I was in the middle of nowhere. It was very quiet except for the dull sound of hooves, the creak of the cart wheels and the low voices of the man and woman. It seemed incredible that I was in Turkestan, that fabled land I had read about by torch under the bedclothes when I was a small child, and later, as an adult burning the 'midnight oil' in New York and London.

After nearly half an hour, we reached a wide metalled road, bounded on both sides by poplars, and on one, by a narrow canal with houses set well back behind more trees. Finally we pulled up before the huge iron gate of the Shin Bin Gon. Knowing I was being charged far too much, but too tired to haggle, I paid the requested five *yuan*.

Following the man who had unlocked the gate, I was taken across a large courtyard from which a number of paths led off between lawns and flower-beds, and into a very large reception hall, at the end of which stood a semi-circular desk. Behind it was a woman hardly out of her teens. She smiled pleasantly when I asked for a room.

The expected reply of 'No' came immediately. I put my bag on the floor, leaned my elbows on the counter, smiled sweetly and asked again. Still no, but there was a bed in a dorm. Again, I smiled and stated that I was tired (understatement), and I really did need a room. Again, she smiled. We were really outdoing one another with politeness. She was sorry, but there was no room. Impasse. I tried another tack. I was also hungry and thirsty. She brightened a little. There was no food but would I like a beer? That was a delicious idea, but food and a room were of more importance. Then I tried yet another angle. If there were no single rooms, how about a double? She looked at me, sighed, and went through her list, which she had already done at least a dozen times. She pondered for a moment, looked at me again, and then said I could have a double room and then change it for a single in the morning. Would that be all right? Relief! I followed her out into the courtyard, down a long path between the lawns and flower-beds, beneath a colourful awning and into a large building where a spiral staircase wound up from an elongated lobby with a reception desk and souvenir counter at one end, and several couches and armchairs. Up the stairs, along the carpeted landing to an open door, from which came the loud sounds of running water, I glanced in to find a man, in shirt sleeves and overalls, standing in the bath-tub knee-deep in water, trying to stop the shower from gushing.

The receptionist, and the room attendant who had joined her, looked at me hesitantly. 'Shower big problem but very good basin and nice bed. You want room, yes or no?'

'Yes!' I said quickly, and went back to my favourite topic. Again came the answer the kitchen was closed. What time I asked. Ten-thirty. I glanced at my watch. It was exactly ten twenty-five. Triumphantly, I showed her my watch. She smiled even more broadly. "Yes, ten twenty-five Kashgar time. But twelve twenty-five Beijing time!'*

With resigned acceptance I said 'Okay, I'll settle for a beer.' The words 'Beer finish!' really came as no surprise, and, as I closed the door, hugging a bag of noodles and a packet of biscuits given to me by some Hong Kong Chinese in the rooms opposite, I counted my blessings, especially when I sat down on the bed and discovered some green tea next to the thermos of boiling water. The sound of the shower in the bathroom would not, I felt, disturb my sleep that night.

---

*For travellers coming over the Khunjerab, there are four times zones with which to cope: Pakistan, Sinkiang, Kashgar, Beijing. Buses and hotels work on Beijing time which is two hours ahead of local Kashgar.

Bond of Sympathy

Very early next morning, still carrying all my valuables, as I had not yet been given a key for the room, I made what turned out to be an abortive attempt to rescue my baggage. An hour getting there and then two hours of frustration at the bus station had rewarded me with the information that unloading would not be until four o'clock in the afternoon.

Returning to the guest-house, I thought I'd better sort out my room. After a slightly shortened action-replay of the night before, the receptionist led me to another part of the hotel where the rooms had china spittoons, not unlike chamber-pots, outside every door. For some reason, I was to find out later, I had been placed in the Chinese wing. The room was not a single but a double, and was comfortably furnished with twin-beds that sported gaily-coloured pink sheets and eiderdowns, and was complete with television and telephone. It was the best I had seen since leaving my friends in Abbottobad, but when I asked for the key the receptionist smiled enigmatically and mumbling something about the room-attendant, left without giving it to me.

I stayed in the room to revel in its unexpected luxury a little longer before leaving to find the attendant. She was a pretty young woman wearing a brightly-coloured blouse, and a dark skirt beneath which stockinged legs appeared. I noticed her high heels and wondered how she did her job in such fashionable and uncomfortable footwear. I uttered the word key and went through the motions of unlocking a door. She gave a half-smile and said simply: '*Maeo!*' Advice from Mali Wan and travellers in 'Pindi and Gilgit rang in my ears and I asked again. The girl looked at me uncertainly. Then, to my astonishment, drew up her skirt, and showed me a five *yuan* note tucked in the top of her stocking, just below the suspender. I drew out my wallet, handed her five *yuan* and immediately received a key. No, it was not a bribe, as I then thought, but a deposit.

Having only breakfasted frugally on miniature doughnuts and figs at the bus station, I was delighted to find the dining-room open for lunch even though it was only 10 a.m. local time. It was a large cheerful room holding about ten round tables, each seating a dozen or so people. Within minutes of sitting down, a middle-aged woman, with almost white curly hair, was shown to the seat next to me. Although I can usually detect where a person comes from the moment they speak, she had me puzzled—but by the time the soup and omelette arrived, I had found out that she came from Washington DC and had been born deaf. She had learned to communicate through signs, finger spelling, writing and reading and had begun speech training at the age of ten. Although she was only able to hear high pitched sounds, she had managed to master speech through her early use of finger signs and was now a devoted exponent of the idea of total communication in the treating of the deaf.

As we finished our lunch, I decided that not only did I admire this woman but I liked her, and, when we strolled into the courtyard together, I was most sympathetic when she was told by the passing receptionist that she would have to stay in a dorm as there were no more rooms available. Leaving her talking to a fellow American, I returned to my haven of privacy and debated with myself. Moments later I offered to share. We went back to the room together and I showed her round. The bathroom wasn't pretty like the bedroom, being painted in institutional green and brown, and the toilet didn't flush, but other than that she was most impressed as was I when she showed me how to make the toilet work. Apparently, she had once lived on a remote farmhouse, and had learned to do her own plumbing jobs there.

As four o'clock approached, I left for the bus station in the hope of retrieving my rucksack. This time, when a donkey-cart appeared, I started haggling, but I was still far too tired to fight beyond four *yuan*. I climbed onto the cart which was wet and muddy, but my clothes were so dirty by now that it hardly seemed to matter. As we trotted along, I watched the passing scene in much the same way a commuter looks out of a train window, as he mulls over work or family problems; looking without seeing. But, as we passed a group of children on a canal bridge something did catch my eye—surely they had something furry in their arms? I looked again and was just in time to see them swing a large wet puppy into the canal. We turned a corner, the noise of the creaking wheels were mesmerizing me. Still I did not move. Then a hundred feet or so further on, I suddenly told the driver to stop, and, with much difficulty, got him to understand I wanted to go back in the direction we had come. Looking thoroughly perplexed, he turned back, and, as we rounded the corner, I saw a very wet and bedraggled puppy drag himself across the road and slink into the undergrowth beneath the trees.

Back at the bazaar I passed between stalls selling fruit, ice cream and bread, picked my way through merchants squatting on the ground, some displaying multi-coloured hats, others daggers with beautifully worked handles and scabbards, and entered the dark and crowded interior of the bus station. Stepping carefully over the people still asleep on the ground, I went out the other side to the bus park. Suddenly someone shouted and I turned to find a group of my travelling companions. Between us we soon sorted out the baggage problem and after joining them for an ice cream, I set off back to the guest house.

On the way I witnessed one of those cameo-like scenes which imprint themselves on the mind. As the horse slowly pulled the cart up the hill, a boy, leading a dog on a leash, walked off the roadway, stood amidst the undergrowth, and, as the dog turned in a circle, he undid the buttons of his flies, and boy and dog peed in unison.

A hot shower, clean clothes, a full stomach, and a sympathetic and charming companion can work wonders on a person's flagging spirits, and I sat down to have a long talk with Frances.

Frances was, to quote a fellow traveller from California, 'one charming, gutsy lady'. Having learnt not only to lip read but to talk she now, at sixty-two, had the added difficulty of being blind in one eye. She held the post of Associate Professor of Art History at Gallaudet College in Washington D.C., the only liberal arts college for the deaf in the world. Since her mid-forties, she had travelled around the world four times. This was her fifth. She did not travel in tour groups, but, like myself, alone, invariably seeking the wilder and more unspoiled regions of countries belonging to what is now familiarly called the Third World. Wherever she went, she visited schools and promoted the use of total communication in the education of deaf people. This language concept involves the utilization of such modes of communication as formal sign language, gestures, and finger spelling, as well as speech and speech reading in the education of even the very young deaf children. In an article she had written and which she showed me, she also described her struggles and triumphs in trying to convince educators and government officials around the world of the importance of total communication. In her travels, Frances had visited hundreds of schools for the deaf, including some in remote areas of countries like Ethiopia, where she had travelled by jeep for days on end across rough terrain. Her life appeared to have been one long struggle. Added to those physical handicaps, there had been an unhappy marriage, an accident had paralysed one arm, which she now had to exercise constantly, and then at the age of forty-three, with grown-up children, and grandchildren, she had gone to college. After the break-up of her marriage, she had refused all offers to re-marry, for now the world beckoned.

When she was a child, during the depression, her parents had sold up their home and moved to Tahiti. After three years of farming, her mother, a teacher, became very homesick, and the family decided to go back to the States. The Second World War, however, had broken out and they were forced to remain on Tahiti for another two years, until they heard of a hundred-foot schooner which was going to brave it across the Pacific to San Francisco. During this journey, they sailed into a hurricane. When Frances became afraid, her mother told her that if she died, it would not be a terrible thing for there would be blue skies, beautiful silver beaches and blue sea; her bones would become coral, her teeth pearls, and her hair sea-weed. This had the desired effect and Frances was at peace. Shortly after, a huge wave swept down and swamped the schooner as it plunged into a trough, but, because of a well-placed pocket of air, it shot right up again out of the water and all survived.

It soon became obvious to me that Frances was not only a strong character, but also lived by a strong faith, not in God as such, but in a cosmic force and the power of the mind. Whatever else I should learn about her, one thing was for sure—she was a living testimony to her beliefs. By the end of that first day, we had already decided that we had been destined to meet.

Talking about Frances, I digress but often our chance encounters change our view of a place or bring back our perspective.

Next day our travels together in the city took us through the modernized part of Kashgar, where we walked along a wide avenue, its centre path reserved for traffic, the occasional bus, the rare truck and the odd tiny tractor-truck that slowly spluttered past. Although motorized transport was rare, cyclists, however, were numerous and we made the mistake, as so many foreigners do, of walking in the bicycle lanes rather than on the pavement. It was then I came to appreciate fully the difficulty Frances must have every time she is in a town or city.

On both sides of the avenue were small department stores carrying Chinese-made Western-styled clothes, shops selling cosmetics and bath-room soaps, and serendipity stores like those in Pakistan bazaars, but they were very much larger, and had far less merchandise and choice. The Chinese are great stamp collectors and, opposite the very large and efficient post office, there was a shop where you could buy the latest stamps as well as collectors' items. There was really little else to excite the traveller with money to burn.

The efficiency and courtesy of the people in the post office was matched by that of the people in the bank where we exchanged our foreign currency. We had to wait a short while, but no longer than in

150

Europe or the United States. It was a small uncluttered office, where all the clerks were young women, fashionably dressed in traditional, brightly coloured head-scarves, blouses, jackets and skirts with high-heeled shoes. They were really no different from young women in similar jobs at home. Now, looking at them, I came to the conclusion I have come to many times before when travelling, that people the world over are basically the same: they have the same fears, the same joys and the same heartaches. Perhaps, where we differ in the West, and perhaps it is to our disadvantage, is that we no longer treasure the family unit; religion is no longer an institution of morality; and technology is taking over. Modern China, too, has its problems with its one-child families, its increase in technology and its atheism—and, perhaps, stands to lose in its desire for progress. In Kashgar and in eastern Turkestan, however, where most of the people, mainly Uighurs, are Moslem, families are allowed as many as four children which may have a healthy restraining effect on China's ambitions to catch up with the West.

With our business done, we walked on towards the old city, stopping to refresh ourselves with slices of water-melon, while watching leather-workers squatting on the pavement, deftly mending shoes and bags. Farther on, we bought lemon ices sold to us by a woman in a wide straw hat and white jacket, pushing a small white cart; a frequent sight all over Kashgar. (As water is always boiled in China, neither of us were afraid of stomach upsets.) On one side of the road was a large hoarding, advertising the latest blood and thunder Kung Fu movie. Soon after, we heard publicly broadcast martial music, as we walked on past a huge statue of Chairman Mao. Flower-beds and lawns were pleasing to the eye as we made our way to a large square dominated by the Id Kah Mosque, one of the largest in China. Men squatted on the ground carving musical instruments and smiled for photographs. We obliged and passed on by some more water-melon sellers and a kebab stand. On market days the square is even more crowded merchants using the pavements as stalls for shirts, scarves, socks and other goods.

A fellow American, whom we had met moments earlier and who knew Kashgar well, led us round the back of the mosque. Had we realized it was prayer time we should not have ventured in. Above us, with their backs turned, were rows of kneeling men, their coloured skull caps and assortment of dress appealing to my photographic mind, but both Frances and I were hesitant about using our cameras at such a moment and we remained still, our cameras in our bags, embarrassed at even being there.

When the worshippers rose to their feet a few seconds later, I saw that they were nearly all elderly and they looked at Frances and then at our

A musical instrument maker in Kashgar.

companion and myself unhappily. They gestured that they took great exception to Frances' bare arms, and her stockinged legs below her very chaste skirt. No-one could have been more modestly dressed in our Western eyes, but to them she had violated their code—no woman should expose either her arms or legs or wear a low neckline.* In some conservative Islamic areas, for example in Multan, in Pakistan, it is deemed necessary for a woman to wear a shirt or *khameez* down to her knees over her slacks or *shalwar*. Poor Frances. Over an hour later she said to me that she still felt naked. To cheer her up, the American led us to a tea-house which overlooked the city and which thereafter became my favourite haunt.

The next day Frances left and once more I was on my own. I was very

---

*The fact that we were in a holy place made this even more offensive to them.

152

Young metal workers in Kashgar.

sad to see her go. A few medicinal pills had been a poor exchange for the pleasure of her company.

With Frances gone, I fell victim to one of my less brilliant ideas. I decided that to avoid the hassle of haggling with the cart-drivers and disliking their use of sticks to goad the animals on, I would do the sensible thing—copy the Chinese and use a bicycle. Unfortunately, I had not only forgotten that I always come unstuck when I try to be 'sensible', but also that my history of riding bicycles wasn't too clever either. When I was a child, my mother, much against her better judgement, replaced my tricycle with a child's two-wheeler. It was not long before I had run into a brick wall, smashed the front wheel and twisted the handle-bars. In my early twenties, doing a summer job in the Isles of Scilly, I had hired a bike and run into the back of the island's one and only bus. Later still, in Greece, with yet another hired bike, I had spent most of the time pushing it up hill. A wise man once said 'He who forgets history does so at his peril.'

This time around, I didn't get beyond the gates of the guest-house, which was, perhaps, just as well. The bicycle in question was large, with a high seat and cross-bar. Although sensibly dressed in loose-fitting slacks, I was carrying a heavy camera-bag, the result being, that when I mounted, I went straight over the other side and landed smack on the side of my face. The receptionist screamed. A party of Chinese hotel workers rushed across and picked me up, and before I could gather my wits about me, I was hurried through the reception lobby, and, much to my surprise, into a first-aid clinic. The doctor, a very plump Han Chinese woman was most sympathetic and expertly cleaned up the nasty cut over my eye and attended to the bump on the side of my forehead. Both the wounds were beginning to swell, and after an abortive effort to obtain ice from the dining-room, I got into a cart and made my way to the old city to find some. As soon as we passed a dessert stand (ice mixed with fruit sweeteners, and, I think, yoghurt)* where huge dirty lumps of ice were displayed, I jumped down and asked to buy a chunk. The man gave me an enormous piece, refused payment and looked at me with grave concern. As I sat on a nearby bench, applying the ice to my black eye and swollen face, I was approached by children, old men and young women, all wanting to know what had happened. The answer was easy. I simply pointed to a bicycle and mimed someone falling over. Without exception, they 'oh'd' and 'ah'd'; some put their hands to their hearts, while one old woman blinked back the tears. Children were not only just as curious but

---

*In the bazaar there are dessert stands which use ice. These are usually manned by the Uighurs. The Chinese generally drink hot water as they consider iced water bad for the system.

just as sympathetic. Throughout the day, and the next, and for several days thereafter, I could not walk more than a few steps before I would be stopped by an anxious citizen of Kashgar. Even women wearing the *chowdar* would stop, lift up their veils and peer at me in concern. Whenever I finished my now very professional mime with the words '*Il humdu'illah*,' words and smiles of appreciation were added to those of concern.

From tired ambivalence to love; thanks to the company of a rare human a being and an unfortunate accident, my stay in Kashgar proved to be a heart-warming experience. Some cities are evocative because of their history and associations: Istanbul and the cities of Aleppo and Damascus had bewitched me in the days of my youth, but now, because of the kindness of the people, this ancient city had me captivated. To walk in its crowded lanes and ancient bazaar was to revert to a period before motorized transport and to see life from another perspective; therein lies the charm and value of travel. Modern travellers sometimes wistfully bemoan the fact that better communications and modern technology are making the world smaller—for the Indians of Brazil for instance, they are no doubt an unwelcome and evil intrusion. But for many countries of the developing world and their various ethnic groups, it is a different story. To hope they remain isolated in a time warp is to wish to deny them the benefits of progress. To remember the past and one's heritage, and not be seduced by the future, is perhaps the only way people of the remote areas of the world can make the transition without trauma. Kashgar's neighbours in Hunza appear to have managed it successfully. With the opening of the Khunjerab, Kashgar is again at a major crossroads in its history and only time will tell how well the people will adapt.

Kashgar

Sinkiang, of which Kashgar is the southern capital, lies in the very heart of Central Asia, and is a remote land of deserts and oases, divided into north and south by the mountain range of T'ien Shan, the 'Celestial Peaks'. It is surrounded in the east by the great deserts of the Taklamakan and the Gobi; to the north and west by Russia and, to the south-west, the subcontinent of Pakistan and India.

Land not only builds the character of the people, but its geographical position also determines the fate of its inhabitants. Being the place where several empires meet makes the border region of eastern Turkestan a sensitive and volatile area. It also makes for convoluted politics, and the history of Sinkiang* is a veritable labyrinth of uprisings, skulduggery, factional fighting, subversive shenanigans and foreign intervention—a far too long a story to narrate here, but some details are worth mentioning so as to put Kashgar in its political context in the past and present day.

Although Urumchi in North Sinkiang is the political capital of the province, Kashgar, in South Sinkiang, is the economic and cultural centre and covers an area of ninety-six square kilometres, with a population of 200,000.

Kashgar, Kashi or Shule, as it was called in ancient times, dates back well over 2,000 years and used to be described as the 'bright pearl' on what we now call the Silk Road. In 200 BC, Kashgar officially came under the suzerainty of the Western Han Government, and suffered until towards the end of the first century AD, when the Eastern Han Dynasty was esablished. In more recent times, too, Kashgar has experienced a turbulent history.

In the latter part of the nineteenth century there were a number of uprisings, the most famous led by a mercenary from Russian Central

---

*The Chinese call the two parts of Sinkiang by different names—T'ien Shan Pei Lu in the north, which is more Mongol and Siberian in character, and T'ien Shan Nan Lu in the south, which is inhabited by people of Turkish origin.

Asia, Yakub Beg, who successfully set up a Moslem state. His achievements were hailed by the British and it was hoped that he might unite all the Moslem states of Central Asia into a buffer zone against the advancing Russians. Within a decade, however, he was dead, his administration discredited, the Chinese were back in power, and modern Sinkiang came into being. Until 1928, the province remained peaceful and enjoyed complete local autonomy outside the factional politics and fighting that was going on inside China, while at the same time keeping revolutionary Russia at bay.

As in Tibet, the greatest cause for uprisings in Sinkiang was the clash of cultures between the indigenous population—Moslems of Turkish origin—and the Chinese authorities caused by the take-over of eastern Turkestan by the Han Chinese. In 1928 the governor of Sinkiang, Yang Tseng-hsin, was assassinated. Soon after there were again uprisings and a Tungan (Moslem Chinese) general, Ma Chung-ying,* who had been fighting the National People's Army in the north-west China, marched into North Sinkiang, and, allied with the Moslem Turkis of Hami, continued the battle against the Chinese.

Not surprisingly, both Russia and the British were closely watching these events; the heart of Central Asia is truly a place where empires meet. In 1933, the Russian authorities, after White Russian mercenaries* had earlier in the year reinforced Chinese troops fighting the Tungans and Turkis, now intervened. This proved to be a decisive blow to the Moslems, and the Tungan general withdrew his army to the south of Sinkiang.

While the fighting had been going on in the North, local Moslems had overthrown the Chinese administration of Kashgar, but in 1933, the Turkis and Tungans fell out to be replaced in July 1934 by a combined force of Turkis and Manchurians, under the leadership of the Chinese General, Sheng-Shih-t'sai, who became the new Governor of the Province.

With British influence in eastern Turkestan—a valuable listening post—diminishing, and with the need to restore British and Indian trade,* the British were not pleased when, during the battle between the Turkis and Tungans, the British Consulate in Kashgar was attacked, and the Consul General's wife shot through the arm, albeit accidentally. Soon

---

*Nicknamed 'General Thunderbolt' by the peasants and 'Baby General' by his men, he was a fierce fighter – although hardly out of his teens – and his methods of warfare were violent in the extreme. When he rose to power in Kansu in 1930, he terrorized the countryside. In one resisting town all males over fourteen were put to the sword. In another, three thousand corpses were left lyng in the streets.
*Those Russians opposed to Communism, it was in 1934 that the Communist forces began their long march.

after, the British sent a special mission to Urumchi to make contact with the new regime.

From that time on, until 1942, even though the Chinese Nationalist Government had severed its connections with the Soviet Union, Russian influence spread across Sinkiang Province. Trade with the Soviet Union increased and Russian civil, military and scientific advisers were employed. Trade with central China ceased; Islam was ridiculed in the schools; foreign missionaries were expelled; Indian traders persecuted; and the British Consul-General of Kashgar boycotted.

Although there was some resistance, General Sheng continued to remain in power until 1944.

In 1946, new measures were introduced, including a reduction of the number of Chinese troops in Sinkiang and the giving of a certain amount of self-government to the native population, and for a while there was an uneasy peace. The appointment in May 1947 of a Turki Governor helped, but the lack of medical services, poor education and economic development remained as causes of dissatisfaction. The Communist take-over of China* and the final closing of the borders had their effect upon the ancient trading route—the Silk Road—and the town of Kashgar, but, today, as the economic and cultural centre of South Sinkiang of the Xinjiang Uighur Autonomous Region, Kashgar is at peace—and with the opening of the Khunjerab, the city is again an important staging-post.

To describe a city with all its vicissitudes, nuances, sights, sounds and smells is just as hard as describing beautiful or hostile countryside. For me, Kashgar was in many ways a collection of impressions, rather like a series of photographs accompanied by sound and smell.

Restaurants and food stalls always beckon me, as I love to taste new dishes and regard this as one of the delights of travel. The kebab stands, however, always smoky and in tune with the customary Kashgar haze, were not sights for the squeamish eater. Their pieces of fat on a skewer, or chunks of raw liver were not to my liking, nor were the sights of large iron pots with great lumps of offal bubbling merrily away inside them. Small boys would sit before bowls of what looked like intestines, pick them up as though they were balloons and blow into them in order to fill them with the offal.

---

*Since the 1914–1918 European war and the Russian Revolution, a policy of rigorous control was placed on the borders of Sinkiang (China's 'New Dominion'), including its border with China, by its administration in Urumchi; and travellers were harassed by all kinds of formalities which became further tightened with the revolution in China and the Japanese invasion. Armies began to march; trade was disrupted, the desert way of life was changed with trucks by-passing the small watering-holes; old inns closed down and small oases were abandoned.

*The People's Communist Government was set up in Peking on 1st October 1949.

158

Rush hour in old Kashgar.

A street scene in Kashgar.

One sortie into a workman's café, where I stood beside a grubby counter and wood-burning stove with a large oven, rewarded me with a bowl of green tea and a superb view of lunch-time in Kashgar. Crowded on the benches before the long wooden tables were men in cloth caps and jackets and trousers, reminding me of photographs of mill workers in the north of England in the thirties, or some of the workers I had seen in eastern Turkey back in the early sixties. Most of them were eating from large, chipped, enamel cups in which floated a lump of fatty meat, juice and onion. These same cups had been put straight into the oven complete with contents and drawn out only moments earlier. Other customers of perhaps more modest means crumbled up bread into bowls of green tea.

On another occasion, I ventured into a restaurant in one of the main squares. This was a slightly larger affair with the kitchen in the back, out of sight, and a warm-up counter at the entrance. Bowls of noodles and thick, red chilli sauce had lured me in. I don't think many Westerners frequented the place, because every time I patronized it, I was treated as though I were an honoured guest, especially when I addressed the workers with Islamic salutations. One lunch time, a noodle-maker stood in the doorway, 'throwing' the noodles. Excitedly I drew out my camera, but I was too late. In a loud chorus, the patrons called out to him to give a repeat performance, so that I might take his photograph.

Kashgar is 1,289 metres above sea level and has an annual rainfall of below 100mm. In winter, the temperature can fall to 24 degrees below zero, and, in summer, rise to 40 degrees above. The fertile oases provide a plentiful harvest of fruit, and every day I nearly made myself sick on luscious green figs and slices of water-melon. Lemon ices and bowls of yoghurt were also a favourite and my whole day seemed to be one long meal.

It was not, however, only food which occupied my mind. My favourite haunt became the tea-house I had visited with Frances which had a balcony overlooking the street. Here on large wooden platforms, from which the waiter would brush the crumbs with a broom before his customers sat down, I could look out on the life of the city. One morning, I watched as a large affluent-looking European tour group aimed their cameras at some women who frantically waved at them not to do so.

Television, too, provided me with much entertainment and interest. One evening, I watched a competition-cum-exhibition of Kung Fu and other forms of martial arts. As I hold a purple belt in Tae Kwon Do and belong to a club in Aylesbury, it is a subject dear to my heart, and I watched in awe as both men and women participated. I have never seen such agility, speed and acrobatics—all performed with beauty and grace. Another evening, I watched a Turkestan song and dance show and

A restaurant kitchen in Kashgar.

A Youth blows up the intestines of a goat in preparation for putting in the offal.

delighted in both the music and the costumes. Even the weather report, at the end of the news (the marriage of Prince Andrew and Sarah Ferguson was one of the items), was a show in itself, and, as a detailed analysis was given, colourful pictures of each climatic region were shown.

My sojourn in Kashgar also afforded me a brief friendship with a young Han Chinese geologist who was billeted in my building at the guest house. His dazzling smile and my interest in martial arts had brought us together, and in his free time, he liked to make sure I and other foreigners enjoyed his country and its people. Blessed with a sunny day, he and his driver took a group of us to a village a little way outside the city. It was a pleasure driving into the desert, and I enjoyed the sandy wastes, the dazzling blue sky and the green of the oases and the ever present poplar trees.

Once I saw with delight some of the silver leafed trees I had seen on the bus. On returning to the U.K., I discovered they were probably the silver-leafed sand jujube tree for which Kashgar is famous.* On reaching our destination, some villagers invited us into their farmhouse and then showed us around their property taking us along shady, leafy lanes and through sunlit orchards, and bestowing upon us fresh yellow figs, hand-picked in our honour as we went. Inside their simple house, we sat on a large *k'ang* covered in hand-woven rugs, with our backs against a wall that was covered in red-patterned material and looked onto white-washed walls and bright blue shelves that framed doors and windows. As bowls of tea were passed around, we were called upon to take numerous photographs of the family. A visit to a local ancient mosque with a beautifully embossed wooden ceiling ended a delightful day.

One of the many delights of Kashgar is its children. I am not one of those people who coo over babies and melt like butter, when naughty little boys or girls in frilly dresses are introduced, but every time I hired a donkey or horse-cart and was driven through the narrow lanes, I would see groups of children. Often they would run after the cart, crying out 'Bye, bye!' How they had come to learn that and not 'hello' was a mystery that many of us remarked upon. On one of my rides into the city, a small girl, clad in the habitual scarf, jacket over skirt, and trousers, ran after us laughing, with a long wicked knife in one hand and a huge meat cleaver in the other. Naked children played in the dust by the side of the road or on the edge of stagnant pools while others, oblivious to the interested stares of the foreigners, defecated beside open doorways where mud and water oozed from morning ablutions. Boys too old for nudity were young imitations of their fathers. All wore long pants, with

---

The Gobi Desert by Mildred Cable with Francesca French.

Boys in Kashgar were young imitations of their fathers with their long pants (often with flies undone) and dagger at their waists. Potato selling is a popular pastime of the young.

the buttons on the flies missing (some with a slit down the back of their pants), and the famous Kashgar dagger at their waist, while the girls, in pretty dresses, or in the customary attire of their mothers, scooped up their baby sisters and brothers away from the wheels of passing carts.

There was a vibrancy about the streets that I liked; the city was never quiet. Drivers cried out to clear the way, the jingling of their harness bells reminiscent of the Russian troika; the sound of the anvil mingled with the hammering and tapping of metal workers; except for the funny little tractor-trucks, there was no honking of car horns to spoil the ancient market sounds—only the constant ring of modern bicycle bells.

One morning as I walked towards the old bazaar, the haze lifted and the city was bathed in a mantle of glorious colour. In the distance, the sandhills and the mountains stretched along the horizon. The lanes of the old city, with their tall mud-brick houses, were turned almost golden in the early morning light. The fruit market created a big splash of colour while the hat-seller happily set out his maroon and gold decorated skull caps among the red and green ones, knowing they would surely catch the eye of a tourist. Every so often, a man carrying a cheap plastic bag would brush past me and whisper in my ear 'changes money?' Easily the word 'Maeo' would come to my lips. As changing money on the black market is the only way a foreigner can come by local currency, it is an unavoidable necessity,* but I preferred to change my money in a shop, even if I did have to sidle down a nearby alley.

By the time I left Kashgar, I would not only remember the poor puppy and the drivers using sticks and the word *maeo*, but would also carry with me such pictures as a boy sitting on a cart beside a calf, cradling its head in his arms, and small boys proudly leading dogs and puppies on a rope.

Like most Westerners, I went to the Sunday market, where most people drive in from all the outlying oases, bringing in their produce, stacks of wood and their cattle, horses and camels. This was exciting, but no more so than Kashgar any other day of the week, for it is one continual, throbbing, bustling market. Even now, as I write, I can smell the freshly-baked bread, incense, smoke from the kebab stand, spices, ripe figs, and occasionally night-soil as the cart passed a pond where children paddled in green slime.

I can still remember, as if it were only yesterday, driving through the dusty lanes at nightfall and seeing an oil lamp burning in a window, a man leaning against a doorway playing a tambourine, and a child running up to me crying out 'Bye, bye! Bye, bye!'

---

*A traveller can only pay for bus tickets and hotels with government money (FEC). In the markets, local currency is needed.

164

The Road to Baltistan

Having survived the bus journey over the Khunjerab to Kashgar with relatively few physical and mental bruises, I was now faced with returning the same way—a prospect I was not looking forward to with much enthusiasm.

Thinking about the return trip gave me cause to analyse why I and fellow seasoned travellers had found this journey such heavy going. I have undertaken many journeys by public transport in remote regions, which have been equally tiring and where facilities have been poor and food a problem—a bus ride across Turkey and a trip down the Nile from Aswan to Wadi Halfa and by rail to Khartoum, come instantly to mind—but for some reason that journey to Kashgar was particularly tough. Trekking on foot, horseback or camel is also far more exacting in physical terms, although it brings its own reward, for you soon learn to appreciate the most elementary of things: food for instance, however meagre and plain, in these circumstances tastes more delicious than the grandest French cuisine; water is sweeter than wine, the sun's shadows become a blessed relief, and the desire and pleasure of rest are almost as satisfying as a sexual encounter.

Without doubt, the lack of food, the infrequent stops and the unsprung seats had made that journey uncomfortable, but that was only part of it—perhaps the answer lies in the one-to-one relationship between the traveller and the people of the country. Although I had made friends with the Pakistanis on the bus crossing the Khunjerab, my encounters with the local population, except for officials, had been few, unlike on other journeys. Then, too, in China, not only does the usual language barrier and scarcity of information make travelling difficult, but the barrier of 'no' to every question or request can become very frustrating. Those Westerners I met who had spent a year or more in the country, either as students or teachers, expressed an obviously sincere liking for China and the Chinese people, but found moving about the country a hassle. Apparently the Chinese Government wants only tour-groups. If

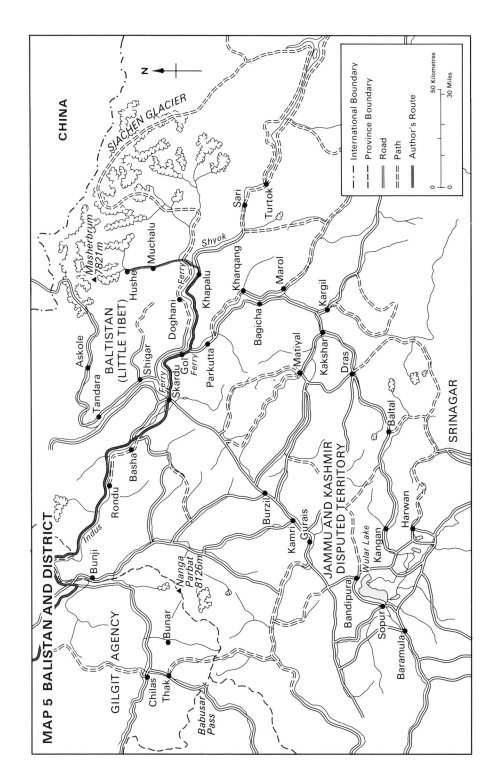

MAP 5 BALISTAN AND DISTRICT

CHINA

SIACHEN GLACIER

Masherbrum 7821m

Muchalu

Hushe

Shyok

Sari

Turtok

Doghani Ferry

Khapalu

Askole

BALTISTAN (LITTLE TIBET)

Shigar

Ferry Ferry

Skardu

Gol Ferry

Parkutta

Kharqang

Marol

Kargil

Tandara

Bagicha

Matiyal

Kakshar

Dras

Basha

Baltal

SRINAGAR

Rondu

Indus

Burzil

JAMMU AND KASHMIR DISPUTED TERRITORY

Harwan

Bunji

Nanga Parbat 8126m

Kamri

Gurais

Wular Lake

Kangan

GILGIT AGENCY

Bunar

Bandipura

Sopur

Baramula

Chilas

Thak

Babusar Pass

Legend

- International Boundary
- Province Boundary
- Road
- Path
- Author's Route

50 Kilometres
30 Miles

N

this is true, it seems a pity, for it is the individual traveller who is likely to spend more time in the country getting to know the people. They are the ones who will go home and write about the good things. For my part, I had seen enough and enjoyed my sojourn in Kashgar sufficiently to wish to return to China and its people.

The return journey to Hunza, blessed this time with bright sunshine, was more cheerful, and a small sackful of food made it less physically demanding. When the bus fell into a ditch and we had to wait a couple of hours for it to be hauled out by the baggage truck, I felt quite relaxed about it; and when on the Pakistan side, just before Gulmit, the road and river became one, I enjoyed, along with my companions, a short trip by bulldozer.

But it had been another tiring journey, and I decided it would be wise, before undergoing the three-day jeep ride across the Shandur to Chitral, to take a rest. Mindful, too, that during my time in China, I had had relatively little exercise, I decided to go to Skardu for a short and easy trek in the high mountains north of Khapalu in Baltistan.

As I believe in omens, I guess I should have taken note, for, although the journey by wagon along the Indus Gorge between Gilgit and Skardu was uneventful, except for a blow-out, arrival at my destination boded ill.

It was nearly eleven o'clock at night, when the wagon crossed over the long bridge beside Katchura Lake and entered the outskirts of the dusty, lonely town of Skardu. It is always eerie entering desert towns at night, but Skardu seemed almost sinister. Not a person, not an animal was to be seen; hardly a light flickered in the darkness. The only illumination was from our headlamps and the only people we eventually came across were some policemen who appeared out of the shadows and flagged us down. Driving into the still, silent town, we were again stopped by some policemen but no explanation was given to us. In the light of a street lamp, I noticed the centre of Skardu bazaar seemed even more broken-down than ever. It was all very disquieting. What I had been unable to see, because of the lack of light, was that what I took for broken-down shacks were the gutted remains of shops that had been set on fire by a mob of rioters earlier that day.

The next morning, having camped out on the lawn of the K2 Motel, which was full of stranded mountaineers, I was to discover what had happened. Two men of rival political parties and ethnic backgrounds had had opposing political views over some matter. One of them had tricked the other into going to his house and had shot him. The murder had led to rioting the next day and a number of shops were set on fire in the bazaar. The flames had quickly spread, causing much damage and a curfew had been imposed. It was into this I had arrived the night before.

Except for the ex-Rajah's dilapidated palace and deserted Askandria Fort,* both of which entail a perilous climb for the visitor, there is not much to see in Skardu itself at the best of times. Its bazaar is poorly stocked, and, being mostly inhabited by Shiahs, the atmosphere is not so relaxed as in other areas. Now with everything closed, I did not even have the joy of seeking out a little custard shop.

Skardu serves as a centre for all the trekking and mountaineering expeditions in the Karakorams, and the K2 Motel is the hub of their activity, so I felt sure that I had come to the best place to find a guide. After poor old grumpy Murad, who had guided me across the Shandur, and inexperienced Arlem, I decided that I should do the 'sensible' thing this time and hire a professional guide. Yes, I should have known!

I will not give you indigestion by supplying a detailed account of my trials and tribulations in the company of the charlatan I eventually chose, but will write sufficient to allow any armchair travellers to congratulate themselves on their wisdom in journeying vicariously through to others. In my reading of travel books, I have often chuckled over the difficult situations that sometimes befall the traveller, but when it happened to me on this occasion, I found humour at times to be in short supply!

Wanting to know what lies around the bend in the road has often led me into both curious and difficult situations. My desire to know what lay around the bend in the river, and around a huge outcrop of rock in Khapalu, certainly led to a memorable trek.

Baltistan, 'Little Tibet', lies in the basin of the Upper Indus, and, before Partition, was connected by a trade route to Tibetan Buddhist Ladakh. The Baltis, who have been Moslem for over five centuries, may have originally been Tibetan agriculturalists, and they still speak a form of

---

*The Askandria Fort was built by Kashmir's Zowar Singh's Dogra forces after their victory over Ahmed Shah in 1840.

*In 747, when the Tibetans had control over Gilgit, a Chinese general crossed over the Baroghil Pass and imprisoned the Tibetan vassal king. Two years later, when an ally of the Tibetans was interrupting communications between Gilgit and Kashmir, he returned and again drove them off. It is believed by some academics that these Tibetans may have been the original Baltis, and that Balti society has probably been multi-tiered from the middle of the eighth century, with the ruling class of alien origin. According to Filippo de Filippi's book *The Italian Expedition to the Himalaya, Karakoram and Eastern Turkestan*, Baltistan was known to ancient geographers who believed these people are the Byltae of Ptolemy and were Dard in origin. Ujfalvy, however, suggests that the Baltis are descended from the ancient Saci who were driven southwards by the Mongols in the second century and subsequently mingled with the Dards and Tibetans. Here, as elsewhere in northern Pakistan, there are those who claim to be descendants of Alexander the Great.

archaic Tibetan.* The country itself is arid with hard-won terraced fields set amidst rocky gorges—rewards for intensive irrigation.*

The terrain between Skardu and Khapalu, formerly the largest principality of old Baltistan, is relieved here and there by picturesque houses built in the traditional style of the Baltis—the lower section, built of bricks and mud, being both the winter quarters for the family and the animal byres, while the upper storey, serving as the summer quarters, are whitewashed with gaily painted window frames. The flat roofs of the mud and stone one-storey houses were spread with orange, red and brown drying apricots. In Kashgar, the predominant fruit crops were figs and melons. Now, back in Pakistan, it was apricots for which Khapalu, along with Hunza, is famous.

After crossing the Skardu plain, we travelled through a narrow, desolate ravine beside the River Indus. At one point after we had passed the confluence of the Indus and its tributary the Shyok, where the two currents crash headlong, sending up angry waves seemingly flowing in all directions, we passed a *ghari*—one of those chair bridges which is nothing but a box drawn on a pulley to take both goods and people across the river, a common feature in many parts of northern Pakistan.

It was at Khapalu, a small ancient kingdom on the banks of the Shyok that my trek began. Leaving the fertile oasis behind us, my guide, Masood, and I came to a stop on a rocky shore lined with willows and poplars. In front of us was a broad stretch of water, at least a mile across where, like the Indus at Skardu, it filled a basin hewn out of the mountains, at the foot of a rising pyramid of peaks. There was a sudden shout behind us. Turning around, I saw four men (two crew and two passengers) carrying a *zaq*, a wooden raft kept afloat by inflated animal skins. I could see sweat pouring down the men's faces, as they passed by searching for the best departure point, and no wonder: Masood told me it weighed two hundred kilos.

Once the *zaq* had been lain down at the edge of the water, with the tyres and skins facing upwards, one of the crew checked it over. The tyres were firm but the skins, apparently, told a different story. As he and his helpmate knelt down to blow in the necessary air, Masood said helpfully 'This river is very dangerous. Many men die crossing it!'

He then went on to tell me there had once been another community on the other side of the lake, higher up the Shyok Valley, which had been cut in half by flood waters with the loss of many lives.*

Once the skins passed examination, the *zaq* was thrown over, to land

---

*Balti villages are regarded as an hydraulic society. After a basic canal is built and an irrigation system constructed, the soil is prepared by grazing. The land is then divided into plots for private management and terraces are constructed.

with a heavy plop into the water. No doubt because of my weight, I was placed in the centre towards the front. Just sitting down and keeping my balance was difficult in itself.

The two passengers sat squashed against me, until one of them was handed a long pole and he moved to the rear. Now the four 'oarsmen' (Masood had also been commandeered) took up positions on the corners of the *zaq*, which, perhaps, measured five feet by five. Slowly they punted out into the main flow of the river, then, with shouts from the leader, thrust the long poles hard into the water as though paddling a canoe. I could feel, as well as see, the water splashing up between the branches of the *zaq*, and every so often a sheet of spray would sting my face.

We had travelled about a hundred yards or so when we came to a long sandbank, where the *zaq* was beached. As the men carried it across the sandy surface, I stopped to take photographs. Carrying on across the sand flats, I heard a shout. The *zaq* had been put down at the edge of the next stretch of water, and they were gesturing to me wildly. At that moment I felt myself sinking. Quicksand! I looked around me. I was some hundred feet behind the others, and, on every side of me there was nothing but waterlogged sand; nowhere did it look firm and there was not a rock in sight. I gestured wildly, asking which way I should go, but I was not understood. All I could hear was '*Jaldi! Jaldi*' Quickly! Quickly!

I tried to run, but running across quicksand in heavy hiking boots, carrying a rucksack cannot be done speedily, and I found myself plunging along in a series of hops and jumps, with my feet sinking up to the ankles in the sand. When I moved, the water gurgled and swished as it oozed around my·boots. When, panting for breath, I finally caught up with the others. I saw the two crew men kneeling on the sand, blowing up the tyres. It was incredible they could find enough air in their lungs to blow up those heavy monsters.

Once more we boarded the *zaq*. This time the older crewman

---

*In Skardu and Gilgit, there are a number of stories relating to floods. One incident, reported to have taken place in the 1830s, tells of a woman, dressed in strange clothes and speaking an unfamiliar dialect, being swept three hundred miles down the Indus on a raft. This was probably due to the break-up of a glacier dam on the Shyok. The most often-repeated tale concerns the tragedy in 1841. During the previous winter, near the confluence of the Astore and Indus Rivers, part of a mountainside had collapsed into the Indus Gorge, damming up the river and eventually forming a thirty-five mile long lake reaching almost to Gilgit. Six months after this enormous landslide, the dam broke. The local inhabitants, perceiving the danger, had acted quickly to prevent a catastrophe, and, although valuable farming land and property were destroyed or damaged, there was little loss of life. Farther down the river, however, a huge wave swept along the Indus, causing many fatalities. Nowadays, the Pakistan air force keeps the danger spots under constant surveillance.

The *zaq* which weighed 200 kilos was a heavy burden for four men to carry.

In Hushe, the leader of the *zaq* crew blows up the animal skins to help it float.

appeared tense. He no longer looked at me with a smile. He was muttering to himself, what, I could not tell, until Masood started doing the same. Suddenly I recognized the first sura of the Koran. I knew from past experience, when travelling with Moslems, that if the Koran was recited, there was danger ahead.

I hung on grimly to the branches which were now almost under water beneath my crossed legs. As the *zaq* bounced up and down where two different currents met head-on, keeping my balance became more difficult. The 'oarsmen' shouted directions to each other, and called on Allah to protect us, as the the *zaq* urgently tried to swing down river, while the men sweating profusely strove to keep heading for the distant shore. It was a battle. There was no doubt in my mind that we were in danger. If the combined strength of the crew was less than that of the grey surging water, we should be washed down river, and, in the speed of that current, I gave us a slim chance of survival.

To the sound of muttered cries of '*Il humdu'illah!*' we passed into calmer waters. Soon we reached the shore, but the discomfort wasn't over yet—in front of us stretched a vast beach of pebbles and sun-bleached stones, completely without shelter, and the mid-morning sun was now beating down.

Remembering that Fosco Maraini,* faced with the members of his team collapsing from dysentery, heat exhaustion and dehydration, had instituted a rule that the longest day's trek should be no more than fifteen to sixteen miles and should begin at first light, I now viewed our intended day's journey of two stages (it was now eleven o'clock) with dismay, and wished I had not agreed to Masood's suggestion. It is, perhaps, just as well I did not realize it would be some twenty miles I should have to travel on foot that day!

With the beach behind us, the path lay between bushes and under-growth, permeated with sand and rocks—a veritable desert. We passed a knoll where a single whitewashed house with a flat roof stood defiantly in that sun-bleached landscape. Not for the first time, I was reminded of Greek island homes. Farther on, I saw a few more scattered dwellings in between the poplar trees. Then, gradually, the sand, stones and rocks gave way to fields of wheat and vegetables, and orchards of trees weighed down with apples and golden apricots. On through shady tracks along the banks of water channels, past animal byres and houses with flat roofs loaded with fruit being dried for winter. With everything shining so colourfully in the sun and with a canopy of leaves above, I would have been content to have stayed there for the rest of the day, but pride and a

---

Where Four Worlds Meet by Fosco Maraini.

desire to go closer to the really high mountains, drove me on.

Underfoot, the ground was carpeted with fallen apricots, which squelched beneath my boots. It was a shame so much of the crop went to waste. In the days when the trade route between Baltistan and eastern Kashmir flourished, whole 'sweet almonds' (apricot kernels) were used by cooks in Indian hotels to decorate cakes, and ground ones were used in numerous recipes.

Now, in the afternoon sun, we were to leave the village and its surrounding fields of freshly harvested wheat behind us, and start up a mountain track; a trail, which, like the one leading to the Babusar, wound on and on, ever upward around the mountainside. Looking back, as we began to follow the Hushe River, I could finally see what lay beyond the bend. There was, as I had glimpsed briefly from the *zaq* departure point, more river and more of the Ladakh Range of mountains, separating the parallel courses of the Indus and Shyok. Perhaps one day I would take that path, even if only for a little way. Just a few months before, there had been fighting on the nearby Saichan Glacier,* and, according to some soldiers I had spoken to, many on both sides had died. From Khapalu it was only a four-day trek to Srinigar in Indian-held Kashmir.

Baltistan is the poorest area in that whole vast mountain region, and, with its trading links with eastern Kashmir cut, it stands isolated in a political vacuum. Perhaps, eventually, the opening of the Khunjerab will provide some material benefit, but that is doubtful, unless the problem of Kashmir is resolved in Pakistan's favour. Pakistan came out of Partition badly, both in the distribution of money and land, thanks to the arbitrary drawing of the border. Aside from being divided into West and East Pakistan (now Bangladesh), the state of Kashmir was split up with part of the Moslem majority left on the Indian side. The problem of Kashmir is too long and involved to go into here, but suffice to say, it is still a festering sore between Pakistan and India as witnessed by the soldiers dying on the glacier which marks the frontier.

After we had passed through the attractive village of Muchalu, where we had a brief stop (at my insistence), we walked on and through a small

---

*Baltistan covers an area of ten thousand square miles, and the UN Cease-Fire Line, which runs south-east from the Chinese frontier, forms the uneasy border between India and Pakistan. The Saichan Glacier, known as 'The Glacier of Wild Roses' is the second largest in the world (forty-five miles long and three to five miles wide), and lies in eastern Baltistan, sandwiched between China and Indian-held Kashmir. To the west is the Soltoro range through which lie the ancient passes to the Glacier. To the south of the Glacier, Chulung Pass leads to both the route into Indian-held Kashmir and the one through the Goma Valley into the Pakistan side. Since ancient times, the Saichan Glacier has belonged to Pakistan, as shown by its Balti name.

village where the children came running up, offering me big white radishes to eat. Towards evening, the weather began to change, and it was spitting with rain and almost dark when we crossed a perilous narrow log bridge over the river and sought refuge with a former high-altitude porter, with whom Masood had often worked.

After a night in which I was first eaten alive by bed-bugs and then drenched with rain (the last time I was to take my guide's advice), I decided to hire our host, Mohammed Ali, to accompany us. He was only too willing to earn himself a few rupees, and his lean, smiling presence and his care and attention were to make up for all the defects of my now completely superfluous guide.

The next morning, there was still rain in the air and the closer we drew to Hushe which lies at the foot of Masherbrum and is the most northerly village in the far north-eastern region of Pakistan, the colder and damper it became. The huge sandstone cliffs that had risen perpendicular from the valley floor had disappeared, while the river ran below us on our left. The high mountain peaks I had come to see were lost beneath grey clouds, but their black rocky bases, looming at the far end of the valley, commanded the horizon. No longer did their hidden icy summits, seen from a distance at Muchalu, entice my flagging spirits.

Hushe itself was situated on a level plain. It was not like the other villages we had come across which had been neatly set among poplar and fruit trees, climbing up the mountainside or straggling over uneven ground. Hushe was a settlement of clustered houses, some two hundred feet or so above the river and surrounded, except for the way we had come, by high cliffs and higher mountains. It was a cold, wet place when we arrived that afternoon. Nevertheless, when the first green and signs of habitation appeared, I was very thankful. The end of a journey, even the most pleasant or exciting, always has its own kind of joy. I was hopeful that after a rest, I might find the energy to go closer to the mountains which had been my goal.

On the outskirts of the village, youths and children came to greet us, all apparently fascinated to learn I was 'only one member'; previously they had only come into contact with expeditions and trekking teams. Now they led us along a narrow lane between small, single-storey, stone and wood-built houses, with, sometimes, a wall made from woven reeds or thin saplings attached to wooden beams and lintels, and the occasional window. Most of the time, I could not tell whether they were homes or animal byres or a mixture of both—all had flat roofs. Then we entered a tunnel which led under the houses. It was dark and dank and mud oozed around my boots. Everyone, except for the young, had to bend low to pass beneath the wooden support beams. The ground continued to squelch beneath my steps, as we came into a small quadrangle where two brothers kindly put us up in a newly built storehouse. The village had what I can only describe as a Dickensian atmosphere.

I cannot honestly say I enjoyed my brief sojourn in Hushe. It was cold and wet. I was cold and wet, so was poor Mohammad Ali, who was sent out by a healthy Masood to chop wood. My stay, however, was not without incident.

Often I am asked by friends, acquaintances or tourists how I 'manage'—it is a subject which seems to hold a certain perverse fascination. The answer is, generally, 'with difficulty,' except in the Kalash valleys, where the accepted cornfield is agreeable, if not overused, and provides a means of fertilization. The over-polluted river banks allocated for tea-houses, *chai* shops and *dukans* pose a problem, as does the foreigner's wretched toilet paper (bright pink in Pakistan and imported from China). More than once, I have caused great amusement by going around with shovelfuls of cedar-wood chips. Few ablutions, however, could have been more memorable than those in Hushe.

In answer to the question 'where', I was led down a treacherous mountain path from which I fell headlong into waist-high wet grass (while my teenage guide fell off a large rock) to a small natural rock bowl, filled by a spring gushing from the mountainside. As I filled my plastic bucket, I looked up to see a line of children standing on the edge of the cliff, watching me gleefully.

It was the return journey, however, that was the most eventful. As I made my way back up the perilous mountainside, I was uncertain which way to go. Usually, I take note of my surroundings and have no trouble finding my way but the village of Hushe, although small, is like a labyrinth. At the entrance to one lane, my way was barred by a group of children, some of whom I recognized. I returned their greetings and with gestures and mimes, tried to make them understand I wanted to return to the storehouse. But the arrival in their midst of a lone stranger was an opportunity too good to miss.

With animals, unless chromosomes are such that no matter what the environment, they will turn out savage, I am convinced they are born with the impulse of 'good', but I am not sure that I can apply the same premise to children, and never did I believe this more than at that moment. A girl of about ten was determined to have her sport. She kept touching me as with a Machiavellian look upon her face she then darted behind me, laughing with high pitched screams. The others joined in and surrounded me. I kept gesturing. The boys, whom I recognized, continued to point this way and that, saying 'Yes! Yes!' in English and jumping up and down laughing, while the girl, her eyes wild, ran around me.

175

176

The storm clouds continued to gather. I started shivering and not just from the wet and cold. There was a touch of evil in the air. A look of cruelty was etched on those young faces. The instinct that sends man chasing after his frightened prey was emanating from them, like some intangible weapon. For a moment I felt a twinge of panic. I felt trapped. They sensed it, and, like hunters about to kill, their voices became more shrill. Gathering my wits and pushing back the pangs of claustrophobia and panic, I swept forward without glancing in either direction, until I came to a small open space where a number of adults were gathered. My tormentors quickly dispersed and I breathed easily once more.

On the outskirts of the gathering was the longest and strangest loom I have ever seen. An old man was sitting astride it, while another, seated beside a wall nearby, spun wool. I brought out my camera and looked hesitantly around me, but I was greeted with smiles and urged to take everyone's photograph. Before I left Hushe the following morning, I felt as though I were leaving friends behind, in spite of the incident with the children.

Although I most emphatically had informed Masood, to whom Mohammed Ali always deferred on decisions, that I was not about to undergo another double stage, the very next day I was tricked into doing just that—another twenty-mile stint. By now ill with suspected dysentery and suffering from a bad cold and cough, I wished only to return to Khapalu. This last and final day was, perhaps, the most exhausting of all.

It had only just gone eight when we left Muchalu, but already, the sun, that I had welcomed an hour before, was threatening to be merciless. Our way was along the exposed mountainside above the Hushe River, which raced far down on our left to join the Shyok. The bare rock face to our right bounced the sun's rays down upon us. Along with all my ailments, I was soon to become plagued with thirst and had to stop every so often to take a sip from my water bottle. Because of nausea, I waved Mohammed Ali on in front (Masood was, as usual, barely visible in the distance), but, now and then, I saw him standing in the track, looking back.

I staggered on, taking more and more sips from my bottle, for my mouth was continually dry; my stomach cramps were becoming worse and the calves of my legs felt like lumps of lead. The sun was unbearable and there was not a vestige of shelter anywhere; nothing but rock and sand and another one of those seemingly endless trails. Every upward curve was sheer torture. Never before in my life had I experienced the agony that the continuous, unprotected glare of the sun can produce. Only once, on the island of Delos, had I suffered sun poisoning, and the sun there was nothing compared to this furnace. For the first time ever I

177

A street in Hushe.

found myself hating the sun, for I could literally feel it destroying me; the sun I had always worshipped had now become my enemy. All I wanted to do was escape. I hated it and feared it, but escape I could not.

I continued on, with the river gleaming far below, grey and silver between grey sand banks. At last the trail stopped winding and just went straight on down to the edge of the river, where, among some trees, I saw Mohammed Ali and Masood sitting on a mound of earth. It was then I remembered the salt powders, but by this time I had no water.

The trail began following irrigation channels on the edge of fields, for we had now entered the village opposite Khapalu on the other side of the river.

Masood once again pulled ahead, but Mohammed Ali, when I waved him on, refused and walked behind me—whether to catch me if I fell, I didn't know, but I found his presence reassuring nevertheless.

Every couple of yards, or so it seemed, I had to sit and rest. Mohammed Ali never strayed more than a few feet away and he seldom took his eyes off me, which became a little disconcerting and embarrassing.

Finally, we came to the end of the lane and branched off past the last fields, again beside a water channel. I was now forever looking down as I felt unsteady and was afraid of tripping. The soft footfalls behind me gave me comfort. How thankful I was that Mohammed Ali had appeared as I was en route for Hushe. I turned to smile at him, but he was not there. Yet I had distinctly heard his foot-falls following me. I turned back and there he was, about fifteen feet ahead, waiting anxiously. I wondered if I were becoming delirious. I had most certainly heard someone walking behind me. I had not dreamt it. Finally, I staggered into a *chai*-house to await the crew of the *zaq*.

Late that afternoon we arrived in Khapalu. For the next three days, I placed myself in the care of two Western medical missionaries who ran a small clinic. These remarkable women soon put me back together again, and, out of my illness, I made two new friends. My list of extraordinary human beings I had encountered on my travels was growing.

Shangri-La

The early morning sun was pleasantly warm on my face, the leaves on the fruit trees in the nearby orchard whispered gently in the breeze, while the hum of insects and the smell of roses almost lulled me back to sleep as I finished my breakfast on the lawn of the Mountain Inn. It was so good to be back in Chitral, I thought, as I lazily gazed out past the orchard to the mountains beyond. Behind them lay the valleys of Birir, Bumburet and Rumbur—home of the Kafir Kalash, 'Wearers of the Black Robes'—an ancient tribe whose history is shrouded in mystery and whose people are reputed to be pagan and given to sacrificial rites.

It had taken me three long, tiring days by jeep to cross the Shandur from Gilgit. Although I had arrived in Chitral only two days before, I had already seen all my Chitrali friends and acquaintances (including the old man who constantly gave me apricots) and had acquired my permit for the Kalash valleys. Now Abbas, the manager of the hotel, and Haider Ali Shah had told me that, according to the bush telegraph, Saifullah was coming in from Rumbur to meet me.

I glanced at my watch. The weather was clear in Chitral, and, if the same applied to the Lowarai Top, the small Fokker aircraft should soon be skimming in low over the hotel on its way from Peshawar. No book on the mountain region of northern Pakistan would be complete without mention of these breath-taking mountain flights that run from Peshawar to Chitral and from 'Pindi to Gilgit and Skardu. I had done the Peshawar to Chitral flight many times, and I never tired of going up into the cockpit as the plane skimmed the Lowarai Top and then watch as, in the early morning light, the pinkish white peak of Tirich Mir suddenly appeared on the horizon, becoming more beautiful the closer we flew towards it; then a left turn and down we would go flying into the Chitral valley with the mountains hemming us in on both sides. But of all my mountain flights, none could surpass the one I took from Skardu—a flight reputed to be the most dangerous and spectacular in the world, a reputation which for me only added to its appeal. Even the take-off is breath-taking as you

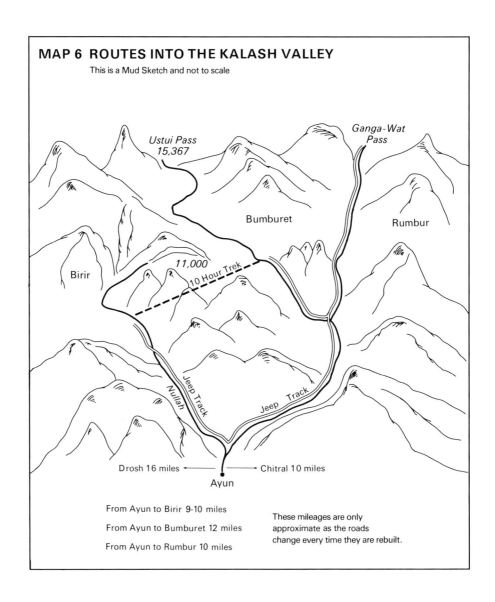

MAP 6 ROUTES INTO THE KALASH VALLEY

This is a Mud Sketch and not to scale

Ustui Pass
15,367

Ganga-Wat
Pass

Bumburet

Rumbur

Birir

11,000

10 Hour Trek

Nullah

Jeep Track

Jeep Track

Drosh 16 miles ← — → Chitral 10 miles

Ayun

From Ayun to Birir 9-10 miles

From Ayun to Bumburet 12 miles

From Ayun to Rumbur 10 miles

These mileages are only
approximate as the roads
change every time they are rebuilt.

seemingly head straight into a narrow valley and only soar upwards and over the mountains at the last minute. The flight path runs over the edge of the great Nanga Parbat massif and as we flew over, we were so close to those lofty ridges I felt I could reach out and touch them. Everyone was transfixed by those glistening slopes—everyone that is except for the young man who sat through the whole flight with his eyes firmly shut and reciting the Koran.

As we came in over the alpine slopes of the Khagan Valley, I asked to go into the cockpit. I watched the dials as we gradually lost height from

180

15,000 feet to 9,000 feet. Now we were flying through the mountains rather than over them, and I listened with open-mouthed astonishment as the pilot issued his instructions to the co-pilot: 'Turn left', 'Carry straight on', 'Mind that mountain peak!', 'Follow that bend in the valley', and as we started to descend still farther, 'Look out for the tops of those houses!' But when the pilot brought out a map that looked suspiciously like a road map and began debating which valley we were following, I found my incredulity stretched to the limit. The excellent safety record of these mountain pilots, however, testifies to their ability. Obviously they are highly skilled—but still it is disconcerting to say the least, when, just before landing, the pilot (as they all do), announces *Insha'Allah* (God willing), we shall be landing in five minutes.'

I suddenly sat up straight; I could hear the approaching hum of engines. Again I glanced at my watch—bang on time. I stood up and there was the small aircraft coming in low, straight over the Mountain Inn. As always, I waved. Only those who live in a place such as Chitral, which is snowbound for six months of the year, or on an island where the daily steamer is a big event, can really appreciate how much the arrival of such transport, from what is almost another world, means to the inhabitants.

I ordered another pot of tea. I was becoming impatient—impatient to see Saifullah. It had been five long years. I wondered if he had changed. When I first knew him he was only twenty-two, full of fun, dynamic and resolute. I was also longing to see Tak-Dira, my Kalash 'mother' who had invited me into her home. How had the years treated her? Kindly I hoped.

Just as I was about to pour the tea, a man came onto the path, bounded up the few steps to the lawn and came towards me with purposeful strides. First the strong handshake and then the warm embrace. For a moment we stood looking at one another. Yes, Saifullah had changed. His fair, almost chestnut coloured hair, a little darker now than I remembered, fell over his high, receding forehead and was cut short with small sideburns. His usually intense bright green eyes were now warm and soft with greeting. We seated ourselves and I noticed that he now sat in European chairs with ease, whereas when I first met him, he would prefer to squat on his hunkers on the lawn in the eastern way. His periodic trips to Peshawar and Islamabad to further the cause of the Kalash, as well as his long association with foreigners, had sophisticated this man far beyond his own culture.

As he turned his face from mine to pour the tea,* my gaze centred on his high cheekbones and strong cleft chin. I noticed his cheeks were fatter as was his figure and there were lines about the eyes and mouth that had not been there before. The problems of the Kalash weighed heavily upon his shoulders. At twenty-seven, he was young to be their leader (especially in a gerontocratic society), but, according to Gillian Darling, a Canadian anthropologist whom I had met, because of his fluency in English and his knowledge of law, the elders were placing more and more responsibility for the welfare of the Kalash upon his shoulders.

Saifullah is the only Kalash to have had any real education, for when he was born many of the parents were reluctant to send their children to the valley schools for fear of conversion* (some still are), and simply chose not to send them to the other more advanced school in Ayun,* ten miles away and along treacherous narrow mountain paths. So the Kalash kept their children at home, that is, all except Saifullah's father, who realized that the Kalash culture would be finished unless they had an educated leader willing to fight on their behalf. So, with the mantle of responsibility on his shoulders, Saifullah had done the long hazardous trek there and back each day to Ayun. Later, he had studied law for a year at Peshawar University. Today he is the tribal representative—a sort of roving ambassador who also advises the Kalash on their dealings with outsiders; the internal politics of the Kalash are still governed by the elders.*

Saifullah caught me looking at him, blushed, and then smiled. We both started to talk at once, catching up on the past. His wife and family were well and now he had three more sons, besides Yassir, his first born. As I sat listening to him in such peaceful surroundings, breathing in the scent of roses, it seemed incredible that this gently-spoken man was the leader of a once warrior people reputed to be the descendants of Alexander the Great's army, and that now he was fighting for their very survival.

As I listened to Saifullah, it did not take me long to realize that many of the problems of the Kalash still existed. His biggest problem at the moment was his battle for forestry rights.

In the spring of 1981, some of the local people from Ayun went in to Rumbur and cut down trees for firewood. When the Kalash asked them

---

*Throughout my travels in Pakistan when in the company of men, whether it was a hotel, or *chai* shop or in a home, the men always poured the tea—the reason being a combination of courtesy and the custom of purdah.

*In 1895, in Kafiristan (part of Afghanistan) the armies of the Emir of Kabul forcibly converted the Kafirs to Islam. In Arabic, Kafiristan means 'Land of the Infidels' or 'Unbelievers'. The area then became known as Nuristan – 'Land of Light'. At the time of the conversion, a number of people fled from Kafiristan and built villages in the upper valleys of Bumburet and Rumbur, but eventually the newcomers converted to Islam.

*A high school for boys has now been built in Bumburet, and a girls' school is planned for Rumbur.

*At the end of 1987 Saifullah was elected to the Chitral Council.

to stop, their request was ignored. In the autumn of that year, Saifullah took the case to the court of Chitral. The immediate result was that both parties were bound over not to touch the trees until the case was finished. The case still goes on. The written statement of the people of Ayun declares that all the land (including the forests) that is not irrigated is common land. If the Kalash lose their fight, it means that not only do they lose the forestry rights, but, also, the people of Ayun could come in and settle and ultimately drive the Kalash out.

Saifullah sighed and shook his head. 'Also, as you know, we have lost much arable land due to floods.* I lost some of my own fields last year but . . .' his voice trailed off, and then his frown disappeared. His eyes sparkled as he leaned towards me and brought a clenched fist down on the table. 'But I have won back some land and trees in Bumburet! And, Maureen, now that I have four sons, surely one of them must carry on the fight if anything happens to me?' It was obvious Saifullah would never, ever give up the fight.

By noon we were on our way to Ayun, the staging-post for the Kalash valleys. This time I barely glanced at the ancient, doorless and roofless jeep, but I did notice that the cracked windscreen had more plastic flowers and photographs than usual. To the customary sound of Chitrali music blasting out of the cassette-player, we shook, rattled and rolled past the polo-ground. I shut my eyes as children, mounted Afghans, dogs and goats leapt out of the way.

The track to Ayun followed the course of the river, which, for the most part, was very wide with large, greyish sandbanks. Looking back, I could see Tirich Mir* towering above the folds of the valley.

Now Afghan refugee camps lined the right bank of the river—small square little buildings made of stone with canvas roofs.* Except for a few children and women drawing water from the wells, the places seemed deserted in the noon-day heat. I reflected that they seemed better off than the Palestinians I had seen in a camp in the Middle East.

Approaching Ayun, green and yellow fields appeared on the opposite bank as we climbed up and then down the valley, and thundered over the

---

*In Chitrali folklore, Tirich Mir is believed to be inhabited by fairies.

*The government has now given money to the Kalash to build three new water channels in each of the three valleys, thereby increasing the arable land of each valley to approx. 10,000 acres. The government is also financing the laying of water pipes so that each village will have safe, fresh spring water on tap. The government cannot involve itself in the forestry problem as it is a judicial matter.

*Five million Afghans have fled their homeland, with some fleeing to Iran and the majority to Pakistan—over three million.

newly-built bridge to the town. Through the bazaar, up a rough track and round a sharp corner, we suddenly found ourselves in a wide, dusty street bounded on both sides by ramshackle wooden buildings. The street was deserted, save for two small boys wrestling on the ground, a mangy-looking dog lying in the sun, a stray cow, and a donkey tied to a hitching-rail; it was as though we had driven straight into a Wild West frontier town.

We had to stop here for a while as jeeps do not go frequently to either Birir or Rumbur, only Bumburet. In the old days it was just as difficult to get transport to that valley, too, but now jeeps and Suzukis ply back and forth at fairly frequent intervals. As I sat in the *chai* shop, Saifullah went back into the heat in search of a jeep driver to take us to Rumbur. Several drivers, en route to Bumburet or Chitral, came and went, offering me cups of *chai* and bidding me welcome back to the valleys. As I sat there, in that tiny dark interior, sheltering from a very hot sun, hitting out at the flies with the back of my cap, I mused to myself why it was that I was drawn so irresistibly to the Kalash valleys. Was it their beauty? Or was it just a question of deja-vu—a feeling that that I had lived there before? Perhaps it was because of the relationships I had formed there—first the young Afghan boy refugee, then Saifullah and then Tak-Dira. I thought back to my very first encounter with the Kalash.

It was in 1980 that I first arrived in Bumburet, the widest of the three valleys and thought by many to be the most beautiful, with its sparkling streams, shady meadows, groves of mulberry, apricot and walnut trees, and yellow and green fields. As the jeep had passed up the valley, small boys with catapults slung around their necks had run alongside, making us feel welcome.

My first contact with a Kalash woman is a moment I remember clearly because it marked the beginning of a strange bond that I feel for these people, something that runs deep yet is indefinable and inexplicable.

It was late afternoon and I had been following the jeep track down valley, when an inviting path beckoned me through a glade and into a peaceful grassy area that was shaded by walnut trees and crossed by a fast flowing stream. I paused here for a while before following the stream alongside a walled-in cornfield. I wanted to cross to the other side of the stream to explore a village sprawling up the mountainside, and as I stood wondering just where to ford, something—a sound, a sudden movement caught out of the corner of my eye or perhaps just a presence felt—made me look up and turn my head. There, before me, was a tall, slim, dignified woman standing amidst the ripening corn. Her eyes met mine; our gaze held. Unlike other Kalash women I had seen, she wore a veil that covered most of her face; her eyes were all I could see. As I smiled a greeting and turned away to try to negotiate the stream I could feel the woman watching me.

There was a rustle of corn. I looked up. She was coming towards me, one hand holding the veil in place, the other pushing aside the corn. Again, her eyes held mine. It was almost as if I were hypnotized by her gaze. She motioned for me to climb over the wall into the field and pointed to a spot where the stream narrowed and I could cross. As I hoisted myself up onto the heavy smooth stones, I missed my footing, and, involuntarily, my hand shot out to take hold of a young sapling. The woman, realizing it would give way under my weight, instinctively caught my arm. As the veil slipped from her face, I could see what it was she was hiding: her forehead and cheeks were a mass of ugly pink and black scabs.

Strangely enough, I did not recoil; I just stared at her, horrified. That meeting made an impression upon me and a few days later when I went to Chitral where I bought some medicines and ointments and returned to the valley to treat her. The satisfaction I felt the following year when I saw her happy, healthy face undoubtedly helped to plant the seed of desire to learn medical work.

I was startled out of my reverie by the return of Saifullah, announcing he had found a jeep willing to take us to Rumbur.

Nowadays, the old jeep track from Ayun to Bumburet over the mountains (from where one took the road for Rumbur) has fallen into disuse, due to landslides and the re-building of a wooden bridge. I had done that journey several times and they had been breath-taking rides on a spectacular and dangerous road that had wound round and round the mountainside up and up almost above the treeline. Below had been a landscape unaffected by change that I had been told still supported the ibex, bear, the rare snow leopard (now a protected species) and markhor. It was there that Saifullah had once explained the significance of the markhor in Kalash folklore. The Kalash believe in fairies (or supernatural beings) and since they believe also that the mountain fairies regard the markhor as sacred, and the markhor feeds on juniper trees, so the Kalash people hold the juniper tree sacred. 'It plays an important part in our purification ceremonies,' he had added.

Now the new track, which hugs the river, is still perilous, as it is twisting and narrow, full of shale and muddy troughs and subject to landslides. As we turned off to Rumbur, the afternoon sun was low in the sky and we had no time to lose; these were not roads to drive along at night.

Soon the track began to wind, climb and then drop down: from time to time, high jagged peaks appeared tantalizingly on the horizon, only to be quickly lost from view behind a bend. Often the narrow track was deep in shadow, with only the tops of the ravine glowing in the late afternoon sunshine: sometimes its dirt and stony surface gave way to shale and troughs of mud and the occasional big pool of water. Once, we travelled beneath a large overhang of rock, scarred with huge frightening cracks, a rockfall on the edge of the cliff, testifying to its vulnerability.

As we reached the outer edges of Rumbur, the valley opened up and the jeep track left the river which thundered towards Ayun. Kalash women were still working in the fields, even though the sun had gone down and now only shone on the far side of the valley. They waved, their bare faces held high. The Kalash valleys constitute one of the few places in rural Pakistan where a man can behold the unveiled face of a woman who is a stranger to him. Little wonder then that young male tourists from the big cities of the plains descend upon the valleys with thoughts far from pure and holy.

We sped past a newly-built double-storey wooden hotel and on beneath low, overhanging branches. In front of us lay the end of the jeep track which was bordered by the Kalash 'Hilton' hotel and two small *dukans* on one side, and, on the other, by the dispensary with its ugly, iron roof and a small Moslem tea-house. At the very end were the old school and the tiny mosque guarding the footpath that led over the strong wooden bridge.* The Kalash Hilton. (I again wondered which tourist had suggested this name), where I had stayed previously, still put me in mind of one of those historic saloons so lovingly preserved in the Western United States.

As the jeep lurched to a stop beside it, some young boys who had been sitting on the hitching rail jumped down to greet us. At the same time several elderly men, resting on a wooden bench on the porch, cried out in welcome.

The confusion and noise of our arrival gave way to the peace and tranquillity of sipping *chai* on the hotel verandah. I was content. I was back among friends and to my joy I had been given my old sleeping quarters on the open-sided verandah where I could sleep out.

Considerably narrower than Bumburet, and without that valley's numerous shady meadows, Rumbur is rugged and majestic; the mountain ridges higher, the river much wilder. As there are few tourists, the Kalash are less shy and less nervous than those in Bumburet. No-one objects to having their photograph taken or charges for posing. Only seldom does the sound of jeeps destroy the peaceful silence of the valley,

---

*Built by the government to replace a series of planks from which a young girl was swept away by the floods of a few years before.

The Kalash Hilton in Rumbur, one of the three Kalash valleys.

The Kalash still use old methods on their farms.

and it is here that I could feel the true strength of the Kalash culture. If I had broken the taboo crossing over the boundary of the Bashali House* in either of the other valleys, the chances are? I might have been excused, but in Rumbur, Kalash custom is still strong and hence the need for the sacrificial goat. Here their taboos about religion are strictly observed.*

Every morning Saifullah would arrive after the sun had appeared over the mountain ridge to the east. By then I would be seated on a small chair, made from walnut and strips of animal hide* enjoying my second pot of tea. Here, by the crude wooden table, Saifullah would sit and talk to me and soon I began to acquire a quantity of notes to add to those gathered on my previous visits; his knowledge of the history of his people and tales of the present-day struggles made fascinating listening. Not being an anthropologist, I tended to concentrate on those aspects of Kalash culture which interested me the most, but Saifullah would, from time to time, add information which he thought worthy of note.

Like other foreigners, the subject that intrigued me in particular was the history of the Kalash. When we had first met and I had asked Saifullah if his people were really descended from the deserters of

---

*The Kalash menstrual hut, the Bashali House, is one of the most fundamental Kalash institutions, for, according to Gillian Darling, the Kalash divide their world into two domains—the pure and the impure, 'each of which is relative to, and defines the other'. In this patriarchal society, the sacred realm, 'Onjesta', is associated with gods, men, and goats. This encompasses altars, mountain habitats, animal sheds and corrals and ritual activities. The major events in the human life cycle, birth, menstruation, sexual intercourse (if not followed by a ritual bath), and death, are regarded as the impure domain, 'Pragata', which is intimately associated with women, either biologically or culturally, hence they are considered as agents of pollution, particularly their mouths, hair, genitals and undergarments.

*The Kalash religion, which, according to Gillian Darling, is based on the strict separation or 'controlled contact' between the pure and impure realms, is a complex and convoluted subject full of ambiguities, and is based on oral tradition. Although most anthropologists consider it to be polytheistic because of its many deities, fairies, evil spirits, strange rites and animal sacrifices, the Kalash themselves, according to Saifullah Jan of Rumbur (where people are more progressive and there is a stronger belief in the monotheistic concept of one single creator), the Kalash do believe in one supreme God—one creator of the universe. This god goes under various names such as the Persian Khodai (Imra is the name used in old Kafiristan), and, most commonly, under the name of Dezau. (As Peter Parkes believes, a good deal of their present day religion may well have been borrowed from Islam.) There is also an intermediary named Balamahin who rides a horse and is a messenger of Dezau.

Horses are very symbolic for the Kalash, who are believed by some anthropologists to have originally been horsemen from the grasslands of the Central Asian Steppes. They used to carve effigies of their dead riding on horseback. Most of these are now in Peshawar Museum.

*The Kalash are one of the few peoples of the subcontinent who traditionally sit on chairs instead of the ground.

188

Alexander the Great's army, he had responded with an enigmatic smile and had replied that he could only repeat what the elders had told him as they had no written language* and all their history was handed down by word of mouth. Later, however, he confirmed that the Kalash had been descended from a General Shalaksha, in Alexander's army, who had come from Tsiam (not to be confused with present-day Thailand) and settled in Chitral. It is also believed that some of Alexander's army deserted in Kabul, in what is now Afghanistan.

Another point of special interest to me was the way in which the Kalash governed their affairs. As it is a gerontocratic society, the elders of the clans dictate the laws, and, if there is trouble between one valley and another, the elders form a council to solve it. To illustrate this, Saifullah told me of an incident some years ago, where a feud existed for twelve months between Rumbur and Bumburet, due to a boy from Rumbur being attacked and beaten over the head by a youth from Bumburet. This had led to fighting among the people, whereupon the elders from the two valleys had stepped in to discuss the matter. The elders of Bumburet had resolved the problem by taking a peace offering of a bull to Rumbur, its meat being distributed among the inhabitants.

According to Saifullah, there is virtually no crime in the valleys, but should a person be tempted to steal or show disrespect for the culture, he is punished by being confronted by the whole community and made to give or pay for a male goat to be sacrificed.* Inside the Kalash community, unlike in Pathan society, where blood feuds still exist, killing is forbidden, and on the rare occasion such a crime is committed, the perpetrator is banished from the valley.

Within a couple of days I found myself falling into a certain rhythm. Like the Kalash, my day began at dawn and ended with the eating of the evening meal shortly after the sun had set. At noontime, when the sun was at its highest and the men and women took a break from their labours, I, too, would rest awhile. Again, like the Kalash, the only day of the week which seemed different to me was Friday, the Moslem holy day. For the few Kalash children who went to school in the valley, Friday was

---

*The Kalash language (closely related to Khowar, purported to have links with Sanskrit) is only spoken and belongs to the Indo-Iranian branch of Indo-European languages, commonly known as the Dardic group—a term applied to the archaic languages of the Hindu Kush.

*If there is a theft and the culprit is unknown, certain 'wise men' among the elders will hold a bracelet, or a bow, made of twigs, between their hands and call out to their ancestors. The Kalash believe that if the instrument shakes, the name of the guilty party will be revealed. His relatives will then have to cast bread upon the graves of the ancestors as an act of atonement. It is also believed the culprit will be struck with sickness and pain.

a holiday as the teachers were Moslem. For me, it meant missing the children's youthful spirits as they passed below my verandah.

The Kalash have no set calendar as we know it. Their year begins around March with the month of the spring sacrifice, and all the succeeding months are decided by the phases of the moon and become synonymous with natural events. Hence there is the 'Month of the Teats', denoting the birth of animals, the months associated with the festivals of the four seasons, and those which bring forth the various crops. When all the harvesting is over, there comes the 'Month of the Leaves Falling', followed by two months of winter, divided into the first forty days called the 'Big Cold' and the next twenty called the 'Little Cold'. Then comes the 'Month of Melting Snow', followed by the 'Moon Month', heralding the beginning of the new cycle.

As my notes expanded, so my interest in the Kalash grew, but, although called upon frequently to attend the sick in the absence of the very able and dedicated dispenser of Rumbur who was on one of his rare visits home, there was a part of me that remained restless. I was eager to see 'my family' again in Birir, and before I went there, I wanted to spend a few days in Bumburet to take some photographs and see old friends.

I had been in the valley about a week when Saifullah greeted me with the news that he must return to Chitral to carry on the battle over the forestry rights. Because of the proceedings, he doubted he would be able to spend time with me in Bumburet or accompany me to Birir. As I looked at his sad face, I saw on the outside, only a ghost of the man I once knew—a man who now stood alone, even among his own people, for the elders who supported him and came with him to Chitral had little understanding of the world outside the valleys. For Saifullah it was a lonely life—gone was the youthful devil-may-care attitude. Instead there stood a mature man passionately dedicated to saving his people from extinction.

The Home-Coming

I spent only a few days in Bumburet, for although I had fallen in love with this valley six years before, I now found it spoiled. The road which opened up Bumburet in the seventies soon brought this, the widest of the three valleys, to the attention of visitors, and before long unscrupulous entrepreneurs from outside the valley, ventured in, tricked the local people out of a number of their walnut trees (one of their main sources of protein), and some of their land, on which they built ramshackle and primitive hotels, and left the Kalash little chance to make even a few rupees from the new and meagre tourist industry.

Now, in 1986, I saw that most of the existing hotels had been enlarged and a new one had been built at the top end of the valley. Ostensibly it was a Kalash hotel, but the Kalash who owned it had been converted to Christianity. Today, due largely to the efforts of a former D.C., Shakil Durrani, it is an offence to convert a Kalash forcibly to Islam,* and the law carries a heavy fine. This law, however, has not been extended to Christian missionaries, and, if it were, it would be a pity as those I've met in Pakistan do not proselytize but teach in schools and help the sick. Unfortunately, though, a group of doubtful origin, and motivation was trying to implement change, but by introducing electricity and modern farming methods they were not benefiting the people. Electricity, although it is undeniably a convenience, would start the Kalash on the trail of becoming a consumer society, while the idea that they should grow hybrid corn would make them dependent on chemicals and fertilizers which they would then have to buy and import—this in a culture where bartering was still the norm.

Chickens, which are taboo among the Kalash,* are plentiful in

---

*Although it is against the koran to forcibly convert, there were such cases in the past.

*When Islam started encroaching upon Chitral, a shaman went into trance and declared, that within a few years, chickens would come to Chitral and this would mean the end of the Kalash. From that time on, chickens have been forbidden food.

Bumburet, because the local Moslem population keeps them, but also because a small Suzuki van tours the valley with battery hens, which are generally served up, all skin and bone, to the tourist at inflated prices.

I chose to stay again at the Hotel Tranquil, where I resumed my acquaintance with Fider, its young owner from Ayun—a shrewd but seemingly decent man.

My stay was anything but tranquil, however, because apart from the jeeps, Suzukis and chicken van passing outside, Fider was building an extension adjoining my room—even though the four-room single-storied building attracted few tourists. Aside from having to contend with these intrusions, I soon found myself caught up with a young teenager in Fider's employ.

One of my many pleasures and sources of amusement when travelling in Pakistan, is derived from my dealings with hotel and rest-house staff. Whereas *chowkidars* are usually elderly and a trifle mad, most hotel workers are young and invariably have some minor defect either physically or mentally. In the hotel in Peshawar, where I had become 'famous' among the staff for my friendship with Habib, the young Afghan refugee I had helped, the youths of the establishment fought among themselves as to who should take care of me. A fourteen-year-old Chitrali at first won the day, and, in the beginning, when I opened the door to order *chai*, he would rush forward. Although lame, he was full of apparently abundant self-confidence, and he would bowl into the room, sprawl out across the clean sheets and pillow slip in his kitchen-stained clothes, and, in his few words of English, try to start up a conversation in a loud hearty manner. His self-assertiveness was so strong, his very presence seemed to shrink the walls. When I finally made it plain to all and sundry that I was not advertising for 'orphans' to adopt, the pressure ceased.

In Gilgit, the young boy who looked after the rooms, also lame, once drove the unflappable Richard into a near stew. The 'little toad', as Richard referred to him, simply had no idea how to clean, and after having asked for our bathroom to be scrubbed for the third time, Richard had gently sent the youth for a bucket and broom, rolled up his sleeves and had done the job himself. On my arrival back from China, I was faced with the same problem and the manager had badgered the same unfortunate young man to put matters right. For an hour I had listened to buckets of water being swilled against the walls next door. When the youth emerged, wet and bedraggled, I had peered in to see a very clean and dripping bathroom. Even the ceiling was wet.

Before departing from Gilgit for Chitral over the Shandur, I had given the cook a tin of cheese and a loaf of Western-style egg bread, bought

192

from the bazaar (I was still suffering from dysentery), and asked if he or one of the boys would be kind enough to make me some sandwiches. Although I had demonstrated what it was I wanted, I had been given, along with the bill, an open but very mangled tin and the bread uncut. No-one apparently had any idea what it was I wanted. When I then set to to make them myself, the manager and cook, plus the rest of the help, looked on, obviously mystified, not, I realized, at what I was doing, but at the logic of it. Why, when I was going to travel on a jeep for three days, should I take the cheese out of the tin and cut it up into small pieces and put them between slices of bread, which would have stayed fresher, uncut? As I continued my work beneath their fascinated stare, I could not help wondering if it were I who was being dumb.

At the Mountain Inn in Chitral, where Haider Ali Shah maintains one of the best and most attractive hotels in northern Pakistan, I found the new bearer to be a constant source of amusement—as well as being humorous he was as absent-minded as me which is, perhaps, why I appreciated this young man. About eighteen, with shaggy, curly hair and a loping shuffling gait, Munshi always brought me my bed-tea*. On my first morning there was a carefully prepared tray with cup and saucer, spoon, jug of milk, sugar basin, and tea-cosy enveloping the tea-pot; unfortunately, he had forgotten to put in the tea. On another occasion, serving me with after-dinner *qawa*, he forgot the cup and saucer. Those lapses of memory, which varied from day to day, were often accompanied by absent-minded physical actions which would send him into gales of laughter; it's not easy to keep a straight face when someone is ambling towards you and they trip over their own feet.

Now, however, in Bumburet, I was not laughing over the predicament of Abdul, whom I had quickly nick-named 'The Nightingale'. The weather was inclement for most of my stay in Bumburet, so I spent more time close to the hotel than I would have done normally. Every day I found myself watching over the youth with growing concern. 'The Nightingale' was thirteen, slight of build, with a pretty, cherub-like face, and if his affliction of two thumbs on one hand bothered him, he did not show it. He was usually attired in a grubby fawn *shalwar-khameez*, which was too short in the legs, making his bare ankles, protruding from his thick high-heeled boots, look odd. He was a great favourite with the jeep drivers—at least he was until night time, when he would give voice to the latest Chitrali love song. For a while I and the jeep drivers stretched out on *charpoys* down the length of the verandah would listen as his sweet

---

*A custom left over from the days of the Raj. Most small hotels still provide bed-tea as well as with afternoon tea. Some even include bed-tea with the tariff for the room, along with the customary welcoming *chai* or soft drink on arrival.

tones rang across the valley. Then, one by one, a sleepy voice would cry out for quiet and 'The Nightingale' would giggle and lapse into silence.

Quick, efficient, and always smiling, he was, nevertheless, an obvious thorn in Fider's side. His continual ill treatment of the boy provoked me to such an extent that I helped 'The Nightingale' to flee back to Chitral, where he obtained a job much more to his liking. Knowing full well that I was on to his habit of ripping off the tourists, Fider suppressed his resulting anger towards me beneath a guise of flattering friendship which had neither of us fooled. My brief relationship with 'The Nightingale' brought Habib vividly back to mind.

For a few short days in 1980, an orphaned Afghan boy had been my constant companion. Although he had been able to speak several native languages, he had known only half a dozen words of English. But it had not seemed to matter. For most of the time our communication had been complete. In the industrial world, man has denied himself the sixth sense. He mistrusts telepathy, intuitive powers are shrugged off disparagingly as women's intuition (sometimes even by women), and silent, instinctive communication is regarded with scepticism. All too often, upon meeting a stranger, we hide behind nervous chatter instead of remaining silent, contemplating the other person, and how dangerous and misleading words can sometimes be, whether spoken or written. With Habib, I found a deep communication that transcended language, culture, age and sex. We were two human beings whose paths crossed for a short while. What each had given to the other could only be assessed by ourselves. What the world saw, no doubt, had a different reality.

Although the Kalash I met in Bumburet were charming and friendly, as they had always been, it was noticeable that, except for the children seeking handouts, they now kept a very low profile and generally stayed clear of the hotels and the jeep track, although this did not stop some of the men seeking me out for medical aid. For me, the magic of the valley was lost. The peace and enjoyment I had once found there belonged to another time.

In Rumbur, where the culture has its strongest roots, and where Saifullah, his father and the other elders keep it alive, the few tourists that wander into the valley see it much the same as it has always been, with just a few necessary concessions to the twentieth century. Now, sad over Bumburet, and longing to spend time with my Kalash family, I returned to Chitral in preparation for my long stay in Birir.

As I journeyed back to that sunlit valley, only some nine or ten miles from Ayun, I wondered what changes there might be.

The road was narrow and mostly on the flat. At one point, near the beginning of the trip, we had to cross a small bridge on which several men were herding donkeys. I asked the driver to stop so I could take some photographs, and promptly caused a 'traffic-jam'. Finally, the donkeys were led off the track and we continued on through a narrow, rocky gorge. After a short distance, we came upon some men clearing a rock slide. By pulling in his side-view mirror, and with the jeep rail scraping the rock, the driver just managed to pass. It was then I noticed the first change. The road was different—it was even more dangerous and hair-raising, for, due to landslides and rock falls, the track was even narrower and more slate-filled than I remembered it.

As we continued on, however, the gorge opened up a little, giving way to fields of tall, yellowing corn. The Kalash still live by subsistence farming and generally apply the old methods.* They still till the soil with wooden ploughs drawn by bullocks; spades and hoes are the only tools; and seeds are all scattered by hand. Wheat, barley, maize, millet and potatoes are the main crops, and some tobacco is grown. Although the men concentrate on animal husbandry while the women are mostly involved in agriculture, they often share the work in the fields, and do the reaping and the heavier tasks, such as digging irrigation channels and collecting heavy logs. They also help in the home, as I had seen for myself.

Until recently, the Kalash did all their transactions by bartering, but since the arrival of the Moslems from outside the valleys and the introduction of small general stores, they are now gradually becoming used to the monetary system, and rupees are used for the purchasing of certain items such as tea and sugar. Although there are those who have more goats and agricultural wealth than others, no-one goes hungry, for feasting is still a mode of exchange, and hospitality and generosity, as always, are considered meritorious in Kalash society. The old are always provided for and so, too, are the handicapped.

Again, until recent times, the women used to weave all their own cloth from which they made their clothes and accessories, but now the more affluent among them buy the material for their black robes—the *chao* and *shalwar-khameez*—from the *dukans*. Women, however, can still be seen spinning yarn on small hand spindles made from wood and pumpkin, with the weaving done on large wooden looms. Another reason, perhaps, why women now tend to frequent the small valley *dukans*, is that they no longer have a large supply of sheep's wool. As the Kalash now inhabit only three valleys, there is precious little grazing land

---

*Recently a motorized harvester has been used in Rumbur to thresh the wheat.

available on which to keep flocks of sheep.

In what seemed no time at all, we arrived in Birir—a narrow valley bounded by tree-covered slopes rising into jagged cliffs behind which, and at either end, are high mountains.

The driver stopped beside a large lawn in front of the government rest-house, situated some thirty feet above the river, and, at my request, sent a small boy scurrying off to find Razak, the Moslem owner of one of the local *dukans*. At first glance, Birir seems terribly narrow and uninteresting, although in reality it is wider than Rumbur.* There are fewer shady meadows here than in Bumburet and the valley is not so open. Moreover at this level, it does not have the majestic awe-inspiring ruggedness of Rumbur. But the narrow rocky valley, with the shallow river running down its centre, is full of 'secret' shady nooks, where the emerald turf is splashed with sparkling rivulets of water. Higher up the mountain slopes, through the branches of the trees, the rugged mountaintops of the Hindu Kush appear stretched out on the horizon, while others loom in close, dark and mysterious or bathed in glorious sunlight.

It did not take me long to discover, to my relief, that there appeared to be few changes other than natural growth for both local Moslems and Kalash. In Birir, the Kalash and Moslem societies are much more closely interwoven than they are in Bumburet (there are very few Moslems in Rumbur), and unlike that valley it had not been taken over commercially by outsiders.

Razak greeted me joyfully, and I soon discovered that this lovable rogue not only now owned a small hotel but was building an even larger one. I admired his industry, but as the few tour groups that venture into the valley generally stay just long enough to grab a few photographs of some poor Kalash woman toiling in the fields, or close-ups of them washing their hair in the river, I couldn't help feeling that his efforts might come to naught, especially as the resthouse had been refurbished. His hotel, really a small tea-house, run by a young, good-looking converted* Kalash was to become my focal point that side of the river. Sharzaman, whom I nicknamed Wali (short for hotel wallah), as his real name was still strange to my ears, soon became a friend.

Now, as I followed the river down the valley towards Guru Village with my new friend behind me, carrying my box of tinned food plus a few gifts and medical supplies, my mind again went back to my first visit, and my first encounter with Tak-Dira.

---

*The valleys lie at an altitude of between 4,875 and 7,800 feet above sea level. Bumburet, the largest valley, is approximately twelve miles long.

*Once converted to Islam the Kalash (then called 'Shaikhs') are considered outsiders, and the woman can no longer wear the black robes.

196

I had been on an exploratory walk following the river to the valley floor. Crossing a wide-plank bridge I found myself in the village of Guru which sprawled up the mountainside,* its wooden houses rising in tiers with the roof of one serving as a verandah for the one above.

By-passing the village, I followed the path along a narrow dangerous irrigation channel which was cut into the foot of the mountain slope. After several hundred yards, I came upon a small cluster of houses built together on stilts. There, a young woman rose from where she had been washing pots in the channel and beckoned me. For a second I hesitated, and then I smiled and followed her onto a long verandah and into a small, partially enclosed space overlooking the river. As she pointed to the kettle lying on the smoking hearth, an older woman, whom I took to be her mother, eagerly placed a blanket over a pile of rags lying on the smallest *charpoy* I had ever seen. Straightening up, she motioned for me to sit. Again I hesitated, but aside from not wanting to give offence, there was something in her eyes which drew me forward.

She sat on a low stool before me, fingering my denim jacket and examining closely the brass studs. She had an oval face with very high cheekbones, and when she smiled I saw she had several teeth missing in the centre of her upper jaw. Her sharp brown eyes, under dark knitted brows, studied me with curiosity. She had wide, flaring nostrils, a generous mouth and a strong pointed jaw pushed forward to give her an indomitable and almost classical appearance. She pointed to herself and said: 'Tak-Dira', and, indicating the younger woman, 'Sainisar'.

While Sainisar boiled up some tea, Tak-Dira rose to her feet, placed a small, crude wooden table in front of me, and, with the back of her hand, brushed off a few grape pips and some squashed tomato seeds. She looked up at me, frowned, coughed, and then, as if a sudden thought had come to her, grinned and turned to the open door of the tiny storehouse which formed part of the dividing wall between her verandah and that of her immediate neighbour. I could hear her rummaging around inside. Something crashed to the floor. Sainisar sat bolt upright and shouted to her mother. Tak-Dira screamed in return, and, moving out through the door backwards, turned to me with a look of satisfaction, as she held up the tattered remains of a piece of what had once been brightly coloured material. Carefully, she laid it upon the table and attempted to press out the creases with her fingers. I cast a side-long glance at Sainisar who was

---

*The Kalash build their homes, made from cedar wood and stones, high up the mountainside, originally for defensive purposes and against floods, now also to conserve valuable arable land. Generally, the houses are ventilated by a small hole over a central hearth, and are just furnished with charpoys and a few low stools. Cooking utensils and bedding are usually the main household articles.

regarding her mother with quiet indulgence. When Tak-Dira finally placed before me a plate of freshly washed grapes and looked at me questioningly, I was torn between laughter and tears. I felt as though I were accepting more than an overture of friendship.

While I drank the tea and ate the grapes, Tak-Dira's dark eyes studied me with curiosity: her gaze was open, direct and without malice or suspicion. She pointed to the *charpoy* and made the motion of sleeping. I found myself hesitating. It was impossible. I could not. I smiled at her, got to my feet and pointed to the rain-filled sky. She came and stood before me, took my hand and clasped it tightly between both of hers, her dark eyes looking into mine, filling me with a weird sensation. It was more than hypnotic, more than a feeling of communication, all of which I had experienced before in the valleys. This was something different, more powerful. It was as if she were seeing right through me, beyond time, into the past. There was a look of knowledge and understanding in her gaze which left me unnerved. Without taking her eyes off me, she released my hand. Slowly, I moved away and crossed over the rough stone hearth, aware that she was behind me. I passed through the open doorway and out onto the muddy slope above the irrigation channel, and turned. She stood in the doorway watching me and then raised her hand in farewell. I waved, jumped over the channel and hurried back to the resthouse before the storm broke and made the going treacherous.

It was still daylight, but rain clouds darkened the sky and without the sun, the high broken windows of the resthouse afforded little light. As I lay in the semi-darkness, listening to the wind gust around the eaves, sending the broken iron sheeting banging against the rafters, I thought back to the day in the winter of 1974 on Mykonos. The wind had whistled around my rented house then, too, as I had tried to come to a decision.

Everyone at some time or another reaches a turning point or a crossroads in their life. Some people are lucky and unerringly follow the right path, but for others the way is not so clear.

I was bitterly disillusioned over a broken love affair, the bottom had fallen out of the market for the gothic novel (I had sold two but only one had been published) and I was broke. My decision then was to go to London (instead of accepting a dear friend's advice and staying with him in New York). My normal optimistic self had completely disappeared, and my grandparents' house, lying empty in North London seemed an ideal retreat.

Turning over on my sleeping bag, as an extra strong gust of wind howled around the resthouse, sending one of the torn curtains flying across my face, I shivered from the cold and crawled inside the sleeping bag. Memories of cold winter nights in that old Victorian house in

London were still fresh in my mind. Dilapidated it may have been, but it had offered me sanctuary from the outside world. In no time at all, I had become a recluse, forced by the crippling re-emergence of that old childhood phobia of dirt, for so many years dormant, to stay indoors. At that time even a walk to the local shops was a journey fraught with peril; a road sweeper, a dustman's cart, a dog, a pile of rubbish—anything in fact, which came within six feet of me, was sufficient to make me hurry home to a bath and clean clothes.

An only child, protected and molly-coddled, I had been, according to my mother, a beautiful baby. Alway dressed in lovely hand-knitted clothes, she would take me out with a small badge pinned to my shawl which read: 'Please Do Not Kiss Me'.

The wind continued to growl and gust around the resthouse as I retraced the passage of years. One can get bored with anything after a time, and being a recluse and playing the part of a writer in an ivory tower soon lost their appeal. Always a great believer in the psychological approach, I worked out my own salvation. I used what, I believe, is referred to as the 'flooding' method, and took my problem to the streets of North London by starting up my own window cleaning business which became a huge success. This led to an equally successful decorating business.

The wind died away, and then the rain began beating down like a shower of pebbles upon the iron roof. I watched as it dripped through the rafters onto the stone floor, forming a pool between the two beds.

As I continued to shiver, I thought of the *charpoy* beside the warm hearth and of the Kalash woman with the high cheekbones and those dark all-seeing eyes. Here I had the golden opportunity I had been looking for. Was I going to let those blasted fears of mine stop me?

When the downpour was over, the sun came out again. Delighting in the aftermath of the storm, as a mass of white, grey and black clouds scudded across the sky and a fresh wind blew, I walked along the cliff beside the river and emptied my mind of the past.

The next day I found my steps irresistibly drawn down the valley.

When I arrived at Tak-Dira's *dora*,* she was beside the hearth and a bunch of grapes, already washed, was lying in a bowl. It was as if she were expecting me. When Tak-Dira again pointed to the *charpoy* and made the motion of sleeping, I smiled in acquiescence. Her face lit up and her sharp brown eyes became soft and glowing. With a sudden movement, she caressed my chin with her fingers.

Two women of entirely different backgrounds, upbringing and con-

---

Dora—house.

ditioning, and yet, for a brief moment in time, we were united. On the surface we had nothing in common, she could never exist in my society, nor I, I thought then, in hers for any length of time, but what did that matter, or that our relationship was only for a second in eternity.

And so began my life with Tak-Dira and her family.

As these memories flooded my mind, my pace quickened. I turned to see Sharzaman smiling broadly, immediately behind me. Carefully, I began walking along the dangerous water channel. With every step, I could feel my heart beating more quickly. I knew from Saifullah that the family were well and expecting me, but five years is a long time. Would they really remember me? Were they still 'my' family? Would that bond between me and Tak-Dira still exist?

As I approached the *dora*, I saw an additional room had been built on next to the narrow gully that ran down the mountainside. The fresh cedar wood and the porch with its trellis work and little gate were most attractive. I was glad. They had not fallen on hard times but were prospering, and I was anxious for news. I knew only that Balan, Tak-Dira's second son, was a member of the Border Police. On my journey out of Rumbur he had been on duty at the bridge where the two roads, the one from Bumburet and the other from Rumbur, converge, and he had called out joyously '*Ishpata, Baba!*' My Sister! My Sister'

All was quiet. I peered through the open door. A woman—a stranger—sat before the hearth. In the second it took me to realize I did not know her, I also noticed that the verandah floor had been smoothed out, a better hearthside and chimney had been built, and, in place of the old broken down slats that had served as a balcony wall, there was now some attractive trellis work.

Before I had time to ask Sharzaman, who knew a few words of English to interpret for me, I heard the rustle of robes and the jingle of chains and bells.* I turned, and a smiling young woman grabbed hold of my hand, put it to her lips and then embraced me, kissing me three times on the cheeks. In five years, Sainisar had grown from a plump, attractive teenager into a very attractive young woman. She had the same oval face as her mother, a long, straight nose and big brown eyes. The joy on her face at seeing me was unmistakable. The manner in which she had greeted me, in the traditional Kalash way, assured me, as nothing else could have done, that I had not been forgotten. One by one, except for Balan, and Mandali, the adopted son, who was shepherding up in the higher pastures, the family wandered onto the verandah and greeted me

---

*The bells are worn supposedly to keep away the snakes.

as though I were indeed a long-lost relative. Sitting beside the hearth with Sainisar were Jumat, the eldest son, his young teenage wife, whom I had seen on entering, and Jafail, Tak-Dira's husband. We talked with Sharzaman acting as interpreter. My eyes were continually on the open doorway, and Sainisar, observing this and knowing full well why, kept chuckling and reassuring me that my *aya* (mother) would be home soon.

Suddenly she gestured with her head to the doorway. Moments later, Tak-Dira paused hesitantly for a second on the threshold, and then with a sweep of dusty robes and the usual accompaniment of bells and chains, grabbed me into her arms and in a rush of emotion greeted me in the traditional way.

When she finally let me go, squatted beside me and wiped her eyes, the rest of the family laughed and Sainisar shook her head. Tak-Dira still clutched my hand, and, as we exchanged news, I reflected that nowhere, at any time in my entire life, had I been greeted so warmly and so demonstratively by a group of people. I truly felt that Tak-Dira and her family were my family. They had invited me in five years before and now they welcomed me back with love and affection. I could not have been happier.

203

The steep slopes of the Birir valley with Tak-Dira's *dora* in the foreground.

Doctor Baba and the Orphans

It was still dark when I awoke to see Tak-Dira lighting the fire. With half-closed eyes, I watched her sift flour through a square-shaped wooden sifter and begin making corn bread, one of the staple foods of the Kalash during the autumn. She flattened the heavy dough between the palms of her hands, fashioned it into the shape of a wheel, pinched the rounded edges and placed it onto a very large, convex iron plate (about a tenth of an inch thick), lying over the part of the hearthside which was shaped into a rocky horse-shoe.

I was fascinated, as always, by everything she did and intrigued generally by the culinary habits of the family. Food such as potatoes and tomatoes were cooked in a heavy iron pot placed on a thin triangle of iron, and sticks of wood were used as stirrers or to flip over the flat bread. Flour was contained in an old paint tin and the sugar in a grimy brake-fluid bottle; grapes and vegetables were kept in a small storehouse on the verandah and milk and cheese, and wine, in a large natural cellar beneath the *dora*; the cold stream was as good as any ice box.

When I returned from the river and my morning ablutions, Tak-Dira pushed me closer to the hearth for though only mid-September, it was cold before the sun rose. She then presented me with a large bowl of goat's milk and some corn bread, which she first blew on, then dusted off on the sleeve of her robes before giving it a final polish on a blackened *khameez*. When I had drunk half of it, she poured in some more. A fly dropped into the bowl, which Tak-Dira removed with a sooty finger, leaving a black trail in the creamy liquid. I watched as the black stream divided and then mixed in until it disappeared altogether.

I spent the morning with her, visiting and renewing old acquaintances. At noon, we returned to the verandah where I sat contentedly beside the hearth, slicing potatoes and watching Sainisar making bread for the mid-day meal. As soon as a few rounds were ready, Tak-Dira, with quick, easy movements interspersed by harsh coughs, took several from the hearth, blew on them to clear off the ash, wrapped them in a large dirty

204

Tak-Dira's old hearthside with Jafail, Sainisar and the young Mandali on my first visit.

Tak-Dira's new hearthside with Garam Bibi.

rag and put the bundle into her cone-shaped basket. With that on her back, her high cheek bones, flared nostrils, black robes and head-dress, I was reminded of childhood pictures of witches (not for the first time among the Kalash), and her croaking voice only lent credence to this mental vision. With her half-toothless smile, she took my hand in farewell and disappeared down the embankment, en route to give sustenance to those working in the fields.

By the open doorway, Garam Bibi, Sainisar's three-year-old daughter and the apple of Tak-Dira's eye, was playing with Arlem Gil, the puny five-year-old son of a nearby neighbour. She was usually a petulant and wilful child, but now she was showing the more attractive side of her nature, as she played happily, continually laughing, with her favourite companion. On a nearby *charpoy*, a neighbour sat crooning a lullaby to the baby in his arms.

Looking over the trellis work, I could see two young bullocks on a grassy slope, battling it out with their horns locked. Over by the flour mill on the other side of the river, four teenage girls were wrestling on the grass, while close by, a group of young women sat beneath the trees, finger-weaving and breast-feeding their babies, their dogs asleep beside them.

A while later, her errand completed, Tak-Dira arrived back at the *dora*, and, ever fearful I should succumb to starvation, ladled out a double portion of potato curry. We had barely finished eating when the afternoon peace was shattered by the arrival of Hush Bibi, who was known as 'The General' by the Kalash. Hush Bibi was a sort of public relations officer in the valley. Apart from the young Kalash man, who had built a small hotel close to the resthouse, she was the only Kalash in Birir I knew of who consorted with foreigners other than myself. As soon as she saw a jeep drive into the valley, she would run up to it with ingratiating smiles, and would pose for photographs for which she demanded to be paid. Often from within her robes, she would produce bits and pieces of jewelry with which to trap the gullible tourist into visiting her house, where she would then invite them to buy head-dresses at exorbitant prices. She and Tak-Dira, who was known locally as 'Little Headache', where arch rivals and constantly moaned about one another, although in true traditional fashion, I had never seen Hush Bibi turned away from Tak-Dira's hearthside. Whether it worked the other way, I don't know, because the only hospitality I ever saw Hush Bibi give was to Kalash elders from the other valleys and visiting officials from Chitral.

Now, before I had a chance to pay her my respects, she ambled in, making Tak-Dira knit her brows together and mutter beneath her breath. Her face took on that self-pitying look I had come to know so well five

206

Above left: **Madame Bibi.**
Above right: **A Kalash elder wearing home-spun clothes.**
Below left: **Sainisar.**
Below right: **Saifullah.**

years before. Then came the tears. I looked at Tak-Dira, who, in the universal way, raised her eyes to the roof. On my last visit, Hush Bibi's husband had fallen over a cliff and had suffered a badly grazed chest and superficial wounds on the legs and hands, all of which I had doctored successfully. Now, through her tears, Hush Bibi told us her husband had again gone over a cliff, this time in a jeep.

Tak-Dira, momentarily forgetting her feud, elected to come with me as I grabbed my first-aid box and followed Hush Bibi along the irrigation channel and up a short, but steep and difficult path to Guru village.

As it was afternoon, there were few people about. Most of the villagers were out in the fields harvesting and only a few youngsters played hide-and-seek among the tiny storehouses. As we passed on up over the rocky ground, two emaciated puppies raced past us to escape a stone thrown by a passing jeep driver.

Hush Bibi's husband sat on a *charpoy* in the gloom of the windowless house. Making sure his head and back were not injured, I gently led him outside to another *charpoy* in the shade cast by a storehouse.

In the light of day, this frightened man was a pathetic and vulnerable-looking figure, as he sat hunched up, trembling uncontrollably, with his face, hair and clothes grimed with oil and dirt. My first concern was to control his fright and reassure him. His wife's tears did nothing to help, which Tak-Dira was quick to realize, and I was relieved when she led her away. I suspected her husband had broken ribs, but, thankfully, there appeared to be no signs of any internal organs having been damaged, for to ferry him to Chitral by jeep was out of the question.

That night I sat writing by the light of the lantern, as Tak-Dira took her turn at making bread and Jafail chopped wood outside the *dora*. I looked up and watched for a moment as Jumat, his lean young face so like his father's, cut up some onions with my pen-knife. I was excused duties because the one and only sharp knife had been temporarily mislaid.

Not for the first time, I reflected upon the notorious reputation of the Kalash. It seemed so inconceivable that they had once been warriors.* There were hardly any weapons in the valleys; a few rifles, one

---

*Although the Kalash are now a peace-loving and docile people, they were once regarded as fierce and warlike. Bravery is highly esteemed, and, in the past, a man achieved rank by being a man or leopard killer, after which, he would celebrate by giving a big feast. Another method of seeking fame and becoming closer to the gods, was to give a feast called *Biramur*, still done to this day. For this a man will kill more than one hundred goats at the religious shrine of '*Sajigor*' in Rumbur, and then distribute the meat throughout the whole three valleys. He will also provide the elders of all three valleys with silken gowns. Then there are two days of feasting and dancing. When a man has achieved rank in this way, he is presented with celebration bands (*Shuman*), symbols of respect and prestige. These are woven for him by the clan daughters, who also make garlands of walnut and apricot kernels—the traditional gifts of the Kalash for guests and men of importance.

208

Kalashnikov, bows and arrows and one spear was the limit of their arsenal. I knew that, during the days of the Raj, the Kalash had escaped the wholesale conversion to Islam which had overtaken the Kafir tribes in Afghanistan in 1895 because of their attachment to the Royal State of Chitral, which was then within the sphere of British influence. In 1895, however, during the events leading up to the siege, the Kalash village of Urtzun was put to the torch by Umra Khan. Until Pakistan's independence in 1947, the Kalash, who for centuries had supplied the royal harem, were virtual slaves to the Mehtar and were subjected to forced labour. In addition, the story goes, they were forbidden to visit the town of Chitral in clean clothes and were required to wear hats with beads and feathers to differentiate them from the Moslems, hence the reason Kalash men still decorate their Chitrali hats.

Not only were they subjugated by the Chitralis, to whom they had to pay a head tax, but they were also held in contempt, which Robertson, in his book on the relief of Chitral, recalls so vividly. When he and his men came to the end of a day's march, they would often be entertained round the campfire. One of the Chitralis' favourite means of entertainment was to play-act. A Chitrali 'Prince' swaggering into the light of the campfire, brandishing a sword, would be set upon by a band of blackened, half-naked Chitralis acting as 'Kafirs' armed only with bows and arrows. The 'Prince' would momentarily capitulate, leaving the 'Kafirs' to dance grotesquely, their blackened bodies indicating they were 'devils'. The 'Prince' would then speedily return to the fray, carrying an enormous sword with which he vanquished the foe. This play was then re-enacted several times, until the most distinguished guest present would announce he had seen enough, whereupon the Chitralis, acting the role of the 'Kafirs', had to seek absolution from the priest so that no stain would be left upon them.

Although the Kalash are no longer slaves, and, since 1969, they do not have to pay a head tax, they still suffer humiliation, for they are often called upon to dance for tourists, visiting diplomats and officials. The Kalash, as is now customary, are paid for their dances, but their lacklustre steps and movements show they take little joy in the occasion.* Perhaps the Australian couple I had met on my first visit to Hunza, who had worked with the Aborigines, had the right idea. They had suggested it might be good to bring in an international team of teachers and doctors to teach the Kalash the pros and cons of modern civilization, and to cut the valleys off from the outside world until the people were sufficiently educated to handle their own destiny.

---

*Saifullah has banned this practice in Rumbur.

Later, when I went out to wash my hands after eating, it was pitch black, rain and dust clouds having hidden the moon. As I breathed in the damp smells all around me, squatting before the irrigation channel, I became aware of an approaching light. I looked up to see Tak-Dira coming towards me, holding a lighted flare in one hand and a water pot in the other. As she went to pass behind me, she smiled. As I turned my head to watch the robed figure disappear down the embankment, I had to shake myself out of the dream-like state into which I'd fallen.

As I rose to my feet I became aware of an unusual smell floating across from the houses. With mounting curiosity, I returned to the silent verandah. The door of Tak-Dira's *dora* was open. By the light of the lantern, I saw Jafail bending over something on the ground. Looking over his shoulder, I noticed a strange object burning in the flames; it was a goat's head complete with fur and eyes—tomorrow's dinner no doubt! I climbed into my sleeping-bag, and stared at the flames and breathed in the smell of scorched goat's hair. I experienced that now all-to-familiar feeling of unreality, which was made all the more acute by its contrast to my sense of being completely at home in the valleys.

Intrigued, I watched as Jafail, now sitting beside the hearth, kept turning the head in the flames. Then, with a stick he levered it out, and, letting it cool for a moment, picked it up and began tearing off tufts of burnt hair. That done, he took the carving-knife and cut through the jaw, splitting the head in two, and scraped out the teeth. I watched in horrified fascination. Next he turned up the head, and, again with his fingers, gouged out the eyes and threw them over his shoulder into the void. Placing the head in a pot, he took a couple of legs from the embers, scraped around the hoofs and placed them on the hearth. From a large sheep-skin, complete with wool, he brought out the rear end of the goat (thankfully already skinned), and, hacking at it with an axe, also put these pieces into the pot. Soon afterwards the fire was extinguished, but it was a long time before I fell asleep.

Although life in the valley seemed much the same as on my previous visit, closer to home there had been some changes. Tak-Dira's immediate neighbour, who had been crippled with arthritis and partially blind, had died. The husband and his four young daughters constantly joined those gathered at Tak-Dira's fireside. In the end house, the young mother of Arlem Gil was now bed-ridden, also with the arthritis. In the next village along the irrigation channel, there were three more young women with the crippling disease.* Sometimes the darker side of the existence of the

---

*Whether all the cases reputed to be arthritis are, in fact, this painful crippling disease, is open to question. A number of such cases I have since been able to diagnose as TB which also can attack the bones.

210

Kalash overwhelmed me, leaving me feeling somehow useless and frustrated.

Within a matter of days, I found myself hurrying hither and thither, up and down the mountainside with either Tak-Dira by my side, or, more often, a small boy in the lead, carrying my first-aid box. On the way back, the same small boy would be accompanied by numerous others carrying bundles of grapes, pears and peaches. It was not long before I found that as many Moslems as Kalash were seeking the aid of 'Doctor Baba', as some of them called me.

The small dispensary,* recently refurbished, had few drugs, as the dispenser spends more time visiting his family outside the valley (unlike his dedicated counterpart in Rumbur) than helping the sick, had failed to travel to Chitral and pick up his medical supplies.

Tak-Dira was not happy I should constantly be on call tending to the sick, ostensibly because it took up so much of my time, but mainly, I suspect because it took me away from her. No matter how much I tried, through Sharzaman or Saifullah, on one of his rare visits (he was still caught up in Chitral, fighting for the Kalash over forestry rights), to explain to her that this was work I had trained for and did willingly, she was not convinced. To my satisfaction though, and to her pride, I managed to involve her by enlisting her help in the distribution of ORS powders for all the babies with diarrhoea that were brought to my attention. Acting as my 'interpreter', for I was still endeavouring to learn the language, she was able to give out the necessary instructions and proved to be a great help.

There was just one problem in having Tak-Dira as my 'aid'. A jaunt with her would either be conducted at lightning speed, which would leave me gasping for breath until, discerning my flushed face, she would slow down, or she would hold me up by stopping en route to chat, scold, scream, lecture or harangue all whom we met. Other times she would pause to bend down to alter the course of the irrigation channel by scooping away at the muddy bank or removing a blocking stone. Tak-Dira, unlike Hush Bibi, appeared to have authority over more than half the valley, and there were many occasions that gave me to wonder about her role in what was a patriarchal society. She was the only woman I saw who obviously held sway over men in a discussion (argument would be a better word as Tak-Dira was not one to discuss), and she seemed to be in

---

*Pakistan is a poor country and in the rural areas, in spite of the government constantly improving health facilities, doctors are reluctant to 'bury' themselves out in the wilds for low pay and poor housing, and thereby condemn themselves to an existence without family life.

*There are several flour mills in each valley.

212

The flour mill at Birir.

charge of the local flour mill,* just below the irrigation channel. On the other side of the river, most of the fields appeared to belong to her family, and wherever she went, she altered the course of the water channels as she thought necessary. She was also one of the few women who chanted the historic legends of the Kalash at the Phoo Festival, a custom usually given over to the elders.

Having medical knowledge made me doubly concerned for Tak-Dira's only daughter who was eight months pregnant, but I should not have worried, for the Kalash take childbirth in their stride. Although separated from her husband, Sainisar still lived as was the custom with his family and his brothers' wives on the other side of the river. It takes time to figure out the relationships, sleeping and domestic arrangements of the Kalash, and my obvious confusion at times was met with hilarity, especially among the women. Wherever I went, I was inundated with *chai* and fruit. When I was not on my medical rounds, Tak-Dira constantly took me visiting, taking pride in showing me off, and it wasn't long before Pakistani visitors to the valley, hearing of a 'crazy foreigner' living with the Kalash, came to seek me out as though I were some kind of celebrity. Haider Ali Shah sent in my mail with his jeep driver, so tourists, too, would wander over. The more visitors that frequented Tak-Dira's hearthside, the more Hush Bibi sulked. Not wanting to be left out of the activity she would arrive almost daily with medical problems—a headache, month-old burns she had scratched, a cough, a sore throat, internal problems, scratches on her arms, cuts on her fingers. Never a day passed that I did not have to bandage, anoint with balm, or reassure her that husband, brother, or nephew would live to a ripe old age. Tak-Dira's air of superiority grew every time Hush Bibi entered, and my own impatience was mingled with barely concealed mirth.

Playing doctor, however, had its serious side, which was illustrated only too well a few days after my arrival. As often happened, the first warning I would have of impending disaster would be the tearful arrival of a friend or family member summoning me to hurry; and so I would rush, not knowing what I should find, or what treacherous path I should have to negotiate to reach the scene of the accident or house of the ailing.

One afternoon, as I watched Tak-Dira cooing over a visiting woman's baby and Garem Bibi running up to her grandmother to grab her around the waist with possessive arms, Sainisar entered, all flushed and trembling. Not one usually to panic, her anxiety communicated itself to us and we left immediately for her house. As we approached we could see a group of women gathered on the verandah. A very pretty woman, whom I had seen several times before, was sitting on a stool, her head cradled in the lap of another. She had been bitten by a neighbour's dog.

214

It had happened a few hours earlier and the local Kalash 'doctor' had attended her, but, now, perhaps, at Sainisar's insistence my help had been called upon.

With my usual audience, this time consisting of a number of women of varying ages, small boys and one old man, I set about what was to prove one of my most challenging cases. The woman, Biroche Bibi, had been bitten on the side of her right calf, and the very deep wound had been filled with mud and (I suspect) cow dung. Cleansing the wound proved to be traumatic for both the patient and myself. Halfway through my endeavours, she gave a gulp and fainted. Her attractive young sister, cradling her in her arms, blew gently into her face, but she did not stir. Making her comfortable and checking that she was not in any danger, I quickly finished cleansing the wound and as I gave a final turn to the bandage, she fluttered open her eyelids and groaned. I wiped the beads of perspiration from my brow with my sleeve, and wished I had the necessary equipment to stitch the wound.

The very next day I was called to Guru Village, where an elderly woman had also been the victim of a dog bite. As I walked down the rocky slope, accompanied by the usual army of small boys and some girls as well, four starving puppies fled to safety beneath the storehouses. I had already discovered that Tak-Dira, who had always kept open house, now fed all the local cats and dogs that strayed in from nearby houses, virtually ran an orphanage as well as soup kitchen for all the field hands and young herdsboys, and to add to this, the verandah now became a surgery, where queueing patients were fed a breakfast of *chai* and corn bread.

One of the biggest problems was lack of medical supplies. Although I had brought in a huge box-load, I soon ran out. Certain items I did not have anyway, and I found that neither did the dispensary. A call to the civil surgeon in Chitral for tetanus vaccine proved futile as medical supplies from Peshawar had not arrived,* and my anxiety for the two victims of the dog bites grew daily. It was not long before I started asking tourists for bandages, dressings (I had been about to cut up one of my two T-shirts) and any medicines they might have, as well as sending in requests to Haider via his jeep driver.

With the harvest in full swing, there were many incidents of infected

---

*On one occasion, when medical supplies did not reach Chitral, an S.O.S. call from the dispenser of Rumbur resulted in a large box of urgent medicines being sent in personally by the former trustee of Minority Affairs, Mr Minoo Bhandara. The influx of Afghan refugees puts a strain on supplies—already hampered by the lowarian and cancelled flights due to inclement weather. Mr Bhandan is now trying to persuade the Kalash to have small stores and better ventilation in their homes which would help reduce respiratory and eye ailments.

Guru village. In the Kalash valleys the houses are made of cedar wood and stone.

cuts among the men, and, with both women and men, burns from hot *chai* and *ghee** were an every day occurrence. One day, though, I was called to a more serious case. I was on my way back from the *dukan* with some purchases for the family, when a Moslem woman, whose daughter I had tended the day before for a head wound, came running up, urgently asking me to go to her house up on the far mountain slope. At that time I wasn't in the habit of carrying my medical kit everywhere so I had to rush back to Tak-Dira's house to fetch it. As we set off I questioned the small boys accompanying me. The victim, a small child, had apparently been bitten by 'something'. Moving on quickly, I climbed the rocky slope to Guru Village and followed my party of young guides up the winding, treacherous rocky paths along the narrow, twisting slippery banks of the irrigation channel. Up and over large mounds of rocks and ducking beneath low branches, we jumped across pools of water and finally arrived at a large verandah where a crowd of men, women and children

Ghee—clarified butter.

216

were gathered around a *charpoy*, on which lay very still a girl of perhaps three or four.

Cries of relief did nothing to dispel my uneasiness. Nor did the eager expectant faces of the small boys hastily assembling. Nervously, I asked what had happened. A man came forward, holding out a stick at arm's length. On the end was the unmistakable body of a scorpion. He indicated the rafters above and pointed at the child. The insect had dropped down on its victim and had bitten her shoulder. As I stared at the tiny mark high up just below the neck, and in a position that made it impossible to apply a restricting band, I racked my brains as to what to do. Turning briefly, I saw those expectant faces staring at me as if spellbound. I asked for a bowl of water and turned back to my task. For a moment I stood paralysed, as I had done five years before, when, in Rumbur, I had been called upon to give medical aid to another young girl—who had suffered a very bad head injury. Now, as then, I was suddenly driven to action by blind necessity. Striking a match, I passed the tip of my knife through the flames and ignoring the gasps from my audience, told the mother to hold the child still. The little girl gazed at me with the tears running down her cheeks. Avoiding the desire to shut my eyes, I stood for a moment with trembling hands above the helpless form. The communal intake of breath was audible as I leaned over and poised the knife just above the bite.* The red mark was so tiny it seemed incredible that this could warrant such alarm. A voice inside me said that what I was about to do was crazy, absurd, theatrical; not the thing to do at all. But what was the right action? My mind was blank. I pushed the point of the knife into the soft skin. A gasp went up all round but the child barely flinched. Gritting my teeth, I pushed it in harder. As soon as I saw a widening red spot, I put down the knife and placed my mouth over it. As I urgently sucked at the wound, all sorts of movie scenes came to mind, Westerns, where some grizzled old timer hacked away at a snake bite—vampires sucking the blood from their helpless victims. It was an extraordinary moment in my life—quite unreal. Another one of those situations where part of one stands back looking at one's actions. Raising my head, I spat out the blood, barely missing the *chaplis* of one of the interested spectators and bent my head once more. When I straightened up, I discovered that everyone, including the mother, was beaming smiles of approval and relief. Relieved myself that the worst

*A few weeks later, I met two English doctors visiting Pakistan, who said that I had done the correct thing. However, the latest idea put forth by the RAF on the treatment of poisonous bites, besides keeping the patient still, is to apply a pressure bandage and immobilize the limb by splintage, a procedure which would have been difficult in this case. Often, snakes and scorpions do not inject a full dose of poison—sometimes none at all. For the victims of such bites it is the psychological shock that is often debilitating.

part was over, I reached in my bag for an antihystamine tablet and finally sterilized the wound by washing it in Dettol and smearing it with antibiotic cream, I then placed a bandaid on the wound and prayed.

With the child taken care of, I now found myself with a collection of patients among the audience, which once dealt with meant a number of return visits to check up on their progress. My Emergency Medical Technician's Course had given me a very good grounding and most of the cases were simple. What was not so simple was travelling up and down the mountainsides all day, especially, when, the very next morning, leaning over from my sitting position on one of the low stools, I broke one of my healing ribs.

One of the many virtues I had noticed among the Kalash was their stoicism in the face of hardship and pain. Men with throbbing wounds went about their work as if nothing had happened; pregnant women did their day's physical chores to the very moment they entered the Bashali House—in Sainisar's case, at literally the eleventh hour. So, much against Tak-Dira's insistence that I should rest, I continued to visit all my steadily growing number of patients, locally, at Guru and villages beyond.

Another virtue of the Kalash is their cheerful demeanour (I constantly came across women singing as they worked in the fields); and their spontaneous and deep love for children is a pleasure to behold. Nowhere in the world have I seen such sibling love nor so many men cradling and rocking their babies to sleep. Generosity and kindness are character traits which are highly regarded by the Kalash and their goodwill is extended to all living things; insects other than hornets or scorpions are rescued from spiders' webs, bees from the honey that has entrapped them, and mynah birds travel upon the shoulders of small children.

Occasionally, though, I would see evidence of cruelty—such as someone throwing a stone at a dog unnecessarily* or a family of emaciated and neglected puppies as I had seen at Guru.

Although I strongly believe in not interfering with other people's domestic and personal lives—a philosophy I take with me when entering another culture—where cases of danger, cruelty or neglect arise I feel that there should be no boundaries. The only problem is to realize what the consequences of one's actions might be. There are certain cultures where the belief is held that a person who saves another from death is thereafter responsible for that life. This is a concept that I can easily relate to, but it does mean that when choosing to 'interfere' with events, gut-reaction has to be tempered with realism—not always an easy

---

*The throwing of stones is often the only way they have of controlling their herds and others arrivals.

achievement.

In the case of the four pups, my gut-reaction to feed them was accompanied by the awareness that they might eventually bite someone, and that I would have to find food for them daily, but that somehow I would be helped by the Kalash.

When I first spotted them, they were about two months old, the offspring of a large, healthy-looking bitch which closely resembled a golden labrador. Two of the pups, one male and one female took after their mother, the other two were brindle in colour, with the male, the largest of the litter and the last to come to my notice, having a big white blaze on his chest and four white paws.

At first, the feeds went relatively quietly, as only the two bitches appeared, but when the two males overcame their fears, more and more children became aware of what was going on, and we threatened to turn the mountainside into a circus. To my cries of '*Doh! Doh!*' (Here! Here!) the children would come out and join me, their cries mingling with my own, until patches of corn would ripple beside us, or a cloud of dust be thrown up at the top of the mountain slope, telling us the dogs were on their way. In seconds they would descend upon me in one leaping bundle of fur and hungrily attack their food. In their enthusiasm the empty tins

The four puppies guard the entrance to Tak-Dira's *dora*.

would go hurtling down the mountainside, to fetch up in the cornfield or the irrigation channel followed in hot pursuit by the children and puppies. Women returning from the fields would stop in their tracks, afraid, perhaps, that the swirling mass of children and pups would hurl them off the slope, but their laughter told me they weren't annoyed and that they were enjoying the spectacle.

Finding the pups sufficient food soon became a problem, for the usual diet fed by the Kalash to their dogs was bread and buttermilk, and these were items I couldn't buy. At first I haunted Sharzaman's kitchen, or armed myself with a 'scrap' bag on my visits to patients or began using my stock of tinned meat given to me by some tourists and rejected by Tak-Dira. Then I had a brainwave. I had already started feeding the pups on powdered milk that I had brought into the valley (and which, together with some eggs—Tak-Dira could close her eyes to convention quite easily—had helped Sainisar overcome her shortage of milk after the baby's birth), and now I decided to try the pups with something else. My contribution to the household was to supply them with tea, sugar, rock salt and most recently rice. I would try the dogs on some rice. Thereafter Tak-Dira would cook extra each day to be shared with the dogs, and both they and the family grew healthier and stronger by the day.

Then came the next problem. What was going to happen to them after I left the valley?

I consulted Tak-Dira. It was she who, when Balan had joined the Border Police, had taken over his dog (similar to a husky) to guard her storehouse. Although she lavished much love on Garda Sher,* it was her large fat goat that was her real passion. She would lead it up and down the valley on a long rope, in much the same way as in the West we would lead our pets on a leash. The goat was usually billeted on the verandah of the neighbouring *dora*, and armfuls of leaves would be brought to the byre by Jumat or Jafail each evening. Other times, when out walking, if there were no leaves within easy reach, Tak-Dira would tie the rope around a boulder and shinny up the nearest tree in her bare feet, leaving me gaping below with hand on heart. If the goat was naughty (she had a penchant for dipping her nose into food pots, and sometimes out on the rope she would stubbornly want to go a different way), she invariably received a hearty thump on her well-padded flanks.

Tak-Dira had obviously been thinking about the problem, too, for she soon told me Mandali and Jumat could each take one to help guard the flocks in the higher pastures, and Sainisar's husband would take the third. The fourth pup was eventually spoken for by an amused and

---

Garda—large. *Sher*—dog.

grateful Sainisar, whose newborn baby I had successfully treated for a very bad eye infection.

It took only a couple of days to entice the pups to the *dora*, where they soon made themselves at home. Now they sat on guard in a row on the banks of the irrigation channel, and those who wanted to pass by Tak-Dira's *dora* after dusk did so with not a little apprehension. One evening I watched some young herdsboys giggling while some hapless girl was chased by Gada Sher and the pups as she tried to drive a couple of forgotten animals home to their byres.

They were constantly in trouble of some sort or another. The golden female got her head stuck between the bars of a gate, while the other was always off exploring and giving chase to anything that moved. The big one who was fast becoming my favourite and whom I was later to call Pooch, saved me from a scorpion and nearly got bitten on the nose in the process; and anything like a garment left lying around was fair game. One afternoon, the pups departed off up the valley along the banks of the river, leaving my laundry strewn in their wake, across the meadow. On another occasion, I saw them having a tug-of-war with Jamat's animal furs, which he wore as a winter coat. As I went to retrieve it, Jumat walked in. He took one look, turned to me with a broad smile and said: '*Ishpata, Baba!*'

Jafail was not quite so phlegmatic when he saw them pulling his bedding off his *charpoy*, just as he was about to retire for the night; but when the four of them grabbed my sleeping bag and dragged it onto the floor, everyone, including all the herdsboys, who were growing in numbers daily, roared their heads off and slapped me on the back.

When they gave chase to Tak-Dira's goat (she was not retrieved until dark), the family laughed, but I was not so amused; there was no milk for the tea that day.

Relationships with animals, as with humans, often stem from strange beginnings. Within a few days of Garda Sher attacking the large pup for pinching his food, he showed favouritism towards his victim, who was still nursing a sore paw, and soon they were happily playing together.

Several times a baby goat, which had been brought down from the higher pastures because of a broken leg and upon whom Jumat lavished much affection, had to be rescued from their curious and noisy attentions, and when Tak-Dira rescued a kitten with a broken hip, the *dora* became a scene of pandemonium. Watching the interaction of the animals with one another, it became very clear to me that, as with humans, it was fear which produced anger and hostility. If the baby kitten ignored them, all was well, but if their nosy insistence got too much, it would arch its back and spit. Then it was a frantic scramble to

Men in Birir transport their grapes in traditional willow baskets.

The Kalash make their own clothes.

separate the kitten and the pups.

One day the house was even more chaotic than usual: the baby goat was there together with the larger one which was not tied up: there were several herdsboys visiting; Hush Bibi had just arrived bemoaning her ailments; Garam Bibi, with tears streaming down her cheeks, was in a truculent mood; I was endeavouring to bandage some youngster's bloody hand, and Tak-Dira was chasing the pups with a pitcher of water. When Jumat and Sainisar's husband walked in from their stint in the higher pastures they just collapsed with laughter.

Now in the valley the cry of '*Aya!*' (when I was out searching for Tak-Dira), was to be replaced by '*Sher!*' followed by gales of laughter, as sometimes, in spite of all mine and Tak-Dira's efforts the pups would come chasing after me on my jaunts to the *dukan*, or would accompany me on visits to my patients. Workers in the fields would stop what they were doing, children would appear from behind every rock and tree, and women sitting beneath the trees, finger-weaving, would dissolve into spasms of laughter. No doubt, our walking in single file across the plank bridge must have made an unusual and amusing sight, as did the spectacle of a foreigner accompanied by a gang of children, rescuing a pup from a Moslem-owned tomato patch.

The pups soon became my shadows and I realized they gave me another link with the people—they provided a diversion, a point of interest, a frame of reference, a topic of conversation, a subject of gossip; they had given me a new insight into the Kalash.

When I returned to Chitral and arranged with Saifullah to send rupees and more milk powder to Tak-Dira, with a promise of money from England (Saifullah is one of the very few Kalash to have a bank savings account in Chitral), I realized that the human warmth generated by the incident of the puppies had worked both ways and that it had brought me even closer to a people I had grown to love.

The Phoo Festival

Slowly the long ears of corn disappeared under the scythe, leaving the fields with a thick yellow stubble. Every day I came across children and men, armed with sticks, thrashing the branches of the trees, bringing the walnuts raining down upon them. The vines were now stripped of their fruit, and the slowly changing umbrella of green, yellow and amber leaves on the branches of trees overhanging the verandah brought with it a feeling of serenity. Soon the Phoo* Festival would begin.

In the half-light of dawn, I watched Tak-Dira, with her miniature witch's broom, sweep around my *charpoy* and carefully replace my boots. I lay quiet, still half-asleep; everything was so familiar, as if it had always been and always would be. For a while I watched Tak-Dira sweeping up the centuries and then fell back to sleep. When I opened my eyes again she was lighting the fire and the feeling that all this had happened before, long ago, was still with me, as though I were awakening from some long dream.

That morning, the water seemed more icy than usual and I stood slapping the palms of my hands against my thighs. In the meadow below Tak-Dira's *dora*, Garda Sher and the pups were chasing one another through the piled up corn. And then above me, a young boy stood on the bank of the irrigation channel, and with his head flung back, he played the flute as if saluting the trees. Even as he played, the rays of the sun reached out from behind the mountaintops to bathe us in light and warmth.

I was on my way to the *dukan* to buy some rice when I heard the distant sound of singing coming towards me. It was a group of women and children playing and running across the lawn of the resthouse. With shouts of '*Ishpata, Baba!*' they called to me and invited me to follow them to the open patch of ground opposite Guru village. Again, they

*In Chitral Phoo is pronounced Phool.

224

began to sing; they were welcoming in the Phoo Festival. They swayed back and forth, their heads held high, their ceremonial head-dresses sparkling in the sun. Then, amidst shrieks of laughter, they gave loud masculine whistles. Soon I saw other women and children hurrying down the rocky slope. As I squatted on the ground beneath a small grassy bank, preparing to take photographs, there was a jingle of bells and the rustle of robes and two more young women, with large pom-poms and brightly-coloured feathers in their head-dresses, jumped down past me, to join the others.

The festival was late this year because the harvest had been late. Nevertheless, there had been bumper crops of both walnuts and fruit, and I had been inundated with gifts of succulent grapes. Everywhere I went, I would be given huge bunches, and soon my teeth became stained with their rich red juice. Even the pups enjoyed a forgotten bunch left on the small wooden table.

That night saw the beginning of the festival, but I knew from before that I, as a foreigner, could not attend. The first time I had been disappointed but now that I knew them so well, I was happy that they still harboured secrets from the outside world.

Both Jumat and Balan's wives, decked out in all their finery, had gone early, while Jafail chopped wood outside and Tak-Dira kept a lone vigil by the hearth. A hush descended on the valley; the sound of axe on wood was stilled. All was quiet, a second in eternity broken by the crackle of a lighted flare, which threw its light up to the blackened beam of the verandah and stretched out to the heavy cedar door, I glimpsed a woman's laughing face beneath her colourful head-dress; the glint of white and red beads as she whirled around, her black robes scraping the dust. Gazing after Gul-Bibi, from the neighbouring *dora*, as she ran to join her companions on the banks of the water channel, and hearing the sound of their chanting made me wonder in which century I lived.

On the second night of the festival, Tak-Dira, with her hair freshly washed and braided said she was going to the dancing. The *dora* became alive with feverish activity and I sat observing the preparations with quiet interest. Being an only child, and close only to my mother and her parents (my father, a workaholic seldom had anything to do with me), the interaction of the members of a family was something that always held my interest.

Now, it was as though I were back in Western society, except that the clothes and location were different. Who was going to the dance? Father had a hangover, much to mother's disapproval; Jumat's wife was too tired from the previous night's dancing and wanted to stay home and Mandali, who had just arrived from the higher pastures, was annoyed his

225

shirt was not dry and mother was not going to let him go in his dirty one. As Tak-Dira held Mandali's shirt over the fire to dry, she cast me a glance and winked as if to say, be patient, this is all par for the course.

Balan, with his hair slicked back and in his uniform of grey *shalwar-khameez*, was looking more handsome than ever, when he arrived on the verandah, with some men and women from a village farther down the valley. Tired of hanging around, Balan took off with his male friends leaving the women behind and putting me in mind of Western men, who, bored with waiting for their womenfolk to stop chattering, impatiently head for their cars. Jumat, however, still sat before the fire. He and Sainisar's husband would not be going to the festival since they had to relieve Mandali's partner, who was guarding their herds up the mountainside, against rustlers from over the border.

Mandali, now busy shaving, was as worried about his appearance as he had been at the age of eleven; then he had kept us all waiting while he had searched for his plastic shoes and catapult (no self-respecting Kalash boy ever went anywhere without his catapult). As I stood up to let Tak-Dira pin some wild berries onto my jacket, Jumat let out a roar of laughter when Pooch climbed onto my *charpoy*, closely followed by the others.

Now we really were ready to leave. That is, all except Jafail, who refused to budge from the warmth of the hearthside. With Tak-Dira holding firmly onto my jacket, I found myself on the bank of the irrigation channel. By moonlight we walked with a group of women led by two boys holding aloft lighted cedar flames. One by one, we travelled along the muddy bank flashing our torches and lanterns before us. We crossed the plank bridge over the river and climbed the steep bank. As the night breeze fanned my cheeks and my foot sent a stone crashing into the river below I felt a touch of unreality as I beheld the eerie scene before me. The women in their black robes with their long silver chains and tingling bells sounding clear in the cool mountain air, presented an unforgettable picture. Unreal. Unearthly—not of this time, this century, this world.

We dropped down again to the valley floor and as we neared a stream, Tak-Dira, remembering where I liked to cross, steered the 'procession' to that point and took me by the hand. Her clasp was comfortably warm and firm, and, through the tingling in her hand, I could feel the electricity in her body. She began chanting and the young women joined in. We passed the small Moslem hotel and the *dukan*, on past the resthouse and the school and up onto the edge of a cornfield. Smash! One of the girls slipped headlong into the corn. With everyone laughing, we continued along the precipitous mountain path, with the river and its bed of rocks some thirty feet below. When it became too narrow, Tak-Dira pushed me in front of her and clutched hold of my elbow or jacket. All the time she remonstrated with everyone not to walk too fast. We crossed and recrossed the river, stepping from rock to rock or walking over slate and log bridges. We passed between and over huge rocks on which, in the semi-darkness, one could easily turn or break an ankle. Then back up the embankment we went, following an irrigation channel. At last we came to the inevitable hollowed-out tree trunk and plank across the void. With Tak-Dira clutching hold of my waist, I inched across the narrow plank, one hand on the rockface. Safely on the other side, she again took my hand. In the light of my torch, with her plumed head-dress, the Afghan blanket around her shoulders, and those dark brown eyes she reminded me of a painting by an old master. Now there came the sound of distant drums, and she again began singing the welcome to the festival—a slow, wailing kind of song that constantly repeated itself.

The drums grew louder; Tak-Dira's hand gripped mine more tightly; the high-pitched singing and the hollow beat sounding strange in the darkness of the night. We marched on, until before us, through the trees, I could see the gleam of firelight. We had arrived at the edge of a large clearing on the banks of the river. In the centre was a huge bonfire, and around it the black-robed figures of the women danced slowly to the incessant beat of the drums. Then the beat quickened, the women broke their formation, and, in twos and threes, began a half-marching, half-running type of dance. The men joined in, letting out loud whistles and wild yells. The faster the youths beat upon the drums, the faster went the dancers until soon the air was thick with dust. I moved back and sat on some rocks.

The drums stilled and the dancers dispersed. It was a moment for gossip and renewing acquaintances, also a time for more intimate pursuits, as, in pairs, boys and girls wandered off into the cornfield,* while the younger ones wrestled on the edge.

Tak-Dira pulled on my arm and gestured towards the bonfire, where the elders of the valley were gathered solemnly around the flames. Leaning upon long staves (supposedly to hold them up should they become too emotional), they stared one by one into the fire as they chanted the story of the ancient history of the Kalash. Tak-Dira, not to be outdone, gave me a mischievous glance, and pushed herself into the

---

*Although virginity among unmarried teenage boys is valued, feminine virginity is not considered to be important. Marriage, which is strictly forbidden within a clan, is usually arranged by the parents, but this is not so strictly adhered to as with Moslems. Betrothal often takes place when both the young man and woman are still children. Love and respect and mutual sexual enjoyment of both partners are regarded as essential.

circle and in true matriarchal fashion, took up a stave, and joined in the refrain.

Then the drums began again and the women joined ranks. Seconds later, I saw Tak-Dira relinquish her place by the fire and allow herself to be swept up into the dance. She swayed past, and, catching hold of me, pulled me into the circle. The steps were reminiscent of those I had learned in Greece and I had no difficulty in following her, as she gestured to her feet. Knowing this was a great honour, for it meant I was truly accepted by the Kalash, I danced happily as the women in the circle called out to me and the men clapped their hands.

Later, as I stood watching the men in the centre, two young women came up and pulled me in between them. Their faces were masked against the dust, but I guessed one was Gul-Bibi. Giggling, she planted her ceremonial head-dress upon my head, and, as I groaned beneath its weight, seemingly heavier than the customary five pounds, the girls giggled even more. Soon the people gathered around us, and it was obvious the picture of me with the *kopas** delighted the crowd. As we danced around the clearing, and I gazed upon the grinning faces before

Kopas—sometimes pronounced Kupis. Ceremonial and winter head-dress for women. The *Shushutre* is the summer and everyday head-dress, a symbol of femininity.

The author dancing with Tak-Dira at the Phoo festival.

me in the glow of the fire, I was struck yet again by those contrasting feelings of unreality and the sense of belonging—weird and wonderful, defying any rational explanation.

The dancing came to an end, and I tried to take some photographs, but I had hardly begun when the drums started up again and the dancing resumed. This time I hung back. Above the smell of woodsmoke, there was an unbelievable stench of urine while all around me, people were spitting. If I moved one pace in any direction, I should most probably be hit, so I stood still and concentrated on taking some photographs.

Then came a lull in the celebrations. Food was being served—Kalash bread and a paste made from crushed walnuts and beans. The stoppage caused dissent, unusual among the Kalash, as some felt the food would end the dancing for the night. They were right. Tak-Dira asked me if I wanted to eat. When I shook my head she gave me an appraising look '*Parik?*'* This time I acquiesced and she went off to round up her flock.

The moon had long since disappeared behind the clouds, and, with only the light from a lantern Tak-Dira had borrowed (the batteries in both our torches had gone), we moved off into the darkness. The going was indeed treacherous. On the edge of a stream, I slipped and went down on one knee, but a jingle of bells and a black-robed arm covered in bangles announced that Tak-Dira was there to help. By day, I had become adept at travelling through this rocky terrain but at night it was a different proposition. All the time I was terrified I should bring Tak-Dira down with me. Often she turned to me, her eyes sparkling in the light of the lantern she was holding, just to check I was okay and to let me know she was glad of my company. What I felt for this woman could only be described as love—not sexual and not really in the sense of a mother-figure. Again, I thought, it was more as if we had always known one another—had always been close; and again I wondered, if, perhaps, in another incarnation, we had been together and had loved one another. How can one interpret such feelings? There was no explanation for the strength of the bond which had grown between us, or for the instant and often silent communication we enjoyed.

When we walked onto the verandah, Jafail, asleep on the *charpoy* next to mine, raised himself on one elbow and stared at us sleepily. The pups hardly stirred, except for Pooch who leapt off my sleeping-bag and came wriggling along the ground towards me. Not wanting to disturb the others I gave him a hug and gently placed him back with the rest. Putting away my camera, I helped myself to some water, thinking that if this were in the West, one would turn on the gas or electricity and make tea or coffee.

Parik—let's go.

But it was not, I reminded myself. As these thoughts went through my mind, Tak-Dira turned to me: '*Chai?*'

I laughed. How I loved her at that moment as she squatted on the hearth and blew into the embers to get the fire rekindled. When the wood was caught, she raised her head and turned. As her gaze met mine, I saw her eyes were full of fun, provocative, almost flirtatious; her craggy, half-toothless mouth set in a crooked grin. There were moments when she was beautiful in my eyes, as at that moment. What is beauty? Skin deep? Or is it in the heart? In the soul?

Supposedly on the last day of the celebrations, the Budalak appears. It is this aspect of the festival which most intrigues the visitor to Birir—the only valley to hold the Phoo Festival. Originally it was instigated by a *shaman* in the face of a decreasing population. The Budalak is a virile shepherd who, traditionally, spends the spring and summer in the mountains, strengthening his manhood and distinguishing himself against other men in feats of physical prowess. On the last day of the festival, he comes down from the high pastures and, in public, he is allowed to have his way with as many women as he can satisfy, in the hope these women will be impregnated. Any woman, whether she is married, single, virgin or not, can be chosen and is thereby truly honoured. A child born of such a union is also epecially honoured, as is the rest of the family including the husband. The day he comes down from the high pastures, the new one will retire to the cattle houses to await the spring, when he will go into the mountains. Since the mid-seventies, however, the advent of the Budalak has seldom been celebrated. A public orgy, for no doubt that is what it would be called in the West, was unwise indeed if orthodox Moslems were present.

Poor Tak-Dira. It was the morning of the most important day of the festival, and she was having a hard time getting the show on the road. Once everyone was awake, the feverish activity of the past few evenings was repeated. What with last-minute laundry, the mending of broken shoes, the weaving of new tassles around freshly washed and braided plaits, the pinning of berries onto caps, and bells and buttons onto head-dresses, it took hours of preparation.

It was well past noon before Tak-Dira, myself and Biroche Bibi, whose leg was still healing, made our way to the dancing ground. En route we picked up others, and, to the sound of distant drums, walked along the treacherous cliff paths, the children dressed in new clean clothes, some with bright silk shawls. Both Biroche Bibi and a number of children were carrying or wearing large cone-shaped hats made from willow and decorated with berries, flowers and feathers.

At first, the celebrations were much like those I had attended on the second night, except there was no bonfire, but, towards late afternoon, young men snatched the festive hats from off the childrens' heads, and, as the women laughed and shrieked, the 'thieves' jumped a high stone wall and fled across the stubble of recently harvested fields.

All around us, the Kalash were picking up their children and belongings and making for a nearby wall. I gave one look at the six-foot barrier of stones and hesitated. Beside me, Tak-Dira jumped up and in two seconds was on top. She reached down and clasped my hand. Six feet of stone wall! For the life of me I couldn't see a foothold. Tak-Dira pulled. Suddenly Balan was behind me. He gave me an unceremonious shove on my rear-end, and I was up.

The Kalash streamed across the fields. Coloured head-dresses and plumes danced before my eyes. Then the people split up. One group followed the river, while the other, including myself and Tak-Dira, headed for the mountains. I had no idea of where I was going. To eat? To see the arrival of the Budalak, after all? Tak-Dira led me up the mountainside at a fast pace, and I had to struggle to keep up with this ageing, indomitable woman, even though she wore only plastic shoes upon her feet. High up on a ridge we rested.

We continued on climbing until we reached a high promontory overlooking the river and lower and upper Birir. Close by were several houses, in front of which a few people had congregated. From the valley

Girls dancing at the Phoo festival.

below came the sound of drums, and I saw the rest of the Kalash moving along beside the river.

The procession, led by two youths beating their ancient, barrelled drums made of wood and animal skins, came into view on the promontory. Within minutes of their arrival, Tak-Dira started off the dancing. Surrounded by mountaintops bathed in the late afternoon sun, the tiny place was filled with magic. The elders gathered in the centre, chanting. Two Kalash men and I moved in close with our cassette-players to record. The women formed a tight circle around us, singing as they danced, while the drums rose to a crescendo. I was filled again with admiration for the people who faced their often difficult lives with such equanimity and gaiety.

Again, there was a sudden flurry of activity as Balan appeared with another group of youths, pounced upon the small children and once more snatched at their recently returned hats. They jumped a fence and fled across the flat rooftops of the neighbouring houses on the side of the mountain.

The dancing stopped. I looked up; soon it would be sunset. Tak-Dira, indicating the sky, said: '*Parik?*'

We started down the path, but, as we rounded a corner, I saw a group of women holding juniper branches. Tak-Dira gasped and put her hand over her mouth. Urgently grabbing me by the arm, she dragged me speedily back to the promontory, where everyone was gathered into a tight, silent group. The drums were still. We all waited patiently; there was a feeling of expectancy in the air. I looked enquiringly at Tak-Dira, but she just smiled.

A Moslem leaned over my shoulder and whispered in English that no-one could go near the approaching women. Just then a young Moslem girl with a goat started down the mountain path, but she was driven back, as were some more Moslems. No-one, not even the Kalash, ventured along the path. As the women came slowly into sight, everyone around me drew even farther back. Solemnly, with funereal steps, the women advanced, holding aloft lighted juniper branches. They reached the large tree, standing about a hundred feet away and surrounded by a high wooden fence, and formed a semi-circle beneath its leaves. Slowly, in solemn ritual, they waved the juniper branches aloft, and, then, one by one, threw them over the fence, bidding farewell to the festival.

As Tak-Dira led me down the mountainside, I wondered if this had really been the final act of the Phoo Festival. What about the Budalak? Had he appeared that first night of the dancing, or was the ritual of the Budalak about to be performed now in some private place shrouded in secrecy and deception?

Reflections

Through the open door of the *dora* I could see Jafail stirring something in a large cauldron. He appeared to be throwing in flour and wine. After much stirring, he lifted out a long coil which somehow looked obscene. Then I realized it was only a necklace of walnuts which would be dried and stored as a sweetened goodie for the winter. Behind me, on Tak-Dira's cast-off robes the pups slept peacefully in a tight bundle.

It was late, and, in spite of the fire, Tak-Dira was cold. I watched as she pulled the robes tighter around her shoulders. She turned away from the open space above the balcony, her eyes closed. Again, she pulled at her robes, clutching them tightly beneath her chin. In profile, with her high cheek-bones, the head-dress and her closed eyes, she presented an evocative picture. On the one hand, she aroused sympathy; on the other, I had the feeling of going back in time and standing before an altar commanded by a high priestess.

My third and longest sojourn in the valleys was coming to an end. Journeys undertaken at different times cannot be compared. Each is a separate entity unto itself, influenced by the person we are at that moment and governed by circumstances beyond our control.

My journeys, though, to Pakistan and these valleys, merged into one. Six years before, I had first ventured into Bumburet and had succumbed to its beauty. The following year, driven by desire to know more about the Kalash, I had returned, and, for a few short weeks, I had found peace with myself and the world. Now, on my third visit, it seemed as if the intervening, desolate and difficult years had never happened. My experience with the Kalash was an ongoing one, the feeling of belonging was overwhelming.

Time was slipping by. I had only one more day left in the valley and those last hours were very precious to me. I did not want them to end. Again, I became aware of how this constant striving for permanence in a transitory world undermines the soul of man, leading only to depression and disillusionment. When his life is nearing its end, is he, who seeks permanence, equipped to take that last transitional step? Yet if he swims against the tide and seeks to live for the present, he is likely to be considered irresponsible—a misfit.

It was a clear autumn morning. Down by the river, I saw a large bird with a white-crested head, black body and deep red tail, alight upon a rock. As the sun came up, I heard the sound of a flute, and there again was the herdsboy standing on the bank of the irrigation channel. I waved and he touched his forehead in greeting, walking on slowly, still playing his flute, until he was lost from sight behind some trees.

With slow steps, I made my way back to the *dora*, the pups playing at my heels. After breakfast, I returned to the river, as I invariably did if Tak-Dira's back was turned, to fill one of the water containers.

Although late October, the sun was gloriously warm. The nearby mill stream and the tiny waterfall above sparkled in the sun's rays. As was my habit, I sat on a rock and watched the pups playing, their young and now much healthier bodies enjoying the freedom of their new vast play-ground. They, too, had won my heart. First Habib in Bumburet, then Saifullah in Rumbur, and here in Birir, Tak-Dira and her family. I turned my head. Coming towards me across the narrow plank bridge was Biroche Bibi, her leg now almost healed. She came bearing gifts of fruit and garlands of walnuts—the traditional gifts of the Kalash. It was not only certain individuals who had won my heart, but the whole of the Kalash people.

Those who have a true abiding faith, whether they are members of an organized religion or have their own iconoclastic beliefs, are, perhaps, fortunate, for those of an inquisitive bent, who spend their days in pursuit of truth, are doomed to a life of perpetual instability. Every 'truth' arrived at lasts but for a short time. Then the next bend in the road will beckon.

There are brief intervals, however, in which peace and tranquillity make the search worthwhile—such intervals I have experienced in the Kalash valleys.

The author sharing a relatively quiet moment with Tak-Dira.

Glossary

Burqa	A tent-like garment, with a narrow opening for the eyes, covered in a type of netting, worn by women in purdah.
Chai	Tea.
Chai-Khana	Tea-house.
Chappatis	Flat, pancake-type bread, common on the subcontinent and usually served hot.
Chaplis	Pathan sandals.
Charpoy	String bed common to the subcontinent.
Chapik	Snack.
Chowkidar	Night watchman.
Dhoti	Loin cloth generally worn by Hindu males.
Dobie	Laundry man.
Dukan	Store.
Ghari	A shallow wooden box worked on a pully system used for crossing rivers.
Ghee	Clarified butter or vegetable oil.
Insha'Allah	God willing.
Il humdul'illah	Thanks be to God.
Jaldi!	Quickly.
Khameez	Pakistani long-tailed shirt worn by both men and women. For the latter, material is finer and more colourful and the garment is longer in length.
Kurta	Long shirt.
Loongi	Puggaree—a type of turban.
Pani	Water.
Parratas	Fried Chappatis.
Powanda	Gypsy.
Puggaree	Turban—usually worn around some other form of headgear such as a domed cap.
Purdah	Isolation of women from men except husband and near relatives.

236

Qahwa	Green tea.
Salaam Alykum	Peace be upon you.
Shalwar	Pakistani loose-fitting trousers worn by both men and women. For the latter the material is more colourful and finer, and the trouser leg is usually gathered in at the ankles.
Tikay	Okay.
Tik tok	Very good.
Zenana	Women's quarters.

Although the national language of Pakistan is Urdu, the country has a number of other languages and dialects, although there are some words commonly spoken by all.

Glossary—Kalash

Aya	Mother.
Baba	Sister.
Bashali House	House of confinement for menstruating and pregnant women.
Doh!	Here!
Dora	House.
Ishpata!	Greetings.
Ma	My.
Ne	No.
Parik	Let's go.
Sher	Dog.
Tu	You.
Garda	Large.

Kalash is not a written language, so I have written the transliterations phonetically.

Bibliography

Arrian, 1971: *The Campaigns of Alexander.* Translated by Aubrey De Selincourt (Penguin Classics).

Boulnois, L., 1966: *The Silk Road.* Translated by Dennis Chamberlain (George Allen and Unwin Ltd, London).

Cable, Mildred with French, Francesca, 1942, 1984: *The Gobi Desert* (Hodder & Stoughton, Virago Press).

Caroe, Sir Olaf, 1958: *The Pathans. 550 BC–AD 1957* (MacMillan & Co Ltd, London).

Clark, John, reprint 1980: *Hunza—Lost Kingdom of the Himalayas* (Indus Publications, Karachi).

Collins, Larry and Lapierre, Dominique 1981: *Freedom at Midnight* (Granada Books).

Darling, G., 1979: *Merit Feasting Among the Kalash Kafirs, North Western Pakistan* (Thesis. University of British Columbia, Canada).

Denker, D., 1981.
'Pakistan's Kalash—People of Fire and Fervor' (*National Geographic* Vol. 160, No. 4. Oct 1981).

Durand, Algernon George, 1899/1908: *The Making of a Frontier* (John Murray).

Emerson, Prof. Dr. Richard M., 1984: 'Charismatic Kingship. A Study of State Formation and Authority in Baltistan' (*Journal of Central Asia* Vol. VII).

Fairley, Jean, 1975: *Lion River—The Indus* (Allen Lane).

Farre, Rowena, 1969: *The Beckoning Land* (Victor Gollancz).

Filippo de Filippi, revised 1932: *Italian Expedition to the Himalaya, Karakorum and Eastern Turkestan (1913–1914).* Translated by H.T. Lowe-Porter from the Italian Edition. (Butler and Tanner Ltd).

Fleming, Peter. 1937, reprint 1941: *Travels in Tartary* (Reprint Society Ltd).

Glassman, Eugene H: *Spoken Urdu* (Nirali Kitaben, 1986 Distinctive Books, Lahore).

238

Hurley, James, 1961: 'People of Baltistan' (*Natural History Magazine,* Oct 1961, Nov 1961, American Museum of Natural History, New York).

Jettmar, Karl, 1974: 'Cultures of the Hindu Kush'. (Selected Papers from Hindu-Kush Cultural Conference held at Möesgard 1970 in collaboration with L. Edelbert, Franz Steiner Verlag, Weisbaden).

Jettmar, Karl, 1980: *'Bolor and Dardistan'.* (A contribution to the ethnological research in Bolor and Dardistan. Publication Section, National Institute of Folk Heritage, P.O. Box 1184, Islamabad, Pakistan).

Keay, John, 1977: *Where Men and Mountains Meet* (John Murray).

Keay, John, 1979: *The Gilgit Game* (John Murray).

Knight, E.F., 1893: *Where Three Empires Meet* (Longman).

Maillart, Ella, 1937, revised 1983: *Forbidden Journey* (Century Publishing).

Maraini, Fosco, 1959: *Where Four Worlds Meet* (Hamish Hamilton).

Mayne, Peter, 1955: *The Narrow Smile—A Journey Back to the North-West Frontier* (John Murray).

Mote, F.W., 1961, (Introduction): *The Travels of Marco Polo* (Del Publishing Co Inc New York).

Morgenstierne, G., 1926: *Report on a Linguistic Mission to Afghanistan* (Institute for Sammen Lingnende Kulturfarsknin).

Morgenstierne, G., 1926: *Report on a Linguistic Mission to North-Western India* (Institute for Sammen Lingnende Kulturfarsknin, Series CI-2, Oslo).

Morgenstierne, G., 1973: 'Notes on Kalasha' (*Indo-Iranian Frontier Languages,* Blindern, Norway).

Murphy Dervla, 1977: *Where the Indus is Young* (John Murray).

Murtaza, G., 1961: *Tarikh-e-Citral* (Wazir Ali Shah, translation).

Parkes, Peter. S.G., 1975: *The Social Role of Historical Tradition Among the Kalash Kafirs of Chitral* (Thesis, Bodleian Library, Oxford).

Robertson, Sir George, reprinted 1975: *The Kafirs of the Hindu-Kush* (Oxford University Press).

Robertson, Sir George, 1898: *Chitral: Story of a Minor Siege* (Methuen & Co).

Schomberg, R.C.F., 1935: *Between the Oxus and the Indus* (M. Hopkinson Ltd).

Schomberg, R.C.F., 1936: *Unknown Karakoram* (Martin Hopkinson).

Schomberg, R.C.F., 1938: *Kafirs and Glaciers—Travels in Chitral* (Martin Hopkinson)

Shipton, Eric, 1951: *Mountains of Tartary* (Hodder and Stoughton).

Spain, James, W., 1962: *The Way of the Pathans* (Robert Hale Ltd).

Staley, John, 1982: *Words For My Brother* (Oxford University Press).

Stephens, Ian, 1955: *The Horned Moon. An Account of a Journey Through Pakistan, Kashmir, and Afghanistan* (Ernest Benn).

Suyin, Han, 1942: *Destination Chungking* (Jonathan Cape).

Teichman, Sir Eric, 1937: *Journey to Turkestan* (Hodder and Stoughton).

Younghusband, G.I., 1895: *The Relief of Chitral* (MacMillan & Co Ltd).

Younghusband, G.I., 1896, revised 1937: *The Heart of a Continent* (John Murray).